PROLOGUE TO PERÓN

PROLOGUE TO PERÓN

Argentina in Depression and War, 1930–1943

Edited by Mark Falcoff and Ronald H. Dolkart

UNIVERSITY OF CALIFORNIA PRESS
Berkeley ■ Los Angeles ■ London

University of California Press
Berkeley and Los Angeles, California

University of California Press, Ltd.
London, England

ISBN: 0-520-02874-0

Library of Congress Catalog Card Number: 74-22961

Printed in the United States of America

TO OUR PARENTS
—for all of the reasons

Contents

Preface

Today the Argentine Republic is often regarded as one of the
world's great failures—a country that though endowed with
apparently limitless possibilities, seems incapable of realizing its
potential in a changing and ever more difficult world. For the
last twenty-five years its economy has been afflicted by a
combination of stagnation and inflation; its political life has
been divided between experiments in messianic populism and
bouts of military repression; its society has been splintered by
social and ideological conflict, now increasingly actualized in
assassinations, kidnappings, and random violence. Foreign
embassies are inundated by applications for exit visas from those
who seek to escape what appears to be a terminal sentence
for an entire society and an entire way of life.

The foregoing picture appears all the more apocalyptic
when placed alongside the Argentina that once was. For until
1930 this South American republic was regarded as one of the
most successful of the new countries of the nineteenth century,
a worthy colleague of Australia, Canada, and—with slight
exaggeration—of the United States. Its wealth, its cultural and
social development, its political stability and progress towards
democracy made it one of the great countries of European
investment and immigration well beyond the First World War.

Since 1930, however, the principal themes of Argentine history have been not order and progress, but conflict, frustration, and, latterly, despair.

The Argentine dilemma finds its roots, we believe, in the abrupt disappearance of the conditions that made possible the emergence of the modern republic in the late nineteenth century. Those conditions were the existence of the British Empire as a principal market for foodstuffs, the international division of labor, and the relatively free movement of goods and services across national boundaries. For most underdeveloped countries those props were perceptibly weakening as early as 1914, but for Argentina—thanks to a peculiar constellation of circumstances —they persisted until 1930. Then, under the combined impact of the world depression and the Second World War, they collapsed. The failure of Argentina's leadership to respond adequately to the double crisis explains, we hold, the Revolution of 1943 and the subsequent emergence of Colonel Juan Perón as the dominant figure of Argentina's contemporary history.

The period 1930-1943 thus forms a watershed between two "Argentinas." One was an outpost of Europe in South America, a Latin American nation apparently untrammelled by the heavy hand of Catholic traditions, of unassimilated indigenes, or of insurmountable geographical barriers; a country that was, in the words of a Mexican admirer, José Vasconcelos, "the first firm success of Spanish civilization on the American continent." The other is a nation rent by all the classic cleavages of early industrial society, divisions compounded by a personalistic political movement and the full range of contemporary social and spiritual maladies. Those who would understand *Peronismo* and the broader problems of modern Argentina would best search, we believe, in the thirteen critical years that separate these two Argentinas from one another. To that purpose we offer the essays that make up the present volume.

In recognizing the importance of this period and addressing themselves to it, the contributors are joining a continuing debate that has agitated Argentine letters and public life for more than fifteen years. For although the outlines of Argentina's depression decade may remain obscure to foreigners, the period is painfully familiar to the Argentines themselves, who recognize that they are living out its legacies. It is not surprising, therefore, that nearly half the books published on historical subjects during the 1960s concentrated on the period that is the subject of this book.

Although varying widely in emphasis, sophistication, and quality, Argentine treatments of the 1930s adhere fundamentally to one of two lines of interpretation. One, a "conservative" school, depicts this era as Argentina's last period of effective government by a qualified elite, dedicated to what it considers the inevitable historical destiny of the country: to play a role that is economically and culturally subordinate to that of Europe. Curiously, there are few systematic expositions of this view, yet, for all that, it has remained pervasive in much of Argentine literature, journalism, memoirs, and repeated public statements by representatives of rural interests, of foreign economic concerns, or of their proxies in various Argentine governments since 1955. The most eloquent spokesman for this view is Professor Carlos Díaz-Alejandro, who is neither an Argentine nor a resident of Latin America.

On the other side, the "nationalist" version—whether of the left or the right—has depicted these years as ones of reaction and stagnation, of corruption and betrayal: an "infamous decade," in the enduring phrase of José Luis Torres. In this view, the thirties witnessed a step backward in Argentine history, during which, in a time of crisis, a handful of beef barons seized power and sacrificed the national interest to British imperialism in the service of their immediate economic needs.[*] This interpretation makes the advent of Perón both inevitable and necessary—inevitable, because in trying to turn the clock back, the Argentine leaders of the day were hopelessly condemned to failure; necessary, because the transformations of the world economy during this period required major structural changes in

---

[*] Although both right- and left-wing nationalist historians agree that the fundamental issue of the thirties is national betrayal by the "oligarchy," they derive their analyses from widely differing assumptions. For those of the right, such as Ernesto Palacio *(Historia Argentina* [1954]) and Julio Irazusta *(Balance del siglo y medio* [1966]), the tragedy of the thirties consists precisely in the decline of an elite that had once governed the nation effectively and patriotically; the underlying tone is one of deploration and disappointment, and the cause is attributed to "liberalism," to the too-ready acceptance of the norms of nineteenth-century bourgeois democracy, which failed to serve Argentina in a moment of maximum need. Nationalists of the left—nota-

order for Argentina to survive as an economic entity. For those disillusioned and discontented in post-Perón Argentina—and they have been without number!—this view of the thirties offered both an explanation for the contemporary crisis and guidelines for its solution. Indeed, Perón's triumphant return to Argentina in 1973 and his subsequent apotheosis owed much to widespread acceptance of this version.

Yet a victory (or a defeat) in the court of public opinion is not necessarily proof of historical truth. To be sure, a subject so fraught with meaning for the present could hardly be approached dispassionately, but the Argentines, who are a passionate people, have contributed inordinately larger amounts of heat than light to their analyses of this period. The essays in this book respond to a shared belief by the contributors that Argentine studies of the thirties have fallen far short of providing an adequate understanding of this most critical of decades. Both sides in the argument have, we think, assumed a strident, polemical tone, and made scandalously selective use of the evidence. Both have emphasized the political aspect to the exclusion of nearly everything else—as if economic policy, cultural life, even demographic shifts were but the effects to which the comings and goings of politicians and generals were "cause"; the walls of interpretation are pock-marked with "what if" hypotheses; and both sides, for different reasons, choose to overlook the continuities that link this period to either side of the historical divide, or the discontinuities that give it a life of its own. Those who have credited Perón with qualities akin to those of a savior naturally have wished to liberate him from any association with the "infamous decade," while admirers of the

bly Rodolfo Puiggrós (*Historia crítica de los partidos políticos argentinos* [1956]), Juan José Hernández Arregui (*La formación de la conciencia nacional, 1930-1960* [1960]), and Jorge Abelardo Ramos (*Revolución y contrarevolución en la Argentina* [1957])—use a fundamentally Marxist framework to explain the "sellout" in terms of class interest and the necessary "internationalism" of a "comprador bourgeoisie." The reader may find it interesting, and altogether illustrative of the complexities of Argentine politics, to learn that while Palacio served as a *Peronista* deputy in 1946, Irazusta refused Perón's offer of a major European embassy because he frankly deplored the latter's *"demagogia obrera";* likewise, Hernández Arregui held minor academic and cultural posts, and Ramos served as the European bureau chief of Perón's principal newspaper, but Puiggrós, then a communist, initially fought the regime as "bonapartist and fascist" —passing to the Peronist side in 1947. Recently he was Rector of the University of Buenos Aires (1973-1974).

old Argentina have preferred to exaggerate the differences between it and the new dispensation. Both have failed also to appreciate the truly innovative features of the thirties—the nationalists because they wish to view it as a relapse to the period before the extension of suffrage, a restoration, bag and baggage, of pre-1916 Argentina—which it was not. And the conservatives prefer not to think about the ways in which the hated policies of Peron were foreshadowed in so many of their own. Consequently we have something of a deadlock—a debate between the deaf. The essays in this book are an attempt, however modest, to break that deadlock and generate an authentic dialogue. While together these essays fall far short of being a definitive history of Argentina during the 1930s, they do succeed, we think, in reconstructing its principal features. They also widen the boundaries of the territory to be surveyed and delineate the specific curves and furrows that led up to and shaped the Peronist state. At a minimum, we hope that they will inspire greater interest in the period in the United States, as well as greater rigor in its study in Argentina.

An overview of the period is, of course, necessary in order to introduce the reader to the fundamental contours of the terrain about to be entered. Our guide is Professor Arthur P. Whitaker, dean of North American scholars of Argentina, who draws upon a wide range of materials and the experience of an extended stay in 1937, to produce a broad-brush impression of the society during the Depression decade. His attention is mainly focused upon two neuralgic points: first, the stark contrast between the Argentina of the early twentieth century, suffused with faith in the future, and that of the thirties, characterized by a loss of confidence in the country's physical and human potentialities; and second, the gap between Argentine conditions as they actually were and as they were perceived by the Argentines themselves. Professor Whitaker would argue that what Marxists call "false consciousness" can become an independent variable and shape events to which it does not fully respond.

Although the year 1930 infused virtually all aspects of Argentine life with a sense of crisis, perhaps no single event provided more dramatic evidence of time out of hand than the overthrow by a military coup of the government of President Hipólito Yrigoyen on September 6. Until that date, Argentina had provided Latin America with a model of democratic political development. In 1912 a ruling elite of rancher-*cum*-lawyers had enacted a law of universal manhood suffrage, by which they gracefully ceded power to Yrigoyen's popularly based movement in 1916. Yet in abruptly withdrawing that concession fourteen years later, and by clinging to power through illegitimate means for thirteen years more, that elite prepared the way for its own liquidation—by the very same agency that had acted upon its behalf in 1930. The nature of the Conservative return to power, the origins of the Revolution of 1943, and the impact of both upon subsequent events are the themes that occupy the editors in chapter 2.

To a significant degree economic policies overshadowed political concerns during this period, which was natural enough given the conditions generated by the Depression. Argentina was particularly hard-hit by the collapse of world trade patterns, since its prosperity was so closely tied to the export of agricultural products to Europe. Yet the country recovered rapidly from the effects of the crisis, partly because of the economic policies pursued by the government. A somewhat technical, but no less acrimonious, debate has raged about the significance of those policies. For although willing to go further than any previous Argentine regime in order to ensure continued purchases of wheat and meat by Great Britain, the Conservatives also put an end to the practice of free trade and presided, whether wittingly or not, over a massive thrust forward in Argentina's industrial power. Wending his way through a tangle of technical questions and political controversies, Professor Javier Villanueva has attempted to reconstruct and analyze not only the policies themselves, but the motives of their makers; chapter 3 suggests, among other things, a far greater continuity in economic policy between the Conservatives and Perón than is normally believed to be the case.

The issues of the Argentine economy are difficult to separate from questions of foreign policy, for the latter had been, in large part, determined by the nation's early choice of trading partners. A traditional British connection dating back to 1825 had made the Argentine Republic an unofficial "sixth dominion" of the British Empire, and English economic primacy was still a fact of life for Argentine diplomacy during the 1930s. However, the United States had already become a serious challenger to Great Britain in both trade and investment by the end of the First World War, and during the thirties Argentines increasingly sensed a growing American economic influence. In discussing the resoundingly unsuccessful attempts by Argentina to derive advantage from a sharpening economic rivalry between the two Anglo-Saxon powers, Professor Joseph S. Tulchin presents in chapter 4 a new view of Argentine neutrality during the Second World War. He also establishes the background for what later emerged as the "Third Position" in world affairs of the Perón regime.

The intellectual currents that grew out of these unique conditions reflected an unprecedented alienation from European (actually Anglo-French) civilization as a guidepost to progress, and a consequent search for a uniquely Argentine synthesis. This trend was manifested most characteristically during the thirties by a thoroughgoing critique of the country's past and present. Novelists and social thinkers cast the blame for the Argentine dilemma on every conceivable source—immigrants, politicians, urbanization, liberalism, and imperialism, as well as basic flaws in the national character. As Professor Falcoff shows in his tour through these gloomy precincts in chapter 5, most writers on national problems during the thirties were either immobilized by pessimism or passionately driven to redress the nation's historic grievances. In either case, they afforded scant comfort for those who wished Argentina to remain what she had always been, and provided abundant ammunition for partisans of her radical transformation.

The search for authentic Argentine roots led to a discovery of the nation's popular culture, which during this period became a source of widespread interest and appreciation. As Señor Gustavo Sosa-Pujato shows in chapter 6, before the 1920s it would have been difficult to discuss this question, for the immigrant masses had not been fully assimilated into the society. But by the following decade it was possible to identify certain nascent features of a truly national culture, a distinctively Platine blend of Argentina's European and Latin American heritages. The principal indicators that he has chosen to investigate are the tango and the motion picture—the tango because, having reached its mature and "classic" form during this period, it faithfully expressed the spirit of the man in the street; the film industry because of the extraordinary role it played in shaping a new sensibility and a new appreciation for Argentina's characteristic national qualities.

Any discussion of national identity inevitably intrudes upon the question of the Argentine provinces, for the conflict between the interior and Buenos Aires has often been expressed in terms of two opposing lines of cultural development. In the final essay, Professor Dolkart explores the origins of the "provincial question" and then argues that during the thirties, for a variety of reasons—political, economic, demographic, and cultural—Argentines rediscovered the backward, forgotten regions of their country that had languished in neglect since the late nineteenth century. The interior had always regarded itself as the "authentic" Argentina, untainted by alien influences and by the crass materialism of the port city of Buenos Aires. During the thirties, its demands for a fuller share of the nation's wealth and a larger voice in the political system coincided with the nationalist view that in order for Argentina to become a fully functional and modern republic, it had to incorporate the interior into its society. The convergence of nationalism and provincial grievances thus constitutes one of the principal features of the period, and one of its most important legacies.

None of the problems arising out of the decade of the thirties —neither the questioning attitude of Argentines toward themselves, nor the increasing loss of economic viability, nor the decline of international position, nor the bitterness and cultural ambivalence of the intellectuals, nor the poverty of the provinces —has yet been resolved to the satisfaction of a clear majority. The *Peronato* (1946-1955), so much an outgrowth of this period, represents the most serious attempt that has been made to meet these challenges, yet for reasons that lie outside of this volume, it signally failed. The record of its successors—both civilian and military—has been more dismal still, and explains in a large measure Perón's triumphant return nearly twenty years later.

In a word, Argentina's failure to come to grips with critical problems in a crucial period of transition has exacted a high price, and the issues of the thirties remain—tragically—those of the 1970s. This failure also assures a continuing interest in the "infamous decade," for in the thirteen years prior to the advent of Perón, Argentines of all persuasions still find an abundance of lost opportunities, and much of their subsequent history can be understood as a search to recover the social peace, effective government, expanding economy, and international status to which they feel—and in truth, to which they are—entitled.

For purposes of exposition, the editors have rather arbitrarily divided Argentine reality into six discrete categories. We realize, of course, that in history as in life, the realms of economics, politics, and culture often overlap and interpenetrate one another, and we beg the indulgence of our readers if one chapter briefly recapitulates or touches upon materials covered in another. We initially asked our contributors to write essays that, though meant to be read together, could be capable of standing alone. The picture that emerges through a reading of the work is by no means totally unified, but the dissonances that mark one chapter off from another are extremely useful in raising an entire series of new questions about the period. To take only the most important and obvious of these: chapters 1, 3, and 4 all rest upon the assumption that the much-maligned "oligarchy" had a far better understanding of the nature of the crisis and had far greater success in meeting it than one might imagine from an isolated reading of chapters 2, 5, 6, and 7. The question that inevitably arises is, if the first group of essays is "correct," why should the Argentine elite have been subjected to the pitiless criticism chronicled in the second set? An answer is suggested in Professor Villanueva's chapter: the peculiar configuration of economic, political, and diplomatic interests in Argentina made it impossible for the government to articulate frankly the policy it had adopted; hence it was forced to defend policies it had actually abandoned in practice. The opposition took the government at its word and succeeded in convincing most politically conscious Argentines that the regime had fallen hopelessly behind the times. This explanation may be too sophisticated, or perhaps not sophisticated enough. It is also possible that neither group of chapters fully grasps the essence of this problem. In any event, it is clear that the gap between what Argentines believed the period to be, and what it actually was, provided the opening through which Perón rose to power. For without the achievements of the Conservative Restoration (particularly industrialization), there would have been no *descamisado* (shirtless) masses, and without its failures—in social policy, in political life, above all in moral leadership—Perón would have passed into an obscure military retirement, rather than acceding to a central role in the drama, and now the mythology, of Argentine history.

The editors thank the following friends and colleagues for invaluable moral support, advice, and technical assistance offered at various stages of the project. At the University of California, Los Angeles: Professors E. Bradford Burns and Robert N. Burr; Professor James W. Wilkie and Edna Monzón de Wilkie; Dr. Ludwig Lauerhass, Jr., at the University Research Library; at the University of California, Berkeley: Professor Tulio Halperín Donghi; at the University of Illinois: Professors Andrés O. Avellaneda and Joseph L. Love, Jr.; at Princeton University: Professor Stanley J. Stein and Barbara H. Stein; at the City University of New York: Professors Isaías Lerner and Hobart Spalding, Jr.; at the University of Notre Dame: Professor Frederick B. Pike; at the University of Oregon: John Douglass and Jeffery Blair Kimmel; at Simon Fraser University, British Columbia: Professor Alberto Ciria; at the University of Buenos Aires: Professor Ricardo Caillet-Bois (Emeritus).

They should also like to express appreciation to the Doherty Foundation, the Regional Studies Fund of Princeton University, and the Foreign Area Fellowship Program for financing research in Argentina that led to the conception and execution of this book, and to the Graduate School of the University of Oregon for assistance in the preparation of the manuscript.

M. F. and R. H. D.

Contributors

ARTHUR P. WHITAKER is Professor Emeritus of History, University of
Pennsylvania. His many books include *The United States and the
Independence of Latin America* (1941), *The United States and
Argentina* (1954), *The Western Hemisphere Idea: Its Rise and Decline*
(1954), *Argentine Upheaval: Perón's Fall and the New Regime* (1956),
and *Argentina* (1964).

MARK FALCOFF is Assistant Professor of History, University of Oregon.

RONALD H. DOLKART is Assistant Professor of History, California State
College, Bakersfield.

JAVIER VILLANUEVA is Vice-Dean of the Faculty of Economics and
Social Sciences, Universidad Católica Argentina, and Research Associate of the Instituto Torcuato S. di Tella, both in Buenos Aires. He
is the author of *The Inflationary Process in Argentina, 1943-1960*
(1966).

JOSEPH S. TULCHIN is Associate Professor of History, University of
North Carolina. He is the author of *The Aftermath of War: World
War I and U. S. Policy Toward Latin America* (1971) and co-editor
(with David J. Danelski) of *The Autobiographical Notes of Charles
Evan Hughes* (1973).

GUSTAVO SOSA-PUJATO is an Argentine filmmaker and critic. His films
include *Documentalizando* (1967), *Siete pintores argentinos* (1969),
and *Carriego, misión suburbio* (1970).

1.

An Overview of the Period

ARTHUR P. WHITAKER

... the average Argentine ... has both that jubilant patriotism and that exuberant confidence in his country which marked the North American of 1830-1860.
James Bryce, 1912

The Argentine likes the image he has of himself. ... To belong to this people is a source of pride that animates every Argentine. He is born with a blind faith in its glamorous destiny. ... Rooted in each individual is an idea of the whole [nation] by which he lives and which insures in this people a kind of patriotism that is hard for Europeans, except perhaps the English, to understand.
José Ortega y Gasset, 1929

National pride and optimism were hallmarks of the booming society of Argentina in the generation before 1930. So concluded these two outstanding European intellectuals after visiting that country at different times over a span of sixteen years, Bryce in 1912 and Ortega y Gasset in 1916 and 1928. The traits that impressed both of them must therefore have been strongly marked in the Argentine society of those decades.

Seemingly, all that changed almost overnight under the shock of the worldwide economic depression that began in October 1929. It quickly crippled Argentina's vulnerable export economy and in September 1930 precipitated a revolt that, with only a whiff of grapeshot, overthrew a democratic, constitutional government under a party in office since 1916 and established in its place a military dictatorship. Thus began the so-called infamous decade, which in fact lasted more than a decade and was by no means wholly infamous.

This period spanned first the dictatorship, which lasted a year and a half, and then the Conservative Restoration of rule by the oligarchy under democratic forms until the military took over again in 1943. These years began with a sudden, wide-spread change of mood from pride and optimism to disillusion-ment and even despair. The transformation is no mystery. For half a century, with only occasional ups and downs, Argentina had enjoyed a nearly miraculous growth, and the former step-child of Mother Spain during the colonial centuries had by the time of James Bryce's visit taken first place among the twenty Latin American states in wealth and political and cultural prestige. Now the prosperity supporting this splendid edifice had been shattered, and, to make matters still worse, many people in Argentina, as elsewhere, had lost faith in the whole capitalist system. Similarly, the failure of the experiment in popular government under Argentina's Constitution of 1853 was all the more disillusioning because it shook faith in the long-standing belief in progress and because the very idea of representative republican government was now under heavy fire in many parts of the Atlantic world.

Attacks on hitherto accepted ideas and values—economic and political as well as literary and philosophical—were stimulated by European influences, to which Argentine leaders in all fields had long been highly responsive. Chief among these influences in the present instance were fascism, nazism, and communism, all of which had been domesticated in the Plata area before 1930 but made a much stronger appeal thereafter. To these should be added the influence of men of letters, beginning with Oswald Spengler, the title of whose only remembered book, *The Decline of the West,* is a clue to the mood of most Argentine intellectuals in the 1930s: pessimism. The depth, if not the prevalence, of this mood is surprising, at least at first glance, for in some aspects of Argentine society, as we shall see, the period was marked by a vitality and a capacity for growth sufficient to justify a less gloomy, perhaps even a hopeful, appraisal of the national scene.

PEOPLE AND ECONOMY

Argentina and its two smaller neighbors, Uruguay and Chile, form what is often called the "Southern Cone" because of the shape of this part of South America on maps. In colonial times the peoples of all three countries had much in common with those in the rest of Spain's American dominions, but as time passed they diverged more and more from the general type. By 1930 they formed a group set apart in many ways, including their more rapid economic, cultural, and political development, which gave them exceptionally strong ties with the leading capitalist industrial nations, especially Great Britain in trade and investments, France in literature, Germany in military matters, and, on a lower power level, Italy and Spain through decades of massive immigration from both.

In some respects, however, Argentina differed widely from its fellow members of the Southern Cone. Most important was the flood of European immigrants, most of them Italian or Spanish, that had poured over Argentina since 1880 in a volume which, in proportion to population, was unequalled in any other country. Uruguay had a similar experience, but in Chile the ratio of the foreign-born in the 1920s was only about one-tenth as large as Argentina's. The great majority of the latter's entrepreneurs were of immigrant stock; they were the economic leaders of the middle class, eclipsing the old creole middle class in this respect; but they stayed out of politics and with rare exceptions they did not even bother to acquire citizenship. One result, according to Argentine social historian Torcuato S. di Tella, was the lack of a liberal party representing the middle sectors and offering moderate, legitimized opposition to the old ruling classes. (The Radical party, though middle class, failed in crucial respects to meet this description.) In sharp contrast, he continues, Chile, not engulfed by immigrants, remained under the direction of its old creole stock and "continued to be the Athens of South America" as regards "democratic development and institutional process."

A striking and highly relevant difference between Argentina and its other Southern Cone neighbor, Uruguay, has been pointed out by Aldo Solari, sociologist and social historian of the latter country. Questioning the common assumption that rapid industrialization promotes extremist movements and that it does so because the political system is unable to absorb the change produced in the economic system, Solari says that nothing of the kind took place in Uruguay, though it did in Argentina, where rapid industrialization after 1935 was connected with a rupture of the political system and the Peronist explosion in the 1940s. The explanation he finds mainly in the fact that at this time in Uruguay, but not in Argentina, there were large numbers of workers in the principal parties and that there was already social legislation that needed only to be completed and perfected, with the result that all political parties had to bid for the labor vote.

In the 1930s Argentina's economy, though advanced on the Latin American scale, was still "colonial" in the sense that it was based primarily on exports of agricultural and pastoral products to industrialized countries, which in turn supplied it with manufactures and also controlled key elements of its economy through private investments (mostly British, with the United States far behind in second place but gaining in the 1920s). In Argentina the dominant economic group was an oligarchy of great landlords and their allies in banking and commerce.

The same group also controlled the nation's government throughout the Conservative Restoration, that is to say, during the Depression period and several years beyond. Unwisely, as it turned out, but understandably, they had ignored warnings given them repeatedly in the twenties that the existing colonial economy had exhausted its potential for growth and must be diversified and made less dependent on foreign interests. Instead, remembering only that this economy had served them marvelously well for a generation, they now took the opposite course and intensified the pro-British colonialism of their nation's economy.

Ironically, measures such as quotas and exchange controls, which were designed to protect only the landlords, had the unintentional effect of providing a modicum of protection to manufacturers, while failing to bring relief to the many little people in the lower reaches of the agricultural-pastoral sector.

It was also ironic that such relief as these little people—mainly small farmers, tenants, and peons—did receive came from the growing industrial sector through its increasing demand for factory workers and foodstuffs.

In addition to its direct economic effects, this industrial expansion, which continued at an accelerated pace in the forties, played an important part in shaping the social and political, as well as the economic, development of Argentina for many years to come.

DEPRESSION AND RECOVERY

The first casualty of the Depression in Argentina was the country's vitally important foreign trade. In the international market the prices of its grains and meats plummeted at the start and never recovered fully until the Second World War. As a result, imports into Argentina from 1930 to 1934 were little more than half as large as in the preceding five-year period, and remained at the same low level from 1935 to 1939 in relation to the rest of the economy. The decline would have been even greater if the Conservative government, headed from 1932 to 1938 by President (and General) Agustín P. Justo, had not defended the position of the politically powerful beef barons in the vital British market by negotiating the Roca-Runciman Pact with Great Britain. The terms of the pact, which are discussed more fully in another chapter, also strengthened Britain's trade and investment position in Argentina. This was done at some cost to Argentine interests and at heavy cost to the national pride of the many Argentines who regarded the pact as another sellout to British imperialism by the "*vendepatria* oligarchy"— an opprobrious epithet that dates from this period. Throughout the Depression, times continued hard in the agricultural-pastoral sector for all but a favored few, such as the beneficiaries of the Roca-Runciman Pact.

In some other sectors the impact of the Depression was relatively mild and short-lived. In one respect—the growth of industry—it was beneficent. Unemployment figures apparently did not rise more than 5 to 7 percent, and while such figures should be taken with some skepticism, even twice as high a figure would remain below the corresponding one for some other countries, including the United States. Again, the gross national product of Argentina was as large in the worst years of the Depression, 1930-1934, as from 1925 to 1929, when it stood at its all-time peak. What is more, the GNP showed an impressive 17 percent increase from the first to the second half of the 1930s, and continued to rise at almost the same rate in the next lustrum.

Some of the slack in the labor market was taken up by the multiplying factories. From 40,600 in 1935, the number of industrial establishments in Argentina grew to 57,200 in 1940. A corresponding increase took place in the number of industrial workers: from about 450,000 in 1935, it rose to 557,500 in 1939 and 732,000 in 1943. One-third of these establishments and half of the workers were concentrated in hypertrophied Greater Buenos Aires, which by this time contained 30 percent of the total population of Argentina. Most of the establishments were small, but in 1935 the 93 largest plants employed some 90,000 workers, or an average of 1,000 each. Most of the industry was of the consumer-goods, import-substitution type. The largest plants were mills turning out textiles, sugar, flour, and paper, or oil refineries and *frigoríficos* (meat refrigeration plants, which were also slaughterhouses).

This industrial development had a heavy political impact, the chief beneficiary of which was Juan Perón during and after his rise to power beginning in 1943. Some of his most militant *descamisados* came from these slaughterhouses and other plants, and most of his few well-to-do supporters were industrialists.

Another development of the 1930s continued and expanded by Perón was the policy, already referred to, of government intervention in the economy. Before 1930 the established policy had been one described by Argentine writers as *semilibrecambista*, or semifree trade. Roughly, it was a policy of hands off except for occasional essays in helpfulness, as in furnishing aid to immigrants from Europe in order to provide cheap labor for the big landowners, or in making land grants to railroad companies and guaranteeing a minimum return on their investments. The principal controls—over foreign exchange, crops, prices, and banking—were set up in 1933-1935 by a former Socialist, the very able minister of finance, Federico Pinedo. In the same seminal period, the first income and inheritance taxes were imposed, and internal tax barriers to trade were removed by a measure that, in Pinedo's words, "completed the economic unification of Argentina."

The Conservative Restoration even continued and enlarged a government control agency set up by the Radicals. This was YPF (*Yacimientos Petrolíferos Fiscales*), which was created at the end of Hipólito Yrigoyen's first administration in 1922 and given a monopoly of future exploitation of Argentina's petroleum deposits. Its creation constituted the country's first major departure from laissez-faire. Another new departure was the appointment of a military man, Colonel Enrique Mosconi, to head YPF. He made a great success of it and, as we shall see, by the thirties he was propagandizing zealously in favor of a much wider application of the same military-industrial pattern of state intervention in the country's economy. Also by that time YPF had become a symbol of national independence from "bad monopolies" such as big foreign oil companies.

Argentina's industrialists failed to extract from the Conservative Restoration another exception to laissez-faire in the form of a protective tariff on imported manufactures. Though they tried hard, their failure need not surprise us, for politically they were a weak lot. They had been united in a kind of guild organization, the Unión Industrial, ever since 1886, but that seems to have been a loose aggregation of rugged individualists. What is even more to the point, some 70 to 80 percent of them were of immigrant stock and in Argentina, in sharp contrast with the United States, not one immigrant in twenty was naturalized. Consequently, in the political arena they were mere spectators and lacked one of the main incentives to corporate action. In addition, many of them were self-made men of humble origin, who regarded the native landowning aristocracy with a mixture of awe and envy that was a further impediment to the formation of an effective industrial power group. Nevertheless, recent research suggests that in the 1930s they were beginning to exhibit definite corporate features, including a "managerial mentality," and that in the next decade they functioned actively as a pressure group. If so, this should be set down as one of the favorable results of the Depression decade.

In other sectors of the economy, disunity and mutual hostility were more symptomatic. One of the least unexpected
expressions was the campaign launched in 1931 against motor-
ized agricultural machinery by the prestigious Rural Society.
An organized expression of Argentina's largest landowners, the
Society emphasized (while disclaiming any "sentiment of
reactionary nationalism") that importing tractors would put
money in the pockets of foreigners, whereas the use of horses
would keep the money in Argentina, widen the market for
local products such as alfalfa, corn, saddles, and the horses
themselves, and create more jobs. Since the Society had long
benefited from Argentina's traditional commitment to free trade,
the turnabout was a significant indicator of changing moods
within the rural establishment.

On the other hand, the signs within the landed sector by no
means pointed in a single, unambiguous direction. For one
thing, that sector was divided by a rift that widened considerably by the mid-thirties. This was the schism between the small
ranchers of the interior and the big *estancieros* of the Province
of Buenos Aires, which took the form of a battle between the
new Confederation of Buenos Aires and La Pampa, and the
venerable Rural Society. The main point at issue was the effort
by the Confederation to free its members from domination by
foreign-owned meat-packing houses (frigoríficos), an issue
greatly aggravated by the Roca-Runciman Pact. Members of the
Rural Society, favored by the packing houses and beneficiaries
of the pact, could only lose by upsetting the status quo.* Hence
the Society opposed the Confederation's effort—successfully—to
the end of our period.

MIGRATION AND URBANIZATION

The beginning of the Depression was also the beginning of further demographic changes in Argentina, which had already been
revolutionized in this respect since the 1870s. The flood of
immigrants, which had gone on for half a century with little
interruption and had been concentrated mainly in the cities, was
reduced to a trickle in the 1930s, partly because Argentina was

---

*For a fuller discussion of the Roca-Runciman Pact and its provisions as they
pertain to these comments, see chapters 3 and 4. [Eds.]

no longer the land of opportunity and partly because the
government now restricted immigration. As immigration declined,
however, migration from Argentina's own interior provinces to
the cities increased to such proportions that there was no letup
in the process of urbanization that had been going on apace
for half a century. As always, Greater Buenos Aires led the
race by several lengths. By 1936 it was receiving some 83,000
internal migrants each year, and in the next decade the annual
intake rose to 96,000. One result was that the metropolitan
area's foreign-born element, which had stood at the extraordinarily high level of one half the city's total population from
the 1890s to 1914, was cut in half by mid-century, declining
to 36 percent in 1936 and 26 percent in 1947.

All the while, the cityward trend of the nation's population
continued at a steady pace. From 53 percent in 1914, the urban
share rose to 60 percent in 1940, and Buenos Aires continued
to lead the other cities by a wide margin.* Its metropolitan
area contained 2.0 million inhabitants in 1914, 3.4 million in
1936, and 4.7 million in 1947. This was between a third and a
fourth of the nation's total population, which was estimated to
be 13.2 million in 1938. Some of the other cities were likewise
growing rapidly, but none approached Buenos Aires even
remotely in size. The two next largest, Rosario and Córdoba,
had populations only about a sixth and an eighth as large as
the capital city's. The others—old Santa Fe, Tucumán, and
Mendoza, to the north and west; the newer La Plata, down-
river some 40 miles from the capital; and Bahía Blanca, 400
miles to the southwest of it—lagged far behind.

The disparity between Buenos Aires and the other cities,
though enormous, was not surprising, for Buenos Aires was the
country's economic, social, and cultural as well as political
capital. Any good transportation map of the period would
illustrate and help explain its wide margin of primacy: the city
was the principal focus of the country's railway network, which
was the most extensive in Latin America and the seventh largest
in the world; of the country's vitally important seaborne trade;
and of its international air service, which was just getting under

---

*Figures for the 1930s are my estimates. No national census was taken between
1914 and 1947.

way—even in the late thirties, the regular commercial planes still took four days to fly from New York to Buenos Aires.

By this time the city gave the appearance of having completely recovered from the Depression, and it had much to offer to people of all tastes, especially, as in any other modern metropolis, the well-to-do. Along with its unexcelled beef and lamb served in many fine restaurants, its attractions ranged from horse racing in the elegant hippodrome and soccer football on several fields to libraries and museums galore and the nation's chief university, and from the world-famous tango singer Carlos Gardel (heard on radio more than ever after his untimely death in a Colombian airplane crash) to equally famous European opera singers in the city's mammoth opera house.

The streets and buildings of the city suggested by turns Seville and Madrid, in its older quarters; the United States (it even had a district named Nuevo Chicago); and, especially in its center, Paris. There the city on the Plata had in fact been made over since the 1880s in much the same way as the city on the Seine by Baron Haussmann under Napoleon III. Outstanding features of this part of the city were new parks, new buildings, new avenues hacked through old buildings and opening wide vistas, and a considerable degree of architectural harmony, with French Renaissance most in evidence. Also outstanding, and yet typical, was the 120-foot-wide, mile-long Avenida de Mayo, for which block after block of buildings had been sacrificed so that it might run in a straight line from the Palace of Congress (built in 1910, the centenary of independence), to the Plaza de Mayo, where stands the *cabildo,* the colonial government house, in which, official history says, the independence movement began in May 1810. Across the spacious plaza from the cabildo is the Casa Rosada (Pink House), the executive office building, from the balcony of which Juan Perón was in a few years to deliver the first of his many moving speeches to descamisado hosts packed into the plaza below.

LABOR, THE MIDDLE CLASS, SOCIAL CHANGE

Organized in 1930, the General Confederation of Labor (CGT) was to become in the next decade, as it remains today, a major interest and power group in Argentina. Throughout the 1930s, however, it was weak and ineffectual. For one thing, it was small in numbers. Worse still, it was racked by internecine conflicts. The first major conflict arrayed socialists, representing liberal nationalism, against syndicalists, who were apolitical internationalists. The socialists won out in 1935 and, in the same year, in accordance with the Kremlin's Popular Front strategy, the Argentine communists' hitherto separate federation of labor dissolved to join the CGT. But in 1939 the Hitler-Stalin Pact started another internal struggle that by early 1943 had split the organization wide open—just in time to aid, unintentionally, the military coup in early June of that year.

Consequently, throughout the Conservative Restoration the CGT was quite unable to improve the workers' unhappy lot. It could not even protect the basic right to strike, much less keep real wages from sagging in the latter half of the decade, although the Depression was over for most urban Argentines by this time. The smaller unions that remained outside the CGT were no more successful.

Large numbers of internal migrants from the back country entered the urban labor market after 1935, with far-reaching results for the organized labor movement in the next decade. At first the effect was hardly perceptible, for the existing unions paid little or no attention to the newcomers, and the latter couldn't have cared less. Many of them were illiterate peons fit only for unskilled jobs and, coming from the interior where there had been much intermarriage with Indians in colonial times, they were so swarthy that city people looked down on them as *cabecitas negras* and *negritos*. (The myth that there is no racism in Latin America has little if any foundation in most parts of it, and none at all in Argentina.) Moreover, these migrant workers from the back country were xenophobes and brought with them a tradition of *caudillismo* which in this context may be defined roughly as a tradition of "follow the leader." For all these reasons they were, it seems, made to order for Perón's system of regimented labor unions and populist nationalism.

As one writer has put it, the process of social polarization typical of societies in the decisive stage of industrialization was at work in Argentina during this period. The formation of a working class capped the process. Argentina had had an upper class since colonial times and a middle class of substantial size since the turn of the century. By 1930 the middle class was estimated to make up about a third of the population, and the Radical party, which controlled the national government from 1916 to 1930, might be called its political arm. This phrase could, however, easily trap the unwary into forming a very exaggerated notion of the middle class's unity. In fact, as studies by Argentine sociologists since the 1940s have shown, it was not a class at all but an aggregation of disparate groups, ranging from artisans, shopkeepers, and white collar workers just above the proletariat to successful professional and businessmen just below the oligarchy. All of these middle groups had little or nothing in common with one another except that all stood somewhere in the middle ground between the top and bottom layers of Argentine society.

Two facts about the composition of this so-called middle class in the 1930s merit special attention. One is that at that time it was still, as in earlier years, composed largely of persons connected in one way or another with the export-import economy and hence not disposed to challenge the internationally oriented policies that had passed for economic liberalism during the last half-century. This was particularly true of the more conservative minority wing of the Radical party, the Anti-personalists, led in the twenties by Marcelo T. de Alvear. It was less true of the majority wing, the Yrigoyenists, but that had made little practical difference when the Radicals were in power, for although Yrigoyen talked of economic nationalism and indeed made it for the first time a subject of widespread public interest in Argentina, he did not translate it into a program for political action. It was probably just as well that he did not, for such a program could hardly be feasible without a strong interest group to take the lead in framing and promoting it.

The second noteworthy fact about the Argentine middle sectors is that, as already suggested, such an aggregation in its likeliest form, a national bourgeoisie—composed of industrial entrepreneurs and businessmen—had not yet developed far enough during these years to be effective. Something of the kind did emerge later on, but only under quite different circumstances and as a very junior partner in the Perón regime.

Thus was social change intimately bound up with economic and political change in this period. The important social changes that took place during its course have been summarized as follows. Before the Depression, it had not been unusual for skilled workers and members of the middle class to become small proprietors and entrepreneurs, but now the achievement of such independence in an urban economy was no longer possible, save in very exceptional circumstances. In the agrarian sector, the major change was one we have already noted: hard times stimulated large-scale migration to the cities, where the competition of cheap migrant labor not only held industrial workers back but tended to proletarianize the lower fringe of the middle class. In contrast, the fortunate possessors of capital reserves profited at the expense of the needy. As a result, social mobility was curtailed and the structuring of modern social classes in Argentina became definitive; the middle class increased in size, but declined in independence and cohesiveness; and the urban labor force grew in size but not yet in strength and became less foreign and more native in its composition. By the end of the decade the process of polarization typical of societies in the decisive stage of industrialization was well advanced in Argentina.

Of the many details of social change that could be added, one of special interest relates to the institution of the family. Argentina at this time provided an important exception to the current rule of sociology that the family, being an integral part of the traditional society, is necessarily weakened along with it by the process of modernization. In Argentina the very opposite was true of the numerous class of migrant rural workers. As members of the traditional *ganadero* society they had often lived alone for long periods and as a result their sexual unions had been irregular, and illegitimacy was common; but all this changed with the great exodus from rural areas to cities that began in the thirties, for even in the *villas miserias* (shanty-towns) of Greater Buenos Aires—and still more in its working quarters—members of this group began to develop for the first time the orderly, permanent relationship of the family.

EDUCATION, PRESS, RADIO

In Argentina education, press, and radio were established in that order: education in the colonial period, the press at the end of that period and the beginning of the nineteenth century, and radio just after the First World War. In all three categories Argentina stood in the forefront of Latin America during the 1930s.

Concerning education, three points are to be noted. The first is that the great majority of Argentines were at least literate. The literacy rate of 85 percent at the end of that decade—the highest in Latin America except for Uruguay, where it was about the same—had been raised to that level from an abysmal 22 percent in 1869, when the first national census was taken. It is remarkable that so great an improvement had been made in so short a time—only a little more than half a century—and at a time of extraordinarily rapid population increase. The explanation may lie partly in the source of the increase, that is, in the fact the level of literacy was higher among the immigrants than among the creoles, the native Argentines, but it almost certainly lies in the superiority of Argentina's elementary public school system. Again, alone in Latin America except for Uruguay, Argentina had for many years provided universal, compulsory education at that level. Started in the 1860s by Presidents Mitre and Sarmiento, the school system was still based in the 1930s on a law passed in 1884.

The second point to be noted is that, although this school system was democratic for those times, it had been supported from the start by the oligarchy that ruled Argentina down to 1916 and again after 1930. In explanation of this seeming paradox we are told that the oligarchs gave the public school system their support because, and only so long as, it supported their privileged position by, for example, instilling in the children habits of obedience and a patriotism laden with respect for the status quo. Significantly, as soon as Perón changed the character of the educational system to their disadvantage, the upper classes shifted their support from public to private education. In the thirties, however, they still maintained their long-standing mutual assistance relationship with the public system of education.

That system, of course, included the five national universities; and the third and last point to be noted under the rubric of education has to do with Argentina's famous University Reform. Begun at the University of Córdoba in 1918-1919, the Reform had had a great effect before 1930 and was to do so again after 1940, but in the intervening decade it seemed to be in a state of suspended animation. The long hiatus may seem surprising, for the Reform of 1918 was no isolated event, but rather a continuation of a movement that had led to the founding of the University of La Plata in 1909, and it soon took on a left-wing political character that should have guaranteed its high potential for troublemaking for decades to come. Going far beyond strictly academic reforms designed to modernize faculty as well as curriculum, it politicized the universities, identified educational reform with social reform, and squinted at the formation of an anti-imperialist union of the Latin American states. Surely, one might think, there were enough irritants in the 1930s to activate the Reform's troublemaking potential.

That this did not happen can be explained only in part by the fact that the Conservative government took repressive measures. By the admission in 1926 of one of its own leaders, Carlos Sánchez Viamonte, the Reform movement had already bogged down by that time; yet the Conservative Restoration still lay several years in the future. A more likely explanation is that, during the Depression, students who could afford to make a career of university politics were apparently too few to reanimate the Reform; or that malcontents felt that the universities were still the "bulwarks of reaction" that Sánchez Viamonte said they had become again in 1926, and that it would be a hopeless task to try to reform them. In 1932 a National Congress of University Students, in an effort to revive University Reform by broadening it, defined it as inseparable from social reform; but the response was tepid.

The nearest equivalent in the 1930s of the University Reform was FORJA (Fuerza de Orientación Radical de la Joven Argentina), a left-wing youth group of the Radicals, organized in 1935, which was made up mainly of university students and recent graduates. Yet FORJA was not representative of the academic community, for after it first seceded from the Radical party and suffered a schism, the remnant eventually merged with the Peronist movement, whereas most university students as well as faculty were decidedly anti-Peronist. Disunity by this time characterized the academic as well as most other sectors of Argentine society.

Although freedom of the press began to be curtailed in the 1930s, it was still extensive and all branches of the press flourished. The country's newspaper circulation was much the largest in Latin America and from two to three times as large as that of much more populous Brazil and Mexico. On a per capita basis Argentina stood second only to Uruguay, by a narrow margin. By the early forties Buenos Aires alone had twenty-six newspapers, of which nineteen were in Spanish and seven in foreign languages (two each in English, Italian, and German, and one in French). The two oldest, *La Prensa* (1869) and *La Nación* (1870), were also regarded as the best of the lot and as equal in quality to the best in any other country. Both, however, were widely regarded as rather conservative and stuffy, and, as in more advanced countries, the mass circulation newspapers such as *Crítica,* were those tailored to appeal to the masses. For the intellectual elite there were two magazines, *Nosotros* and *Sur,* which enjoyed international esteem. For Catholics a new weekly journal, *Criterio,* offered discriminating guidance, mundane as well as spiritual; while sympathetic to fascism, it denounced nazism and coupled its appeal to nationalism with a summons to social reform that dissociated it sharply from the right-wing nationalism that was building up throughout this decade.

Thanks partly to the Spanish Civil War of 1936-1939 and the outbreak of the Second World War later in the latter year, Argentina's book-publishing business, already well established at the turn of the century, ended the decade in first place in the whole Spanish-speaking world. Newcomers such as the distinguished Spanish publishing house Espasa-Calpe now stood in the forefront, but already there were well-established *porteño* firms, among them Guillermo Kraft, founded in 1864 by German immigrant Wilhelm Kraft and "naturalized" before the end of the century by publishing the works of the great Bartolomé Mitre and other Argentine classics. By 1940 Buenos Aires was setting the pace for Latin America in both the quality and volume of its book manufacture, exporting several million volumes annually, and numbering among its best customers Mexico, which had formerly been Spanish America's leading maker and exporter of books.

The 1930s were the first decade in which radio was a major means of communication from the start. Its rapid spread since the mid-twenties had carried it all over the country within a few years. In small towns as well as big cities even the families too poor to own a receiving set were reached much of the time by broadcasts from uninhibited loudspeakers that were as often located outside, on street corners or plazas, as inside the cafes or shops of their proprietors. One of the principal sending stations was government owned; the rest were commercial. Here was a new instrument, potentially more effective than the printed word, for reaching the hitherto unmobilized masses, who did not at this time participate effectively in any of the country's most important institutions: in the political parties, in the labor unions, or even in the church. There was conscription, but for the draftees army service was hardly what is meant here by effective participation.

THE CATHOLIC CHURCH

Nearly all Argentines have always been Roman Catholics, but in the late nineteenth century secularizing tendencies and anticlericalism throve so greatly that the church's active members were reduced to a small minority, often said to be only 10 or 15 percent. Since about 1900, however, European precept and example had helped to bring about a recovery that reached its peak in the 1930s. It received a great stimulus from the holding of an International Eucharistic Congress in Buenos Aires in 1934, with Cardinal Pacelli—the future Pius XII—in attendance as papal delegate. In the same year a branch of international Catholic Action was established in Argentina; it soon became an important factor in promoting "vocations" (recruitment for the priesthood or religious orders) and spiritual life and social action on the part of laymen, especially the young.

Special study courses and the influence of *Criterio,* already mentioned, helped produce a Catholic elite; a broader popular appeal was made by the extension of the Catholic labor union movement, begun about 1918 and led by Monsignor Miguel de Andrea, titular Bishop of Temnos, while professional men were provided with "guilds" of their own, such as the Consortium of Catholic Physicians, which had its headquarters in Buenos Aires and branches in six provincial cities. The church also intensified its pastoral activity, creating new parishes and dioceses. Outstanding in all this activity was Santiago Luis Copello, born in Argentina in 1880, who studied and was ordained in Rome, returning to Argentina in 1903. He started as assistant rector in La Plata in 1903 and rose steadily in the hierarchy until he was made archbishop of Buenos Aires in 1933 and a cardinal three years later—the first cardinal ever appointed in Argentina, and the second in all South America.

Under the Constitution of 1853 the church was state supported, but as James Bryce commented in 1912, Argentina was, "of all the Spanish-American republics, that in which the church has least to do with politics" and "that freedom of religious worship which is guaranteed by law is fully carried out in practice." All this was still true in the thirties, but an ominous development of those years was a rift among Catholics over the definition of nationalism and the implied shift toward participation in politics. Of course almost all Argentines, including Catholics, had for several decades been nationalists of one kind or another, but now a particularly virulent right-wing form of nationalism made headway and tended to break down the church's apolitical tradition.

A notable representative of this form of nationalism was a secular priest, Father Julio Meinvielle, who in 1932 published his first important book, *A Catholic Conception of Politics.* The book contained violent attacks on toleration and democracy as well as on Yankee imperialism, Jews, and communists, but its most significant feature was its proposal that those "pests and perils" be dealt with by reviving the traditional Hispanic "sword and cross" crusading spirit—that is, by joint political (and, one might infer, military) action by the Catholic Church and the armed forces of Argentina. This same "sword and cross" theme was played up by Colonel Perón in his rise to power in the mid-forties.

ARMED FORCES AND POLITICAL PARTIES

In fact, however, there is reason to believe that in the 1930s less progress was made toward the union of the sword with the cross than with the toga. Stated another way, Argentina's armed forces became increasingly involved in the political arena during these years, whereas no perceptible change took place in the relation of the military to the church, which remained good but showed no gain in fervor or intimacy.

Politics was quite another matter. It has been customary to take the irruption of 1930 as the beginning of a military domination of the political arena which, whether open or concealed, has continued to the present writing. As a rough approximation this view will serve, but it requires qualification and one cannot accept the corollary sometimes added that during the Conservative Restoration military intervention was made inevitable by the entrenched oligarchy's refusal to permit free and honest elections since it could not hope to win them. By closing the door to peaceful change, the argument runs, the oligarchy's refusal left its opponents, who were a majority, no alternative but to resort to force, and that meant invoking the aid of the military, who held a near-monopoly of force.

This explanation is quite misleading, both as to the role of the armed forces in public life and as to the relative responsibility of the government and the opposition parties for magnifying that role. The fact is that the armed forces had played an important part in Argentine politics for many years past, as in the crucial revolt of 1890, and what was new in 1930 was not that they (or, to be more precise, a handful of them) overthrew a particular government, but that this handful then went on to try to change the whole system of government. They failed, but under the sham democracy of the next eleven years, domestic and foreign influences combined to convert the rest of the armed forces (the great bulk of them) to belief in a thoroughgoing revolution. Herein lies the significance of the 1930s as regards their role in bringing about the failure of constitutional, representative government. As for the role of the political parties in that process, the chief significance of the period lies in its mounting evidence that the intervention of the military in politics was chargeable about as much to the urging of opposition party leaders as to the initiative of the armed forces themselves, and that it was perhaps chargeable most of all to the chief opposition party, which was the Yrigoyen wing of the Radical party.

For political as well as other purposes, the armed forces were never a monolithic unit. (By armed forces, we mean the officer corps; the great majority of the enlisted personnel was made up of draftees, was constantly changing, and had no voice in such matters.) Interservice and personal rivalries divided them, as did widely different social backgrounds. Most of the officers were now preponderantly middle class and came of creole and immigrant stocks in nearly equal proportion. The upper class was still well represented and one of the capital city's two most prestigious clubs was the Círculo de Armas (the other was the Jockey Club). So when we talk about the conversion of the armed forces to the cause of revolution, we are not necessarily talking about the whole officer corps, but only about the decision makers in an authoritarian, rank-conscious, and highly diversified organization. Also, our concern here is not with the completion of this process of conversion, which even the coup of June 1943 did not complete, but only with the factors that contributed to it during the 1930s.

One factor was a combination of a widespread and growing sense of need for sweeping changes in Argentina with the likewise increasing confidence of the officers that they were especially well qualified to provide the new technical skills that an industrializing country needed. Already in the 1920s economist Alejandro Bunge and others were warning that Argentina's agrarian economy was not capable of further expansion and must be diversified by a great enlargement of the minuscule industrial sector. Few civilians heeded the warning at that time, but the armed forces were more receptive. This was understandable, for industrialization, they believed, was essential for national defense and would require technical skills developed in army and navy schools, whereas the civilian educational system stressed the humanities, law, and medicine to the neglect of science and technology. Hence the choice of a military man, Colonel Enrique Mosconi, to head the government petroleum agency, YPF, founded in 1922.

Although its subsequent history was less happy, YPF flourished under Mosconi throughout the rest of that decade, and the officer himself, rapidly advanced to general, became a vigorous advocate of the same kind of economic nationalism with respect to other sectors of the economy. His speeches and writings linked the interests of his own military guild with those of the nation at large and the rest of Latin America. In 1929, for instance, he called for the development of industries needed by the armed forces, justifying the call by tying it to national defense and the integration of Latin America as a counterpoise to the influence of Europe and the United States. And in 1936, after a vigorous statement of the same propositions, he cited the case of YPF as proof that "our country has reached the technical and administrative maturity required to organize and conduct with success the most difficult undertakings that characterize the complex economic structure of modern nations."

The other major factor in the armed forces' conversion was a growing sense of their mission to save the country politically. Many circumstances contributed to its growth. For one thing, the decline of the political parties, of which more will be said below, left the military as the only power group in the country with sufficient strength and prestige to rule it. Perhaps even more influential were the antidemocratic currents flowing from countries with which Argentina had strong ties, particularly Mussolini's Italy, Hitler's Germany, and Franco's Spain.

Italy had been the chief source of the massive immigration from 1880 to 1930, and at the end of the 1930s an important military mission, of which Juan Perón was a member, paid it a two-year visit, from which all participants returned much impressed by Mussolini's regime. Germany had developed strong economic as well as military ties with Argentina since 1900. The uninterrupted successes of both countries' aggressions after 1930 made them seem truly the wave of the future. Yet the main result in Argentina was not so much to promote either fascism or nazism there. Rather, among the people at large, it was to breed apathy and multiply defections from democracy. This was already weakened by the shortcomings of democratic leadership abroad as well as at home and was discredited by the contrast between the calamitous depression in the democratic countries and the contemporary and highly publicized success of the Soviet Union's first Five-Year Plan. All this strengthened the German-trained Argentine army's natural bent towards authoritarianism and a nationalism that was primarily Anglophobe because of England's domination of the Argentine economy.

Another stimulus to the army's authoritarian predilection seems to have come from the Mother Country and second-largest source of immigrants, Spain. There, a military dictatorship under General Miguel Primo de Rivera in the 1920s had achieved some success, followed by a disastrous experiment with republicanism and then, from 1936 to 1939, by a bloody civil war. Starting with a military rebellion supported by the Catholic hierarchy, the war ended in the establishment of a military dictatorship under Generalissimo Francisco Franco, which spread abroad a kind of right-wing Hispanicism, called *Hispanidad,* that dovetailed with "sword and cross" conservatism in Argentina.

Argentina was only one of many countries in the Atlantic world in which, during the interwar years 1919-1939, the public lost faith in the whole system of representative republican government. In addition, however, although Argentina's political parties represented a diversity of economic and social interests, they left without effective representation two new, important, and growing groups: labor and the industrialists. As the thirties wore on, the decline of the party system continued.

After 1931, the government parties, united in an uneasy alliance called the *Concordancia,* were originally three: National Democratic, Antipersonalist Radical, and Independent Socialist. Belying their labels, all three were conservative, the first of them most of all. Some of their members were of the "liberal Tory" type, but they were unable to shape party policy. As a result, Argentina passed through the whole of the Depression decade without any equivalent of the social reform legislation adopted at that time by its next-door neighbors, Chile, Uruguay, and Brazil, not to mention the United States with its New Deal.

Moreover, none of the Concordancia's constituent parties had strong popular appeal. The Independent Socialist party, never more than a splinter group, disappeared in 1937. The very name of the Antipersonalist party, which meant anti-Yrigoyen, became meaningless after the deposed chief executive

died in 1933; and to make matters still worse, the Antipersonalist
party's original head, Alvear, then left it to become head of
the main Radical party, which was also the chief opposition
party. As for the National Democratic party, it was so notoriously elitist that the Concordancia had to call on the less
unpopular Antipersonalists for its presidential candidates in both
the national elections of this decade, 1931 and 1937. Even so,
the Concordancia kept itself in power only by systematic
fraud and corruption ("patriotic fraud," its leaders insisted),
with the army in reserve as a kind of Pretorian Guard.

The largest of the opposition parties, the Radicals (officially
the *Unión Cívica Radical,* or simply UCR), had a long record
of trying to involve the military in politics. They had done so
ever since their party began to take shape in the 1890s, stirring
up military revolts when out of power and playing politics
with the armed forces when in power, which was only from
1916 to 1930. The former scenario was repeated from 1931 to
1934, when several military revolts actually took place. All,
however, were small-scale affairs and were soon snuffed out by
loyal troops. After the last of them, Alvear induced his fellow
Radicals to depart from their traditional rule of "abstention
and revolution" when out of power and to resume participation
in all political activities, including elections. To people in other
countries this would seem a thoroughly commendable course,
but measured on a Spanish-American scale of values it shocked
many Argentines besides Alvear's co-religionists as a gross
betrayal of principle. As a result, it deepened the discredit into
which the Radical Party fell, along with all the other parties,
during this decade. A more tangible result was an anti-Alvear
movement of young left-wing Radicals that led to the formation
of FORJA, an intellectual-political cenacle directed to popular
nationalism and the restoration of Radical "intransigency,"
in 1935. As we have already seen, the hard core of FORJA
ended by merging with the Peronist movement, to which it
contributed a number of ideas, including the importance of
collaborating with the armed forces in structuring a new
nationalism and of taking a third position between capitalism
and communism and between rival great powers.

Only two other parties, Socialist and Communist, need be

noticed here, and little more need be said of them than that neither came anywhere near being nationwide in membership or influence. The Socialist party, founded in the 1890s, had always included some of the brightest and best Argentine intellectuals, but it was strong only in Buenos Aires. The much younger Communist party, too, was small and exclusively urban. Among intellectuals it was overshadowed by the Socialists, and although it made some headway with the workers as the decade wore on, it had little or no success with two groups in this sector: the anarchists, who had long been stronger in Argentina than in any other Latin American country, and the migrants from the interior, who responded more readily to the call of a caudillo than to the doctrine of either Marxist party, Communist or Social-ist. For these and other reasons that have been suggested above, we may agree with Argentine political scientist Alberto Ciria that in Argentina the period we are considering marked the beginning of the end of political parties as that term is under-stood in Europe—and, we might add, in the United States.

THE PESSIMISM OF THE PENSADORES

It has been suggested that Argentina's literary world of the 1930s suffered a loss of vitality, a dearth of new talent, an excess of introspection, and a general decline, and that this was connected with Argentina's contemporaneous political decline. The temptation to make such linkages is strong, but they break down in some notable instances, such as the Golden Age of Spanish literature, which coincided with a decline verging on disaster in Spain's political, economic, and military affairs. And while it is true that Argentine writing in the thirties was intro-spective, the term could be used in a favorable sense signifying a perhaps overdue self-appraisal. Even more important, it is no less true that much of this writing was vigorous and seminal, though often irritating to readers with different tastes; that new writers did appear and established writers expressed themselves in new ways; and that while quality is a matter of opinion, leading authorities have attested to the generally high quality of what several of the writers of this decade wrote—which is about as much as can be said of most decades in the history of any country.

In addition, Argentine literature of the 1930s had two salient features that have not been mentioned so far. One was a profound pessimism; the other, a paradoxical combination of a new, bristling kind of nationalism with continued semicolonial dependence on foreign, especially European, thought.

For an expert appraisal of the literature of this decade, as seen in historical perspective, no work could serve us better than Enrique Anderson Imbert's highly esteemed *Historia de la literatura hispanoamericana* (Buenos Aires, 1961). Here we find preferential attention given to four writers active in the 1930s. The first is Ezequiel Martínez Estrada, a poet who had just turned *pensador* and begun a new career as essayist and social critic. His first book in the new vein, *Radiografía de la pampa* (1933), a highly critical "x-ray" examination of the Argentine people, past and present, is described by Anderson Imbert as equal in profundity to D. F. Sarmiento's nineteenth-century classic *Facundo* and is recognized by all as having had a tremendous influence on Argentine writers for decades to come. The second writer is Jorge Luis Borges, "one of the greatest writers of our times," who in 1930, we are told, had just "repented" of youthful literary follies and was beginning to produce the stories and essays on which his fame has come to rest. He is followed by Eduardo Mallea, whom our appraiser describes as "a great novelist" and who likewise had just turned pensador, though without abandoning the novel. Of his *Historia de una pasión argentina* (1937), which was another searching but less gloomy analysis of the Argentine people, the distinguished philosopher Francisco Romero wrote, in his introduction to a 1940 edition of it, that what Descartes's *Discourse on Method* had done for "total reality," Mallea's book did for "the substance of Argentinity." Fourth and finally, Roberto Arlt was a realistic novelist and playwright, most of whose work was done in the thirties. It expressed the frustrated hopes of the Argentine middle class, we are told, and he was still attracting new readers in the 1960s.

To the foregoing should be added at least Raúl Scalabrini Ortiz, whose two major works were published at the end of the 1930s. They do not come under the rubric of literature in the sense of *belles lettres,* for they are exposés of British economic exploitation of Argentina with the collaboration of its own

oligarchy. Yet they are so well written and so richly documented
that they made Scalabrini Ortiz, in the words of a recent
biographer, Mark Falcoff, "one of the most influential intellectual personalities to emerge in the Argentina of the nineteen-
thirties" and an inspiration to nationalists of all varieties,
including Juan Perón. Scalabrini is also entitled to inclusion here
by his first important book, *El hombre que está solo y espera*
(1931), a psychological portrait of the man of Buenos Aires
that has become a minor classic. The "don't get involved"
spirit of the porteño described in it goes far, we are told, to
explain how the military coup of 1930 developed into a national
crisis that seems to have become permanent.

Established writers who continued after 1930 to produce
books of a kind already familiar, and to provoke lively controversy, were Leopoldo Lugones and Manuel Gálvez; but they
had nothing essentially new to say. What was new was the
journal *Sur,* founded in 1931 by Victoria Ocampo, a kind of
Argentine cross between Madame de Staël and Gertrude Stein.
With Borges and Mallea among the members of its editorial
board and José Ortega y Gasset as one of its foreign consultants,
Sur played a leading part in the intellectual life of Argentina
throughout the rest of the decade. Something of the "pure
literature," "art for art's sake" spirit of the preceding decades
still clung to it, and it specialized in introducing the latest
developments in European letters and arts to its readers, but
soon some members of the group, including Borges, began to
promote interest in the literature of ideas and apply these ideas
to a study of Argentine problems.

One of the group in question, Ezequiel Martínez Estrada,
is the outstanding exponent of the pervasive pessimism of this
decade in Argentina. According to Anderson Imbert, himself an
Argentine, the x-ray picture of "our miseries" revealed in
Radiografía de la pampa makes it the bitterest book ever written
in that country. One must admit that a more bitter book about
it would be hard to write. Like his Old Testament namesake,
the prophet Ezekiel, Martínez Estrada spoke to his people with
the voice of doom. Scanning the whole country (not only the
pampa) and its whole history, he found no merit and no hope
anywhere.

Though less extreme in others, pessimism was widespread among Argentine writers at this time. In addition to such obvious reasons as the current economic and political depressions, there were also some very depressing intellectual influences from Europe, to whose literary as well as political and most other fashions the Argentine elite were always highly responsive. At this juncture they were especially attentive to three European writers, all purveyors of gloom: Oswald Spengler, José Ortega y Gasset, and Count Hermann Keyserling.

Spengler, in a book mentioned earlier, had written impressively about the ineluctable decline of all Western civilization, including, of course, Argentina. Ortega, in 1929, shortly after his second visit to Argentina, had published an article about its men (not, he insisted, about its women) under the title "El hombre a la defensiva," or "Man on the Defensive," which, though partly favorable, was also highly critical of them on many grounds, including their lack of discipline, their narcissism (as reflected, for example, in the country's most famous poem, *Martín Fierro*), their technical and professional incompetence, and other traits that made it impossible for a European to communicate with them and also for Argentina to develop economically, despite the "ferocious appetite" of its men for getting on in the world—an appetite so hypertrophied, said Ortega, that economic crises affect the whole life of Argentina in a way that would be incomprehensible in Europe.

Keyserling, a kind of occidental guru who was taken quite seriously by many people at that time, likewise visited Argentina in the late twenties and then damned it in print—a book entitled in English *South American Meditations* was published in Spanish in 1931, just when the Argentines were already reeling from economic and political shocks. "Frenetic and reptilian sexuality" was one of the lesser counts in Keyserling's indictment of them. Perhaps worst of all in the long view, he condemned them without appeal on the ground of something he called the telluric spirit, the spirit of the soil, which, he declared, would never permit their alien European culture to flourish on American soil. Like Ortega, Keyserling complained that he could not even communicate with any South Americans, including the Argentines. Such strictures were particularly galling to most of Argentina's intellectual elite, who prided themselves on being Europeans, not Latin Americans. Keyserling's primitive formula of geographical determinism nevertheless caught on at once and enjoyed a great vogue. It is a key idea in Martínez Estrada's *Radiografía* and was adopted even by writers such as Mallea and Scalabrini Ortiz who did not swallow Keyserling's "meditations" whole.

To be sure, some well-placed Argentines shrugged off this literature of despair and pointed to the brighter side of things, such as their country's quick recovery from the worst of the Depression and the retention of its primacy among Latin American nations. In its annual report for 1938-1939, for instance, the Association of Labor pointed with pride to the contrast between the "social and economic uncertainty" prevailing at the time of its creation in 1918 and the present-day "period of marked social tranquillity." This association, however, was an employers' organization set up by the Chamber of Commerce, the Rural Society, millers, coal importers, and other businesses precisely for the purpose of coordinating and harmonizing labor relations, so that it was hardly a disinterested observer. More convincing was the testimony of the "grand old man" of Argentine Socialism, Alfredo Palacios, who, as late as 1934, could still declaim with vintage 1910 optimism about "our Argentina" as a "generous land" and about the obligation of every Argentine to "be proud of our nationality" for its "pure, idealistic tradition," which "represents the highest and most advanced tendency in the world today."

Yet the widespread mood of anxiety infected even right-wing intellectuals who might have been expected to take heart from the Conservative Restoration. Thus, in 1937 two of them, Manuel Gálvez and Carlos Ibarguren, speaking at the International Congress of PEN Clubs in Buenos Aires, voiced their misgivings in the troubled terms already made familiar by pensadores from other sectors of society. Gálvez complained: "Europeans can hardly imagine how tragic is our loneliness. . . . We Argentines, as well as other Latin Americans, are indebted to foreign culture for our whole intellectual being. . . . We are . . . a modern Babel." And Ibarguren stressed the "world crisis" resulting from the "terrible collapse" of nineteenth-century culture and the "revolt of the masses" (a phrase taken from the title of the recent and already famous book by Ortega y Gasset, who took part in this congress).

How widely the pensadores' pessimism was shared by their fellow countrymen we cannot say without further investigation. That will not be easy, for even the newspapers, which are the most obvious source because they were numerous and addressed to a wide variety of audiences, are of limited value since, as noted above, their formerly extensive freedom of speech was increasingly abridged under the restored oligarchy.

On the other hand, we need have no doubt about the prevalence of disunity in Argentina at the end of the 1930s. Indeed, disunity verging on fragmentation seemed to characterize all sectors of Argentine society and every aspect of Argentine life—labor, agriculture, industry, the armed forces, academic and literary circles, and even the church. One essential ingredient of the old regime—the creoles' acquiescence in the oligarchy's claim to be a natural governing class—had been destroyed by the long-continued flood of European immigrants who rejected it. Now the Depression eliminated another: the long-standing agreement of the great bulk of the Argentine people in favor of the prevailing semifree trade system. Opinions on economic policy now diverged widely and this rift soon developed into an ideological schism that has not yet been healed. Even the once generally accepted "canonical" nationalism (as Martínez Estrada called it) of nineteenth-century Argentine leaders Sarmiento, Roca, and Mitre had now been pushed into the background by competing nationalist sects. One of these, right-wing and aggressive, even succeeded in getting itself recognized by most people as the nationalist group *par excellence;* but such recognition, far from deterring the other sects, served rather to make it easier for them to disclaim any selfish nationalism and present their own variety as simple patriotism.

Periodization by decades is highly artificial, but in the history of Argentina the decade of the 1930s is less so than most, for it began with the first full year of a catastrophic worldwide depression and ended with the outbreak of the most destructive war in history, and both events shook highly sensitized Argentina to its foundations. Perhaps their most notable combined effect was to speed the social fragmentation of that country. The nearest approach to a consensus that remained seems to have been in the widespread belief that the times were out of joint and that, sooner or later, and whether one wanted it or not, a drastic change was bound to come in an effort to set things right. If this belief was not self-fulfilling, at any rate it helped prepare the way for the revolution that was attempted in the next decade.

2.

Political

Developments

MARK FALCOFF and RONALD H. DOLKART

THIRTEEN YEARS, TWO REVOLUTIONS

On September 6, 1930, a column of cadets from the Military
College and a handful of troops from capital garrisons followed
a retired general to the center of Buenos Aires, where to near-
universal acclaim they ousted the government of Radical
President Hipólito Yrigoyen.[1] Whatever their opinions of the
September Revolution, few Argentines then or later doubted
the historic importance of the event. For one thing, it marked
a sharp break with Argentina's pattern of constitutional development, one characterized by a long tradition of civilian dominance.
The great nation of the Plata had not known a military pro-
nouncement in more than seventy years; for nearly as long her
armed forces had abstained from playing an independent role
in the political arena. During the next decade and for many
years thereafter, these armed forces would be either the arbiter
or balance wheel of national politics. In addition, the Revolution
of 1930 restored to power the Conservative party, expression of
the landed elite that had dominated Argentine public life before
the enactment of a law of universal manhood suffrage in 1912.
In order to retain their reconquered terrain, the Conservatives
found it necessary to tamper drastically with the machinery of
a liberal state. Consequently, politics during the thirties and
early forties rested upon a perversion of the very laws that had

once made Argentina famous as the leading democracy of South America. Finally, the Revolution made possible one of those frequent ironies of Argentine history, a somewhat similar military coup on June 4, 1943, which ended the Conservative Restoration and opened the road to power for Colonel Juan D. Perón. Two military revolutions thus bracket a critical transition period, during which Argentina's fragile constitutional advances of the 1920s were utterly destroyed and the stage was set for an upsurge of messianic populism that would forever alter the rules of the political game.

Because this period is so rich in complexities, we propose to unravel it in sections. First, we shall narrate its political history much as it might be comprehended by an intelligent reader of the daily press. Then, in an attempt to explain its motive forces, we shall move back to the twenties, working our way forward to the Revolution of 1930. Finally, we shall examine the governments of 1930-1943 from the perspectives both of their strengths and of their weaknesses. And in our conclusion we have suggested those factors which during the thirties prepared Argentina for the political transformations of later years. At the end of this chapter we present a chronological list of the events we shall refer to in this discussion.

The leader of the September Revolution and the new Provisional President was Lieutenant General José F. Uriburu, scion of the Salta oligarchy, nephew of a turn-of-the-century Argentine president, and, most recently, Inspector-General of the Army. Although in temperament and outlook utterly unlike the men who ruled Argentina before 1930, Uriburu was no stranger to national politics. He had participated in the first of many attempts by what later became the Radical party to come to power by force in 1890, and although he thereafter professed his distaste for politicians, in 1913 he had been persuaded to serve a term in the Argentine parliament as a Conservative deputy for his home province. During the twenties he was a prime candidate for War Minister and lost this most coveted of service posts only because President Marcelo T. de Alvear was dissuaded by French military authorities from appointing a man of pronounced and public Germanophile tendencies. In March 1929, shortly after Yrigoyen's triumphant return to power, Uriburu retired from the Army to devote himself full-time to conspiracy against the government.

The movement that coalesced around the general was a curious marriage of old and new elements in Argentine politics. It drew support from the traditional parties of the right, particularly the Conservatives and the Antipersonalist wing of the Radical party, both of which had been defeated at the ballot box in 1928 but remained unwilling to accept six more years of rule by the aging Yrigoyen. For them Uriburu's family connections and his prestige in the military held out the prospect of a rapid and successful coup, followed by an equally rapid return to some nebulously defined "normality." But it also included those "new" forces of militarism, fascism, and nationalism at work in the Argentine army, press, and intellectual circles, as well as some sectors of the Roman Catholic clergy. These people regarded Uriburu not merely as an expedient but as a Man of Destiny—a creole Mussolini who would not only end the Radical era of Argentine history, but completely reorder the political system itself. For some time before the Revolution, General Uriburu was known to frequent the editorial offices of two right-wing nationalist dailies, *La Fronda* and *La Nueva República.* His closest ideological mentor was Leopoldo Lugones, one of Argentina's most distinguished men of letters, who since 1924 had been announcing to all who would listen that the "hour of the sword" had struck in Argentine history. As the economic crisis of 1929-1930 deepened, and the incapacity of Yrigoyen to meet it became more apparent, the conspiracy of old and new right was joined by the center and the center-left: by the Independent Socialists, the Progressive Democrats, and—at the end—by both the Socialist party and the students at the University of Buenos Aires.

With so broad a base of support, Uriburu found it easy to topple the Yrigoyen government. But to rule with such a coalition proved impossible, not least because the general was completely uninterested in doing so. He had originally planned his revolution as an exclusively military movement, aimed not just against the Radicals but against the parliamentary system and political parties. It was his intention, once in power, to effect fundamental changes: to repeal the law of universal suffrage, to replace the Congress with a Chamber of Corporations in the Italian fashion, and to substitute a board of "apolitical administrators" for the cabinet. In the fashion of the day, he argued that representation by economic function rather than by numbers would "bring [the] institutions of the nation into harmony with its living socio-economic forces"; talkative lawyers and politicians would be replaced by the "true representatives" of Argentina—spokesmen for land, industry, labor, the clergy, and the military.[2] So central was this conception to Uriburu's thinking that he was persuaded to include leaders of the traditional parties in the movement only after former War Minister General Agustín P. Justo assured him that this was the precondition for full support of the Argentine army.

During seventeen months as Provisional President, Uriburu made few converts to his cause. For one thing, his cabinet was far from the promised team of "apolitical administrators": most of its members were Conservatives exhumed from pre-1916 governments; the aroma of mothballs was strong in the Casa Rosada. For another, the President's deteriorating health and the enormous press of day-to-day tasks left him without energy to pursue a nationwide campaign of constitutional reform. His heavyhanded response to opposition—the liberal use of torture, exile, and arbitrary arrest—aroused unexpected sympathy for the deposed Radicals and provoked growing hostility to the humorless general himself. And finally, he was outflanked by the Conservatives and their allies in the revolutionary camp, who as professional politicians were decidedly unenthusiastic about his constitutional projects. They believed, moreover, that Yrigoyen and his followers had been so thoroughly discredited in office that it was now possible to contemplate elections for the first time in many years with a reasonable hope of victory. It was with this in mind that they and General Justo, their closest ally in the armed forces, pressured Uriburu to convoke elections in the Province of Buenos Aires on April 5, 1931.

The results astounded both the regime and its allies: the Yrigoyen wing of the Radical party, beneficiary of a generalized disillusionment with the outcome of the Revolution, won a resounding victory. In profound embarrassment Uriburu annulled the results and cancelled further ballotings scheduled in Córdoba, Santa Fe, and Corrientes—which in turn unleashed a three-year wave of subversion and abortive uprisings by Radicals in those provinces. At the same time, the Conservatives, now disabused of the notion that Yrigoyenism had been liquidated as a political force, scurried about to salvage what they could of the Revolution. The solution they devised amounted to a working alliance with the Antipersonalist Radicals, a coalition thereafter known as the *Concordancia*. Under the terms of the agreement, in each successive election the latter—presumably the more "popular" of the two—would provide the presidential candidate, while the Conservatives, now rechristened the *Partido Demócrata Nacional* (PDN), would provide the running mate and the finances. Joint slates would be drawn up for congressional and provincial elections.

TABLE 1

Elections of 1928

Party	Candidate	Popular vote
Radical Civic Union	Hipólito Yrigoyen	838,583
Radical Civic Union/ Antipersonalist*	Leopoldo Melo	414,026
Socialist Party	Juan B. Justo	64,985
Progressive Democrats	Lisandro de la Torre	14,173

*The UCR/Antipersonalist ran as the "Frente Único," with tacit Conservative support. The Conservatives did not present a candidate in 1928.

Source: Alfredo Galletti, *La política y los partidos* (México-Buenos Aires, 1961), p. 48.

In reality neither party could count upon a truly broad base of mass support. In the 1928 elections (see table 1) the two combined did not amass 35 percent of the votes, and the Antipersonalists lost much of their constituency when Alvear himself rejoined the parent wing of the Radical party in 1931. Consequently, systematic recourse to fraud and force was necessary in order to establish and maintain the Concordancia in power, together with the occasional use of exclusions and interventions where the instruments of falsification appeared inadequate. In the 1931 presidential elections, for example, fearful of more setbacks, the Provisional Government vetoed the proposed Radical ticket of Alvear-Güemes, seizing upon the excuse that the former president was ineligible, since a full six years had not elapsed since the close of his term in 1928. The Radicals responded by returning to their historic (pre-1916) tactic of abstention, a policy which relieved the Concordancia of a serious challenger at the ballot box until 1935, when Alvear returned the party to a policy of active, if largely ineffective, participation.

The apparent beneficiaries of Radical abstention from 1931 to 1935 were the Socialists and Progressive Democrats, each of which gained additional seats in parliament in the 1931 elections. But, of course, it was the Concordancia that profited most, for by voluntarily removing themselves from the political stage the Radicals vastly simplified the tasks of the regime, and by their willingness to continue participation, the Socialists and the Progressive Democrats (who ran a joint presidential ticket in 1931), gave the entire system a patina of pseudolegality that allowed many Argentines and not a few foreign observers to believe that the country had been restored to constitutional normality.

Nothing nourished the illusion of business as usual so much as the Concordancia's presidential choice, General Agustín P. Justo. For although a veteran of more than thirty-five years of military service, and possessed of immense prestige within the armed forces, Justo was the most civilian of Argentine soldiers. As a young lieutenant he had attended night classes at the University of Buenos Aires, from which he received his engineering degree in 1903. After a brief tour as professor of mathematics at the Military College, he became director of that institution, a post which he held for eighteen years until appointed War Minister by President Alvear in 1922. An ardent bibliophile with a deep interest in Argentine history, over the years he had accumulated one of the finest private libraries in the country. Moreover, unlike Uriburu but like most Argentine army officers, Justo came from a middle-class family, one with strong political interests. A distant cousin had founded the Argentine Socialist party, and Justo's father had been both a congressman from and governor of Corrientes province; the general himself had been a member of the Radical party since

the turn of the century, and by the mid-twenties was firmly
identified with its Antipersonalist wing. During his term at the
War Ministry (1922-1928), Justo had occasion to deal with the
Argentine parliament on military matters, and his contacts with
some of the leading political figures of the twenties served as
the basis for many a shrewd decision during the next decade.

Two of Justo's characteristics attract the attention of the
historian, and go far to explain the extraordinary success of his
political career. One was his deceptively banal appearance—bald,
heavy-set if not obese, he possessed a full face offset only by
rimless glasses and an almost-invisible white mustache. Self-
possessed, kindly, even grandfatherly, he looked not like a
military caudillo so much as a shopkeeper in his lodge uniform.
This placid exterior masked a combination of tenacity and
strategic skill whose effect on political opponents could be
utterly lethal. The other characteristic was a total mastery of
the art of duplicity and dissimulation. There are many who have
seen the downfall of General Uriburu in terms of advice offered
in bad faith by Justo—of which the 1931 elections in the
Province of Buenos Aires is the most frequently cited example.
But perhaps Justo's principal achievement was to lure the
Radicals into playing the role of a loyal opposition once the
Concordancia was firmly established in power. Having benefited
from Radical abstention during his period of maximum vulnerability, Justo in 1935 turned to exploit UCR participation by
promising his old chief Alvear that sooner or later, honest
elections would be resumed. The promise was never fully kept,
but it was sufficient to divide the Radical party by sustaining
the appetite of its professionals and drowning out the protests
of its younger members who favored more violent approaches
to power. In a word, Justo was the perfect leader and symbol
for a profoundly cynical age.

If the principal motif of these years was the restoration of
political order, the two contrapuntal themes were political
violence and political alienation. The first was manifested not
only by the brutalities of the Revolution of 1930, but by
repeated incidents of assault and occasionally murder, perpetrated either by underworld elements unofficially allied to the
PDN or by nationalist "shock" groups. The most spectacular

example was the assassination in 1935 of Senator-elect Enzo
Bordabehere of Santa Fe on the floor of Congress while his
colleague—and the intended target—Senator Lisandro de la Torre
was in the midst of an extended exposure of the government's
collusion with British and American meat-packing houses. The
subsequent revelation that the gunman was a free-lance thug in
the service of one of the Conservative caudillos of Buenos Aires
was disquieting, but not really surprising, for behind its facade
of bourgeois legality the regime held in reserve an entire
repertoire of strong-arm tactics in the event less drastic measures
proved wanting. As conventional political protest increasingly
stood revealed as something of an academic exercise, a climate
of hopelessness and alienation overtook the general public, and
especially that bellwether of the future, the university generation,
for whom extremist ideologies acquired an unwonted appeal.[3]
That alienation, of course, assumed passive as well as active
forms, and during the thirties both were much in evidence. Many
voters probably resigned themselves to the Concordancia out
of a sense of political fatigue—out of a desire, that is, to end
the constant political turbulence identified with Radical rule
in the twenties. And the economic crisis, which pushed many
sensitive and thoughtful people to the left, drove at least as
many more to seek shelter in the familiar—an especially powerful
trend in a country with so large an imperiled middle class. Thus
for much of the period it was unclear whether the growing
alienation of the masses would undermine the regime or whether
the conservatism of despair might sustain it indefinitely.

   Justo himself professed a lack of interest in such matters, but
they were of profound concern to his handpicked successor,
Roberto M. Ortiz, who as the Concordancia candidate "defeated"
Alvear in the presidential elections of 1937. To be sure, nothing
in Ortiz's background suggested that his presidency would be
marked by new departures. The son of Basque immigrants and
a member of the Radical party since his student days, he served
during the 1920s as Alvear's Minister of Public Works and
subsequently acquired a considerable fortune as legal counsel
to the British railroads in Argentina. In 1931 he threw in his
lot with the Concordancia rather than with the reunified Radical
party, and from 1935 to 1937 was Justo's Finance Minister.

Yet, unlike Justo, Ortiz was deeply apprehensive of an increasingly embittered and cynical electorate. His purpose once in power was to blunt the more vocal and active sources of alienation by eliminating fraudulent balloting practices, thus providing an outlet for popular grievances rather than allowing them to accumulate and, he thought, ultimately explode into a revolution.

Ortiz made his first move in this direction a month after assuming office by directing a letter to the governor of La Rioja, ordering him to assure the integrity of upcoming provincial elections. At first this was regarded as a pro forma gesture to placate the recently cheated Radicals, but when a few months later the President used the power of federal intervention to annul the results of a rigged balloting in San Juan and sent special federal missions to Santiago del Estero and Catamarca, his intentions were clear. Then in March 1940, Ortiz took the decisive step of intervening in the Province of Buenos Aires, where Conservative Governor Manuel Fresco had just presided over what was possibly the most corrupt election in its history. This move provoked a serious cabinet crisis; two Conservative ministers resigned, and a few days later, the expected occurred: in congressional elections held in eleven provinces, the Radicals won 76 seats to the 73 of the Concordancia. When combined with other nongovernment parties, the Radicals had an opposition majority of 85, and for the first time since 1930 the Casa Rosada found itself facing a hostile Chamber of Deputies. In the ranks of the Concordancia there was much bitterness, for the man they had placed in office was systematically destroying a laboriously fashioned political machine; conversely, the Radicals were euphoric at the prospect of a return to power after nearly a decade in the wilderness.

The hopes raised by Ortiz were dashed in mid-1940, when the President, sick with diabetes and steadily losing his vision, was forced to take an extended leave of absence for reasons of health and to delegate the executive power to Vice-President Ramón S. Castillo, an unreconstructed Conservative whose political notions predated the Sáenz Peña era. Castillo did his best to undo what Ortiz had accomplished. He appointed a new cabinet and began intervening in province after province to ensure Conservative victories: "interventors," that is, federal agents of the President, were sent to Santa Fe, Mendoza, San Juan, and Buenos Aires. In a matter of weeks it was clear that the "patriotic fraud"—as its advocates referred to it—would remain the unvarying standard of the regime.

Fate and Castillo conspired to prevent Ortiz from consummating his plan, but the Concordancia was never the same again. When in August 1940 Ortiz offered from his sickbed to resign over a scandal involving the sale of lands in the Province of Buenos Aires, it was the Radicals and the Socialists in Congress who defended him against the attacks of his erstwhile supporters, and in February 1941 the ailing chief executive publicly broke with Castillo over both domestic and foreign policy. By the time of his death in July 1942, the government had ceased to be a coalition of two parties and had become—in the words of the new President—"a unanimity of one."

During the thirty-six months that Ramón S. Castillo presided over Argentina, politics, even in the limited sense of the term, gradually ceased to exist. On the pretext of "wartime conditions" —although of course the country was not at war with anyone— the republic was placed under long periods of a state of siege, which the executive interpreted as allowing him to ban meetings, censor publications, and dissolve deliberative bodies. When confronted with juridical arguments to the contrary, Castillo, former dean of the Buenos Aires Law School, dryly replied, "If laws are lacking, there will be no shortage of decrees."

Yet his government was not toally unpopular. By steadfastly refusing to be drawn into the world conflict—and by abrasively rejecting United States efforts to involve Argentina in a program of hemispheric defense—Castillo won qualified applause from sectors of the public normally given over to the opposition. And by nationalizing the municipal gas company in the Federal Capital and the port of Rosario, by beginning the Argentine merchant marine, and by cracking down on speculation in articles of prime necessity, he convinced himself—and probably some others—that his, at least, was a Conservative government that pursued a nationalist line.

In reality, Castillo was less a nationalist than a Conservative; otherwise, his term might not have been truncated by a military

revolt. But in early 1943 he made it clear that in the forthcoming elections, the official presidential candidate would be
not an Antipersonalist Radical, but the Conservative President
of the Argentine Senate, Robustiano Patrón Costas. In so doing,
Castillo had selected one of the least popular figures in the
republic, for in style and substance Patrón Costas was the
quintessential Argentine oligarch. Reputed to own all that was
worth owning in Salta province, he was at any rate its greatest
landlord and the chief stockholder in its sugar industry. To
those who knew the Argentine Northwest, his name represented
"traffic in Bolivian Indians, the shipping of peons in cattle cars,
the company stores that kept laborers perpetually in their debt,
the poverty, the filth, the disease that were the price of great
individual fortunes."[4] Moreover, Patrón Costas had long been
connected with Standard Oil in Salta and was widely believed
to harbor pro-Allied sentiments in the world conflict. For those
who anticipated an imminent Axis victory, or who simply
regarded neutrality as the touchstone of patriotism—many of
them wearing the uniform of the Argentine army—Castillo's
choice was totally unacceptable. And to those nationalist groups,
such as FORJA, that were both anti-Conservative and anti-
interventionist, Patrón Costas was a superexploiter who was also
a stooge of Anglo-American imperialism—a target too good to
be true.

Patrón Costas' liabilities aside, by designating a Conservative
as his successor, Castillo shattered the remnants of the Concordancia and sent many disappointed Antipersonalists knocking
on the doors of the parent Radical party. For a brief period
after the death of Alvear in 1942 it appeared as if the Radicals
would yield to the approaches of General Justo, until death too
overtook him in 1943. Thereafter the Radicals began secretly
treating with members of Castillo's cabinet. On the eve of the
Revolution of June 4, 1943, the President angrily confronted
his War Minister with evidence that he was conniving at a coup
with the opposition. The officer in question, General Pedro
Pablo Ramírez, vociferously denied the accusation, but a few
days later drove the President and several of his ministers out of
the Casa Rosada, ending not merely a government but an entire
era of Argentine history.

THE ROOTS OF THE CRISIS: A LOOK BACKWARD

Hipólito Yrigoyen's overwhelming victory in the 1928 elections and the massive outpouring of public grief at his funeral in 1933 have often been cited by Radical or pro-Radical historians to suggest the "unnatural" aspects of the Revolution of 1930. In the most commonly received version, any government enjoying such high marks of public favor simply *could not* have been overthrown except through outside intervention; hence, the Uriburu movement is habitually laid at the door of the Standard Oil Company, whose properties were threatened with national-ization by a bill pending at the time in the Argentine Senate. Apart from the fact that there is scant evidence to support it,[5] this interpretation of events conveniently glosses over some fundamental weaknesses of the Radical party, many of which had developed during the previous decade and became especially acute under the crisis conditions of 1929-1930.

Although from the First to the Second World War most Argentines regarded themselves as Radicals, a unified Radical party had ceased to exist as early as 1924. In that year President Marcelo T. de Alvear, Yrigoyen's chosen successor, broke with his onetime patron and sponsored the founding of a rival branch of the party known as the Radical Civic Union/Antipersonalist. By "Antipersonalist" Alvear unmistakably meant "Anti-Yrigoyen," for he deeply resented attempts by the older man to control the government once he was out of office. Again, Radical historians make much of supposed policy differences between the two men, and yet here too there seems little reason to accept their views. For the divergences—such as they were—were ones more of style than of substance. Yrigoyen was in many ways a nineteenth-century caudillo in modern dress. He regarded loyalty as the most important qualification for high office, and during his two presidencies the administration was full of deserving unknowns. An autocrat with messianic delusions, Yrigoyen chafed under constitutional restrictions and kept the provinces continually in turmoil by quarreling with and often by deposing their duly elected authorities.

Alvear's approach to government was far more pragmatic and legalistic. A son of the highest porteño aristocracy, his one breach with his class had been his marriage in 1906 to a Portuguese opera singer—an aberration which was quite forgiven by the time he reached the Presidency. Although a man of thoroughly democratic sentiments, Alvear nonetheless preferred the company of men of his own background, and most of his cabinet ministers were recruited from the *Círculo de Armas,* the Jockey Club, and the Rural Society.[6] At the same time, during many years of residence in France he had developed a deep respect for parliamentary government and for the traditions of conservative liberalism, and his presidency resembled less a middle-class revolution than a constitutional monarchy.

Alvear's refusal to take orders from his former chief and his division of the Radical party led Yrigoyen and a host of disappointed office seekers to regard him as an apostate, while for Conservatives, more moderate members of the middle class, and several provinces resentful of Yrigoyen's interference in their internal affairs, Antipersonalism became the tolerable version of Radicalism. A direct confrontation between the two dispensations on the electoral battlefield in 1928 did nothing to heal the breach; after a resounding victory the Yrigoyenists were in no mood for conciliation with the schismatics, and the latter were sufficiently displeased with the results of the contest to connive at revolution with the Conservatives and the Army in 1930.

The overthrow of Yrigoyen was greeted with relief, then, by at least a third of those Argentines who responded to the Radical label. From Paris, where he was serving as Ambassador to France, Alvear hailed the coup as an utter necessity, for, he said, "Yrigoyen, with an absolute ignorance of all aspects of democratic government, seemed almost to take pleasure in defaming our institutions."[7] Yet when he returned to Buenos Aires in early 1931, Alvear became immediately aware that the September revolutionaries had no intention of restoring Argentina to constitutional democracy. Encouraged by the ailing Yrigoyen, a few weeks later he called for a reunion of the two branches of the Radical family. Most of the rank-and-file responded, but many of the leading figures of Antipersonalism joined the Concordancia, and at any rate between 1931 and 1934 Alvear and other Radical leaders spent much of their time in political detention camps because of their inability to restrain revolutionary elements of the party from trying to return to power by force. When Alvear revoked the policy of abstention in 1935, he came under fire from younger Radicals for compromising with a fraudulent regime; yet "abstention and revolution" had proved an utterly sterile tactic, although of course the kind of participation that was possible under Justo was not very productive either. The point is that for much of the thirties Alvear and the greybeards of Radicalism had to spend nearly as much time beating off challenges from the Young Turks of their own party as they did fighting the Concordancia, and by 1940 there were already signs of further schisms. FORJA split off in the latter part of that year to join right-wing nationalists and later enter the ranks of Peronism, while Arturo Frondizi and Moisés Lebensohn were laying the foundations of what later became the Radical Civic Union/ Intransigent. Thus a continual propensity to divide, first manifested in the twenties, rendered Radicalism far more vulnerable in the crisis of 1929-1930 than it would otherwise have been and enervated much of its attempt at a political comeback in the thirties and early forties.

The fact that it was the Argentine army that ejected the Radicals from power in 1930, and, as a principal factor in the political equation throughout the decade, prevented them from regaining it, has led some to regard the UCR as the first victim of what subsequently became the endemic Argentine disease of militarism. Yet the Radicals' dilemma was much of their own making, and here too, the roots of the problem lay in the 1920s and before.[8] For fifteen years after the party's founding in 1892, the Radicals expected to come to power through a revolution, for which purpose Yrigoyen was a frequent visitor at the barracks of potentially dissident regiments of the Argentine army. The abortive Radical revolts of 1893, 1897, and 1905 were all effected with the active participation of army officers, even though a regulation made such activities punishable by immediate discharge. By the time Yrigoyen came to power in 1916 a considerable body of officers had been cashiered in the cause of Radicalism, all of whom were promptly rewarded by legislation that classified their revolutionary activities as "service

to the nation." The officers in question were immediately restored to the ranks and, what is more, were placed on promotion
lists ahead of their less political contemporaries. Yrigoyen's
desire to reward his military partisans posed a serious threat to
the merit system of the Argentine army and constituted a sharp
setback to a tradition of professionalism that had been steadily
growing under the last Conservative administrations. Officers of
professional commitment and standing viewed these moves with
alarm, as they did the tendency to devote an increased military
budget not to armaments and training facilities, but to salaries,
fringe benefits, and pensions to widows and orphans of expired
Radical revolutionaries.

Nor did professionally minded elements in the Army appreciate Yrigoyen's frequent use of their troops for federal interventions in the provinces. Apart from the fact that these officers
saw no reason why the military should be used to make the
interior safe for pliant Radical politicians, they objected to the
diversion of time, energy, and funds from more worthy projects,
such as the training of conscripts. Alvear and his War Minister,
Colonel Agustín P. Justo, put an end to such practices from
1922 to 1928, but the triumphant return of Yrigoyen in the
last-named year presaged their resumption. And in fact on the
eve of the September Revolution, elections scheduled in the
provinces of Mendoza and San Juan, which would determine the
party that would control the Argentine Senate, seemed ready-
made for federal intervention. There was no reason to doubt
that if the result were unfavorable to Yrigoyen, the Army would
be pressed into service. Thus many elements within the military
could support the overthrow of the Radical caudillo not in
terms of abandoning a commitment to civilian supremacy, but
in terms of restoring military-civil relations to their proper
balance. And the same officers could contemplate the continued
use of force, at least during the early thirties, to prevent a
Radical return.

For all its promises to settle scores with the "oligarchy," for
all its committees and conventions, its newspapers and cadre
training schools, Radicalism was from its inception a thoroughly
personalistic political movement. First under the party's founder
Leandro N. Alem (1842-1896), then under his nephew and

successor Hipólito Yrigoyen, the Radical party abjured programs to wait upon the inspiration of a single man. Although the personality cult did not prevent it from capturing and retaining power for fourteen years, it was the principal cause of the schism of 1924. A generalized prosperity and nearly uninter-rupted success at the ballot box throughout the twenties allowed many Radicals to overlook their party's failure to evolve into a more modern political structure, but during the crisis of 1929-1930 one-man rule exacted a fatal price. General Uriburu may have been exaggerating when he told a journalist in 1932 that "in the situation that prevailed immediately prior to the Revolution we were moving headlong towards an abyss with only a few more days to go,"[9] but Yrigoyen's second presidency was an undisputed disaster.

Sustained in earlier years by an exceptional vigor and force of character, the Radical leader returned to power in 1928 over seventy-six years old and probably senile. Even his sympathetic biographer admits that the machinery of state all but ground to a halt for more than two years. Decrees remained unsigned and bills unpaid, while the President, ensconced in the innermost recesses of the Casa Rosada, held audiences for everyone from astrologists to society ladies.[10] Yrigoyen's inability to oversee personally the administration in all its aspects led, we are told, to an unprecedented orgy of pilfering and corruption on the part of his collaborators.[11] Moreover, from the end of 1929 the country was in the grip of a severe economic crisis, and measures from the presidential palace were singularly lacking. Unemployment grew and strikes increased. The President refused to see his own ministers, refused to believe that a military plot was underway, or that if it were, it would succeed. Once it was unmistakably clear that Yrigoyen was doomed, the desertions began; several members of his cabinet solicited posts from the rebels, and even the Vice-President was hoping to jump on the revolutionary bandwagon! The collapse of the regime hard on the heels of Yrigoyen's personal decline seemed to suggest that there was no Radical *party* at all, and in a way this was indeed the case.

From late 1930 to 1933 Yrigoyen spent most of his time as a political prisoner, first on an Argentine warship in the Río de la Plata estuary, and then on Martín García Island. Early in his confinement he designated Marcelo de Alvear his political successor, and from Yrigoyen's death in 1933 the former became supreme chief of the movement—and the cycle began again. While less authoritarian than his departed chief, Alvear lacked something of his undisputed moral stature. Nonetheless, from 1931 to his death some ten years later, he was able to make most of the party's major decisions himself, including the most controversial of all—that lifting electoral abstention in 1935. After his disappearance there was no obvious successor, and the party went searching along improbable paths—first, as mentioned above, to its old persecutor General Justo, and then to the service ministries of the Castillo administration. What was significant was that during fifty years of existence as a political movement, Radicalism had been dominated by three men— Yrigoyen for thirty-six years!—and that with the passing of Alvear, the party was utterly headless. Equally significant were the costs and consequences of the latter's stewardship during the final years of this period. For whatever his personal virtues— and they were many—crisis management was not precisely one of his specialties. In reality Alvear never fully grasped the socio-economic realities and the changed international situation which were the essence of the thirties. And so, persisting in well-worn routines—which were the only ones he knew—he led the Radical party from disaster to disaster. In the process he was unwittingly responsible for an entire generation of young men—embittered, cynical, contemptuous of constitutional procedures and prepared to accept far more drastic solutions than those advanced by his successors. Small wonder that so many of the Radical hosts passed into the ranks of Peronism in the next decade.

THE STRENGTHS OF THE RESTORATION

The Conservatives obtained a second round in Argentine history thanks not only to the limitations of their rivals, but to assets intrinsic to the class they represented. For whatever one may think of the actual policies pursued, during the thirties Argentina was better governed *from a purely technical point of view* than ever before. To say that the Concordancia had a monopoly of political talent perhaps overstates the case, but the leading figures of the period were men of uncommon ability. This was particularly true in the Finance Ministry, where Alberto Hueyo and then Federico Pinedo, assisted by a team which included Raúl Prebisch and Félix Weil, enacted the first Argentine income tax, converted the foreign debt, imposed a system of exchange control, federalized excise taxes, and reorganized the nation's credit and banking system. In general most of the ministers of the Concordancia possessed wide experience in both business and government, in contrast to the deserving unknowns favored with major appointments during Yrigoyen's two presidencies.

Although as yet we have no studies on public administration during this period, impressionistic evidence suggests a marked improvement in the quality of the bureaucracy.[12] Again, given the social bases of the parties concerned, this is logical. For the Radicals, all political issues ultimately reduced themselves to questions of patronage, and during their years of opportunity they had overloaded government offices with the party faithful. The hallmarks of Radical administration had been—and given the size of the party, had to be—a constant multiplication and division of sinecures that rendered the government service ever more costly and unproductive. With a far smaller constituency to satisfy, the Conservatives could afford both to streamline the bureaucracy and to amply reward their followers with the spoils of office. And here too, their appointees were generally a cut above the lawyers-without-clients who constituted much of the rank and file of the Radical movement.

This much said, it must be admitted that much of the strength of the government coalition derived simply from the confusion and disarray that prevailed among the forces of the opposition. The only party large enough to aspire realistically to power was the Radical Civic Union, yet rent with the internal divisions discussed above, and led by men long past their prime, it was incapable of making an effective assault on the citadels of authority. The other parties, the Progressive Democrats and the Socialists, were simply too small and too limited in geographical influence to do anything more than criticize, a task they performed with signal distinction. Although a combination of the three might have presented a formidable challenge to the regime, a traditional Radical repugnance for coalitions ruled this out as a practical possibility. Moreover, by the 1930s relations between the UCR and its rivals had been hopelessly poisoned by the vicissitudes of political life. The Progressive Democrats had been formed out of an early split within the UCR, and their leader, Senator Lisandro de la Torre of Santa Fe, nourished a lifelong hatred of Yrigoyen that manifested itself in support of the Revolution of 1930. Disillusioned with the results of that movement, de la Torre ran unsuccessfully as the Presidential candidate of the Civil Alliance (in coalition with the Socialists and with unofficial support from some Radicals) in the 1931 elections (see table 2), and after several years of further disappointments, he committed suicide in 1938. His disappearance not only deprived the Progressive Democrats of their only possible leader, but left the opposition forces in Congress without one of their most eloquent tribunes.

TABLE 2

Elections of 1931

Party	Candidates	Popular vote
Concordancia		
UCR/Antipersonalist	Agustín P. Justo	
Partido Demócrata Nacional	Julio A. Roca, Jr.	606,626
Civil Alliance		
Progressive Democrats	Lisandro de la Torre	
Socialist Party	Nicolás Repetto	487,955
Radical Civic Union	In abstention	————

Source: Alfredo Galletti, *La política y los partidos* (México-Buenos Aires, 1961), p. 99.

The Socialists, too, represented an early break-off from the Radical trunk, and for two decades before 1930 they had competed with the latter for the working-class constituency of metropolitan Buenos Aires. Although their support of the September Revolution was more tentative than that of the Progressive Democrats, their willingness to profit from Radical abstention from 1931-1935 was the source of endless recrimination. With much bitterness the Radicals pointed out, quite rightly as Table 3 illustrates, that most of the Socialist seats in Congress (and for that matter, those of the Progressive Demo-

TABLE 3

Congressional Gains and Losses of the Socialist,
Progressive Democratic and Radical Parties from 1928 to 1938

Year	Deputies Socialist Party	Deputies Progressive Democrats	Deputies UCR
1928	2	1	87
1932	43	14	—
1935*	42	13	—
1936	25	6	44
1938	5	0	63

*The UCR did not lift abstention until December, 1935.

Sources: Alfredo Galletti, *La política y los partidos* (México-Buenos Aires, 1961), p. 101; Malcolm H. Davis and Walter H. Mallory, eds., *Political Handbook of the World* (New Haven, Conn., and New York, 1929), p. 2; Walter H. Mallory, ed., *Political Handbook of the World* (New York, 1937), p. 3; Walter H. Mallory, ed., *Political Handbook of the World* (New York, 1939), p. 3.

crats), really "belonged" to the UCR. Moreover, long led by men with a propensity for facts and figures, the Socialists during the twenties had delighted in exposing the inadequacies and ineptitudes of the Radical administrations, especially those of Hipólito Yrigoyen. And on many an occasion they had joined hands with the Conservatives to defeat UCR-sponsored legislation, including, curiously enough, a 1927 bill which would have placed all petroleum exploitation under the exclusive control of the YPF, the state agency created by Yrigoyen in 1922. Although the Socialists applied their critical faculties to the Concordancia as well, their transgressions against Radicalism were neither forgiven nor forgotten—much to the advantage of their common enemies.

Simply by being in power, of course, the ruling parties were able to consolidate their strength. In spite of budget cuts made during the crisis years 1930-1934, the regime still dispensed considerable federal patronage, and as the economic situation improved in the second half of the thirties, was able to grant ever-greater favors, including some rather useful public works projects and a national road network. The government enjoyed the support of much of the mass media, particularly what right-thinking Argentines referred to as the "serious press," *La Nación* and *La Prensa* of Buenos Aires. It had effective control over the educational system and the airwaves, and the cordial good wishes of both the Roman Catholic hierarchy and the foreign business community. And for much of the time it enjoyed the steadfast support of the armed forces, particularly the Army, which was the recipient of many favors after 1930. General Uriburu had used government funds to cancel all private debts of active-duty officers, and President Justo, himself a distinguished career soldier, saw to the logistical needs of the military with a sympathy unequalled until the advent of the Perón regime some years later. Finally, the economic recovery after 1934 could not fail to benefit the administration in power, whatever the actual causes of improvement. These factors, combined with the Concordancia's iron determination to remain in power at all costs, made it a formidable enemy indeed.

THE CAUSES OF DECLINE

Behind its facade of invincibility, however, the Conservative Restoration was afflicted with serious structural weaknesses that became more critical with the passage of time. The most significant of these was provoked by the unfavorable outlook for world trade during the early thirties, a situation that resembled not at all the halcyon days of 1910-1916 when the Conservatives had last held the reins of power. In order to survive in a new and more difficult international economic order, the regime abandoned its traditional commitment to free trade for restrictive bilateralism and jettisoned a century of laissez-faire to embrace a policy of state intervention in the economy. The former was symbolized by the Roca-Runciman Pact, concluded in London in 1933; the latter was perhaps best embodied in the production control boards created shortly thereafter. Because both measures so transparently expressed the priorities of Argentina's great landed interests and their foreign partners, the government responsible for them was faced with heavy criticism and even vilification.

For if the London accord saved Argentina's place in the British meat market, it did so at a cost—in tariffs, in exchange quotas, and in "benevolent treatment" of £420 million worth of British investment—which many found excessive. Those who felt cheated or neglected by the new economic arrangements were quick to cry betrayal, a charge that those who wished to score points against the regime for purely political reasons were pleased to repeat, and by the end of the decade the Roca-Runciman Pact had become the *causa prima* for all that afflicted the nation, and proof positive that the Conservatives who signed it were servile instruments of a voracious British imperialism.

To such attacks the regime simply had no reply. For more than a century Argentina's economic life had rested upon an informal relationship with England, one which perhaps justified the statement of Vice-President Julio A. Roca, Jr., in London that "from the economic point of view [Argentina] is an integral part of the British Empire."[13] For most members of the traditional elite, with their deep roots in the rural sector and their close connections with the grazing industry,[14] the alternatives to Anglo-Argentine complementarity were virtually unthinkable. Unfortunately for them, during the thirties it was not the possibilities of a continued share of a stagnant or shrinking export market that captured the popular imagination, but the opportunities for economic independence. This, combined with the shortages produced by the Second World War, made the Concordancia's international economic policies seem even more shortsighted than they really were.

Much the same held true for adjustments in the domestic economy. In order to stabilize the price of major agricultural commodities, a series of production control boards was established to limit the harvest through a system of quotas assigned to ranchers and farmers. Although similar to contemporary practice in Europe and the United States, this measure in Argentina generated a perpetual chain of grievances. The smaller producers of meat and grains, wine, cotton, or sugar claimed favoritism in the distribution of quotas, and city-dwellers could easily be persuaded to believe that articles of prime necessity, particularly foodstuffs, would be vastly more accessible were it not for irregularities in the administration of assignments. And because of the intimate ties between the government and the greatest landowners, the accusation was thoroughly credible.

The Concordancia's penchant for arousing opposition to its economic policies even led to the defeat of one of its few truly innovative projects, the so-called Pinedo Plan, sent by President Castillo to the Argentine Senate in late 1940.[15] Ostensibly a temporary measure to cushion Argentina from the full impact of the Second World War by enhancing its economic self-sufficiency, in reality the Pinedo Plan was an omnibus program of reform which encompassed crop financing, industrial development, and some much-needed low-cost housing. Here, apparently, was a belated response to a decade of criticisms; yet for political reasons it was one that the opposition refused to take seriously. Embittered by Castillo's resumption of electoral fraud and recent provincial interventions, the Radical minority in the Senate staged an all-night filibuster on December 17-18, 1940, in an attempt to talk the bill to death. When this tactic failed to prevent its passage in the Upper House, the Radical effort shifted to the Chamber of Deputies, where an opposition majority prevented the project from ever reaching the floor for discussion.[16]

Of course, the controversies surrounding its economic policies were part of the price the regime was compelled to pay for its lack of a broad popular base. Had it rested upon anything like a genuine mandate, many of its disputed actions might have been accepted as distasteful but unavoidable responses to a situation for which, after all, no Argentine was responsible. But for a people who had known fourteen years of a relatively open political system, the "patriotic fraud" was a step backward in a nation accustomed to progress and was sufficient reason to believe the worst of those who had perpetrated it. Moreover, as the period drew to its close, the ruling circle closed ever more tightly. As a distinguished Argentine sociologist has shown, between 1936 and 1943 "the group that ruled . . . reduced cooptation to a minimum because almost all of the ruling team came from within the upper class. There was little cooptation; one simply belonged to the government by right of adscription. In any case, positions were usually filled by a limited number of peers."[17] In practice this meant that during Castillo's years at the Casa Rosada, Conservatives increasingly assumed posts traditionally reserved for Antipersonalist Radicals, whose participation had been the only basis for wider public support. At the same time, the average age of ministers rose nearly ten years.[18]

Consequently, not only younger Radicals but younger Conservatives were increasingly attracted to one or another of the many nationalist groups, and even the son of Foreign Minister Enrique Ruiz-Guiñazú was writing a book on Argentina's "necessary revolution."[19]

Finally, after a decade of extraordinary discipline and unified purpose, the regime fell victim to internal divisions. Perhaps it is no exaggeration to say that the men who governed Argentina in the thirties constituted "truly a complete ruling class, one of the few cohesive, functional ones the country has had," sharing as it did "identical visions of the country . . . attitudes towards economic development . . . and . . . views on foreign countries."[20] But this unity was shattered by the Second World War, which divided the Conservatives much as it did the rest of Argentine society. Castillo's firm adherence to neutrality was sufficient to separate him from important elements of his own party, yet not enough to win meaningful support from the anti-interventionist sectors of the Radical party or the nationalist groups. The coalition upon which Castillo thought to base his government could not be formed by him or by any Conservative; such a constituency would be available only to someone untainted by participation in the fraudulent decade. Least of all could it be unified behind Robustiano Patrón Costas, whose nomination cost Castillo the support of his last resort—the Army. By 1943 the regime had already spent much of its accumulated political capital with the military in a new cycle of provincial interventions, and the prospect of yet another imposition—to install a candidate apparently inimical to Army interests—exhausted its credit and ultimately brought it down. For all its advantages, then, the Conservative Restoration had failed to construct a permanent political structure, and so under stress it proved as ephemeral as the Radicalism which it sought to replace.

THE CONSERVATIVE LEGACY

After the fall of Perón in 1955, the new Argentine government ordered the Ministry of Education to create a syllabus and text on "democratic education" for all secondary schools. The underlying assumption was, of course, that the Perón experience was an unnatural, a pathological occurrence in Argentine history which "interrupted" the country's progress towards stable democracy.* Such a view, like so many others of Perón's successors, was self-serving to a fault. Above all, it was ahistorical.

For in reality the *Peronato* was very much a product of all that had preceded it. Its populist political style, its rhetoric, even the mood of fervent expectation which it aroused could be directly traced to Yrigoyen, whose presence in Argentine politics was more pervasive than ever after his death in 1933. Its commitment to economic independence and cultural autonomy echoed an entire generation of Argentine writers, artists, and public men. Even its repressive aspects, while carried out on a larger scale and with increased ruthlessness, could find ample historical precedent.

But it was from the Conservatives, and particularly those who ruled between 1930 and 1943, that the Peronist movement derived its richest legacy. For the PDN and its allies had proved, as no one else could, that by the mid-thirties the Radical Party had lost its original motive force and existed in a state of utter political bankruptcy. The logical deduction for the Concordancia and its supporters was that it was high time to return Argentina to the stewardship of those who "really knew" it, but for many disappointed Radicals (and not a few Socialists) the lesson was quite another—that a new political movement was needed to replace the old.

Secondly, the Conservative governments of the thirties seemed to illustrate that a distinct congruence existed between the class nature of the Argentine government and its international economic policies. The fact that it was the Justo government, representative of sectors with important economic interest outside the country, which had signed the Roca-Runciman Pact, led many to infer—and of course, they were helped to infer it—that only a popularly based government, such as that of Yrigoyen, could trade with foreign powers without compromising Argentina's national independence. Thus a fundamentally internal political struggle assumed all the trappings of a crusade for national sovereignty, much to the embarrassment and discomfiture of Argentine Conservatives with "historic" last names, who were used to being called scoundrels, but not traitors!

---

*One of the first acts of the government of Héctor J. Cámpora (March-June, 1973) was to abolish this obligatory course.

And finally, in their contempt for democratic procedures and their high-handed treatment of the opposition, the Conservatives created a mood of cynicism and alienation that is, as so many revolutionaries know, the next-door neighbor to anger and rebellion. Passive sentiments of disaffection become active elements of political action when combined with the ingredients of hope and possibility. It was merely Perón's peculiar genius to see this fact and to act upon it.

SOME EVENTS REFERRED TO IN THIS CHAPTER

1912—President Roque Sáenz Peña secures passage of a law assuring universal manhood suffrage.

1916—President Hipólito Yrigoyen of the Radical Civic Union (UCR) elected to a six-year term.

1922—President Marcelo T. de Alvear, also of the UCR, elected to succeed Yrigoyen.

1924—Alvear sponsors the founding of the UCR-Antipersonalist as part of a break with Yrigoyen.

1928—Yrigoyen re-elected against both Antipersonalist-Conservative and Progressive Democratic tickets, handily defeating also the Socialist candidate.

1930—Yrigoyen overthrown by Lieutenant General José F. Uriburu.

1931—Elections in the Province of Buenos Aires are won by the Yrigoyen wing of the Radical party and subsequently annulled by the Provisional Government; Uriburu vetoes the proposed Alvear-Güemes ticket of the UCR for the presidential elections of late 1931; the Radical party declares its abstention; the Concordancia ticket, General Agustín P. Justo and Julio A. Roca, Jr., elected.

1933-1934—Various Radical leaders in the provinces attempt the forcible overthrow of the regime; Yrigoyen dies in 1933.

1935—Alvear, reunited with the parent wing of the Radical party as Yrigoyen's successor, lifts electoral abstention.

1937—Roberto M. Ortiz and Ramón S. Castillo of the Concordancia elected to succeed Justo and Roca; UCR candidates Marcelo de Alvear and Enrique Mosca defeated by electoral fraud.

1938—Ortiz begins a series of interventions in the provinces to reverse the results of fraudulent elections.

1939—Second World War breaks out; Argentina declares her neutrality.

1940—Ortiz intervenes in the Province of Buenos Aires and is then required because of ill health to turn over the reins of the Presidency to Castillo; the latter immediately reverses Ortiz's policy on the fraud.

1942—Alvear dies.

1943—General Justo, in discussion with Radical leaders about the possibility of being their candidate in the 1944 elections, dies; Castillo announces the candidacy of Robustiano Patrón Costas as his successor and is overthrown by the military several weeks later.

3.
Economic Development

JAVIER VILLANUEVA (translated from the Spanish by
Mark Falcoff)

THE ARGENTINE ECONOMY BEFORE 1930

From the 1880s to the First World War, the Argentine Republic
underwent remarkable economic expansion based on the simul-
taneous development of her agricultural and stock-raising
industries, her railroads, and her network of roads and ports. At
the same time, massive European immigration, heavy capital
investment from abroad, and the opening of new lands to
agricultural exploitation converged to produce a prosperity,
particularly for its landowning classes, that led British economist
James Hobson to place Argentina in 1914 among the richest
countries in the world.[1]

This achievement rested principally upon a close bilateral
association with the British Empire, then at the apogee of its
power. For by specializing in the production of foodstuffs for
England's urban and industrial population, Argentina's rural
producers acquired a huge market that lent the country an
economic impulse whose full magnitude can only be suggested
by statistics. Exports increased in physical volume at an average
of 4.7 percent a year between 1865 and 1899, and then from
1900 to 1929, at an annual rate of 3.6 percent.[2] At the same
time, Argentina's railroad network grew from 10 kilometers of
track in 1857 to 33,478 in 1913, largely with the help of
British capital investment, whose presence in the country rose

from £2,605,000 in 1857 to £23,060,000 in 1874, to peak at £291,110,000 in 1910.[3]

Although neither especially nor systematically promoted, manufacturing activities, too, experienced considerable growth— in 1900-1904 and 1910-1914 at the rate of 7.7 percent a year.[4] These included the processing of products for export (principally meat) as well as the manufacture of meat byproducts and derivatives.[5] Import-substituting industries grew far more slowly; although not the recipients of direct government favor, they benefited indirectly from a tariff created principally for revenue-producing purposes.

Historians and economists alike agree that it was the incorporation of Argentina into the British trade and financial structure that made possible her rapid expansion during this period. Yet that overseas opening was circumscribed by two interlocking factors. One was her limited possibilities within the international division of labor, under rules of specialization dictated by economic complementarity with England. Second, and very much related, the country's economic and even political destiny was often shaped in accordance with the imperial will of the British Crown, acting through its influences upon the Argentine elite.

For much of the late nineteenth century, the potential conflicts enclosed within these two conditioning factors provided Argentina's leading groups with no cause for apprehension. But after 1900, and most especially after the outbreak of the First World War, Argentina's economic life slowly ceased displaying the characteristics that had so recently made it the object of widespread admiration. Although a postwar boom in the 1920s led many Argentines to exclaim that the times had never been better, other analysts who plumbed more deeply into national problems pointed out a loss of dynamism[6] and argued that it was time to replace the economic model of the "generation of 1880" with another, newer one more in accord with the changed economic and political conditions of the postwar world. These critics observed that the confluence of factors that had originally propelled the country forward was rapidly losing strength. Railroad expansion had slackened; the zones most suitable for agro-export activities were all but completely employed; and the

British market showed no signs of increasing sufficiently to stimulate additional Argentine growth. To be sure, the expansion of industry and the entry of foreign captial (especially from the United States) in the twenties provided some new sources of growth, but in any event they were insufficient to restore to the country the conditions that prevailed before the First World War. Prestigious Argentine analysts such as Alejandro Bunge[7] argued that Argentina should develop a new model of economic development, one that—without abandoning her foreign trade or existing international connections—would afford to industry the possibility of acting as the principal motor of a new process of growth.

In a larger sense, Argentina was confronted in the postwar period by the decline of British power. Even before 1914, it was apparent that the traditional partnership with England was being challenged by the United States—a country whose agricultural economy was competitive with that of Argentina, and which was more inclined than Great Britain to the export of newly developed goods, industrial equipment, and raw materials, but unlike the latter, persistently unwilling to absorb Argentine imports. Thus, the predominantly two-way exchange with Great Britain was becoming a triangular relationship that rested upon the convertibility of the pound sterling.

Naturally England saw no reason to accept graciously the intromission of a third party into her South American sphere of influence, and during the 1910s and 1920s lost no time in trying to stem the rising tide of American competition by placing increasing emphasis upon the imperial aspect of her relationship with Argentina. As early as 1910, for example, British interests affected by the competition of American meat-packing houses requested the intervention of the Argentine government to stem the "undesirable competition."[8] And in 1925 the British hand was strengthened by a rumor that pressure from the Dominions, particularly Australia and New Zealand, would compel London to establish commercial preferences within the sterling area and impose heavy duties on articles imported from outside the Empire. The Balfour Committee (1925), the later visit to Argentina by Lord D'Abernon, and the Roca-Runciman Pact all increasingly confirmed that British economic policy was operating within a new frame of reference. Nonetheless, Argentine authorities, overwhelmed by the weight of forms long established, seemed unaware of the need to find a way out of the *cul-de-sac* into which the country was slipping. In this sense, for the first three decades of the twentieth century, there was a delay in the search for an adequate response to the changing conditions of the world economy and the international power structure.

ON THE EVE OF THE CRISIS

Argentina's tardy awareness of these harsh facts was in part due to a period of economic recuperation that began in 1922 and peaked in 1927-1928. For in spite of the transformations in the international context and the tendencies toward a long-term stabilization of economic growth to which we have referred above, the economic recovery of the twenties imbued many Argentines with a sense of euphoria. The literature of those years abounds in testimonies that tell us as much; typical also is the recent recollection of one writer that "those of us who passed our youth in that period know that 1922-27 were perhaps the most brilliant years in the nation's history."[9]

The crisis of 1930 put an end to the air of celebration. But only the passing of the years would reveal that not only had an era come to an end, but that the very conditions that had once made it possible were extinguished. By an ironic twist of history it fell to an essentially popular political movement, the Radical party of Presidents Yrigoyen and Alvear, to guide an economic system created by the Conservatives through its apogee and then through the beginning of its definitive crisis. And by an even stranger turn of events, it was the Conservatives who during the thirties conceived, or perhaps merely accepted, a new economic plan adjusted to the narrower economic conditions that prevailed thereafter.

Some of the problems that would confront Argentina in the crisis of 1929-1930 were already taking shape in 1928. For in the middle of that year there was a sudden exodus of capital, and exports began to decline sharply. Instead of reducing imports, as traditional practice dictated, the government chose to increase state expenditures, broaden credit, and reduce interest rates. As a result, imports were not adequately restrained and the peso began to slide downward, leading to an additional flight of the short-term capital that had entered the country a few years before. This ultimately compromised the value of the Argentine currency, already burdened by an exceptionally heavy foreign debt that prevailing conditions made increasingly difficult to refinance. Between 1928 and 1929, Raúl Prebisch has written, the country witnessed the departure of all the gold that had entered during its bonanza years.

Far more significant for long-term economic prospects was an event that reflected the underlying tensions of Argentina's relationship with the outside world. In the final months of 1929, Viscount D'Abernon, accompanied by a group of British businessmen, visited Argentina to consolidate the economic links between the two countries. The visit was actually prompted by an invitation from President Yrigoyen, who hoped to use it to counteract growing United States influence in Argentina—but the British were pleased to accept the opportunity that was so graciously made available.

Shortly after his arrival in Buenos Aires in August 1929, the British peer pointedly declared that "up to now England has abstained from introducing commercial restrictions on Argentina . . . but there exists a strong current of English opinion which favors concentrating our economic activities within the Empire." On various public occasions he emphasized that "the decisions that may be taken on this question depend not only on conversations between London and the major Dominions, but also in a certain measure on the action taken by foreign countries with which we have commercial relations. Trade with these countries depends in a good measure upon the facilities which these countries offer us . . . the more liberal those facilities are, the more diminished are the chances of preferential moves in detriment to their interests."[10] To even a casual listener, the intended message was quite clear.

The D'Abernon mission culminated in an accord which, in general lines, committed the Argentine state railways to purchase from England the materials and supplies they would need during the following two years. For its part, Great Britain promised to buy the quantities of meat that Argentina normally exported in any event. Not surprisingly, Lord D'Abernon departed from Buenos Aires in a euphoric mood, declaring that "the results of the British Mission in Argentina are not only satisfactory but astonishing; at any rate, they astonish me."[11]

The draft protocol was quickly signed by the President and sent to the Argentine Congress. It was approved by the Chamber of Deputies, but before the Senate could act upon it, Congress was dissolved by the Revolution of 1930. In any event, it established a precedent for the later Roca-Runciman Treaty, which so much resembled it.

THE STORM BREAKS: THE CRISIS OF 1930

From the end of 1928 to 1931, Argentina slipped down the abyss opened by the world economic crisis. But after the "golden years" of the twenties, her directing elites persisted in hoping for a return, sooner or later, of the conditions that had made possible the earlier boom. In 1930, for example, the *Revista Económica del Banco de la Nación* commented complacently that "we have entered. . . in the course of 1929 . . . a downward phase of an economic cycle. . . . What we are experiencing is a passing phenomenon which characterizes the economic evolution of any country." Consequently, it is not surprising that much of the economic policy-making between 1929 and 1931 consisted of nothing more than a series of ad hoc responses dictated by traditional economic policies—a reduction in the salaries of government employees, the creation of a 10 percent tariff surcharge, and the mobilization of the country's gold reserves to prevent further deterioration of the peso.

Yet the crisis of 1930 was a heavy, if not precisely catastrophic, blow to the Argentine economy. The prices of agricultural products, especially cereals and flax, dropped considerably. At the same time, exports contracted between 1929 and 1930 in the amount of nearly 800 million pesos, while imports were reduced in the same period by only 300 million. Apart from considerations of a poor world market, the country's economic leadership also had to contend with increasingly unfavorable terms of trade for Argentine exports (see table 1).

The delay in stemming the tide of imports was especially serious at a time in which the possibilities of obtaining foreign loans were practically nonexistent. The balance of payments problems that emerged from these conditions were naturally critical and, given Argentina's position as a debtor nation, were inevitably translated into heavy pressures on the peso.

TABLE 1

Impact of the World Crisis

(a) Average Prices Paid for Argentine Products, Taking 1926 as Base 100.

Year	Cereals and flax	Meat
1929	100.8	111.8
1930	82.5	109.7
1931	55.9	90.3

Source: *Revista Económica del Banco de la Nación,* January 1932, p. 11.

(b) Terms of Trade, Taking 1926 as Base 100

Year	Index
1929	108
1930	96
1931	73

Source: Jesús Prados Arrarte, *El control de cambios* (Buenos Aires, 1944), p. 48.

(c) Argentine Balance of Payments in Millions of Pesos

Year	Balance (+ or −)
1926	−21
1927	+140
1928	−65
1929	+24
1930	−262
1931	−2

Source: Prados Arrarte, ibid., p. 21.

Two events on the economic horizon reduced the field of manuever of Argentina's governing groups. One was the fall of the pound sterling at the end of the twenties; the other was the marked flight of capital, the responsibility for which was partly that of cereal exporters who retained their foreign exchange outside the country in anticipation of a further devaluation of the peso. Both added to a deterioration in Argentina's trade balance, and the rigid burden of the foreign debt left the government no other choice but to intervene directly in the foreign exchange market. Thus on October 10, 1931, an Exchange Control Commission was established to supervise the foreign exchange operations of local banks. In principle the system had two basic objectives: (1) to reduce the demand for foreign exchange by limiting imports through a system of exchange permits at a fixed price and (2) to reduce the supply of foreign exchange in private hands by forcing exporters to hand over currency obtained in their commercial operations. The system also established an order of priorities in the assignment of exchange permits, which were (1) the public sector, the payment of the foreign debt; (2) raw materials for national industry;[12] (3) fuels; (4) indispensable consumer items; (5) remittances of immigrants; (6) luxury consumer items; (7) cancellation or amortization of debts. Obviously the intention was to improve Argentina's balance of payments position; at the time there did not exist— as there would later—an attempt to discriminate in the granting of currency permits according to the origins of the imports themselves.

In the view of the leading groups, recovery largely depended upon the arrangements that could be made with the British Crown, and it was with great apprehension that the Argentine economic community learned in June 1932 that at a special conference on imperial preference in Ottawa, Canada, London had apparently made good Lord D'Abernon's veiled threats— the British had committed themselves to a policy of expanding their foreign trade within the sterling area. The Argentine response to this move can well be imagined; on one hand, the agro-export sector feared the loss of its portion of British trade; on the other, local industrial interests, many of them connected with international capital of non-British origin, were worried that the Ottawa agreements would goad Argentine policy-makers to reduce duties on British finished goods.

A year later, the Argentine government, responding to the pressures implicit in the Ottawa Accords, accepted the conditions outlined in the Roca-Runciman Pact. It is difficult to know to what degree the country had no alternative but that of surrendering to local cattle interests and British pressures, or to what degree it was thought that in so doing other important objectives would be accomplished as well. To know the answer to this we would have to have precise information on the true importance of the meat trade with Britain at that time and the actual political weight of those groups involved in the production and

exporting of beef and its by-products. One might argue that—
given the actual record of economic performance in the thirties
—the government had somehow managed to satisfy the grazing
interests while attracting foreign (non-British) investments in
industry. It serves no purpose to exaggerate the possibilities of
such a complex strategy from the beginning. What is more
probable is that initially the only thought was to save the
cattle-export sector, leaving to existing industry a supplementary
role. Later, the idea of balancing the two may have become
more deliberate, partly through ad hoc formulations, and partly
by an acceptance of the facts themselves. What we can say with
some assurance is that as the thirties drew to a close, that
strategy became increasingly explicit.

THE TREATY OF LONDON (THE ROCA-RUNCIMAN PACT)

Shortly after assuming office, President Justo sent a high-level
mission to London led by Vice-President Julio A. Roca, Jr.,
an important figure in Argentine ranching circles, to obtain an
improvement in the country's place in the English meat market,
and, if possible, control of the Anglo-American meat-exporting
"pool."[13] After three months of negotiations with Board of
Trade President Walter Runciman, Roca signed an agreement on
May 11, 1933.

The Treaty of London, better known as the Roca-Runciman
Pact, established an arrangement with Great Britain that was
very much in the line already established by the D'Abernon
mission. It also established new grounds for an Anglo-American
conflict over Argentine foreign trade that would bring this
country additional tensions for the remainder of the decade.
After a prolonged and abrasive debate, the treaty was approved
by the Argentine Congress in July 1933.[14]

The terms of the agreement were as follows. On one hand,
Great Britain guaranteed to Argentina a fixed, but relatively
smaller, quota of participation in the market of chilled beef
(not less than the quantities purchased between July 1931 and
June 1932, that is, 390,000 tons). Besides that, it promised to
eliminate tariffs that had been placed on cereal imports into
the United Kingdom.

For her part, Argentina committed herself not to increase the number of goods subject to the tariff surcharge.[15] And she assured England of a downward revision of duties on a great number of manufactured goods. Until such revision was implemented, Argentina would retain tariffs on all goods at levels prevailing in 1930, with the exception of a group of articles, such as coal, which would be included on the duty-free list. Additionally, Argentina committed herself to spend all the sterling sums earned from British purchases to pay for imports from that country, financial services, and other remittances, except for a relatively reduced figure initially set at £3,000,000 a year to cover servicing of the foreign debt.

The signature of the Treaty of London[16] constituted the point of departure for the economic team that managed the country's affairs from 1933 to the end of the decade, and whose direct influence persisted to the early years of the 1940s. The team's complete strategy included reform of the banking system through the creation of the Central Bank, the introduction of production control boards, establishment of a system of exchange control, and price supports for cereals.

THE ECONOMIC REFORMS AND THE PROGRESS OF THE ECONOMY
During the latter part of 1933, the government introduced an entire package of economic reforms based both on a greater understanding of the nature of the crisis and an acceptance of the changes in British economic policy. One of the most important of these was a revision of the system of exchange control. Two currency markets were now established—one free, one official. Exchange on the former was considerably more expensive than on the latter,[17] and since import licenses were granted in relation to the availability of foreign exchange, the state was in a position to discriminate among importing countries by allocating to the free market currencies—such as American dollars—from countries whose commercial relations with Argentina did not produce an exchange surplus. The bifurcation of the currency market and the manipulation of exchange control were plainly discriminatory; indeed, they were intended to be, as an integral part of the new system of Anglo-Argentine bilateralism established by the Roca-Runciman Pact.

Between 1933 and 1934 the Argentine economy showed clear

signs of recovery. The level of economic activity rose, the balance of trade resumed its favorable position, and international capital returned, both in the form of short-term investments (which subsequently quit the country at the first sign of economic difficulty in 1937) and long-term investments oriented essentially toward industry.[18] By 1936 it was generally accepted in Argentina that the crisis was a thing of the past. As the Central Bank optimistically declared, "The regime of crisis has come to an end."[19]

Argentina's agrarian sector was chiefly responsible for the recuperation. As two economists have written, "world [agricultural] prices remained low at the beginning of the cycle, for they rose only 2.1 percent, but due to the devaluation of currency and the establishment in 1933 of the Grain Regulating Board, the prices paid to producers increased 22 percent."[20] Gradually, the price of cereals in the world market improved until the last quarter of 1937, when they began another sharp decline. Meat prices rose until 1936 and remained stable thereafter. The quantity of meat exported maintained a rather stable volume (from 1933 to 1936) as the result both of the London Treaty and a general upward movement in the world economy, and the quantity of cereals sold abroad also rose until 1938. At the same time, industrial investment rose to levels similar to those of 1927, and although real wages dropped, unemployment at least was sharply reduced. In short, from 1933 to 1937, Argentina showed signs of having learned how to navigate through the waters of the crisis.

ARGENTINE INDUSTRIALIZATION DURING THE THIRTIES: MYTHS AND REALITIES

One of the principal features of economic development during this period was industrial modernization achieved with the help of foreign investment. This was attained mainly through exchange control and, to a lesser degree, by quantitative restrictions on imports. Both were major elements of a policy that saw in industry an "additional wheel" that would counteract the effects of the world crisis with new activities and greater employment opportunities.

One important incentive to direct investment from abroad was provided by discriminatory exchange rates. Since United States firms—and those of other countries not favored by preferential trade treaties—found difficulties in exporting their manufactured goods, the only means of surmounting this invisible tariff wall was to fabricate the items they wished to market *in situ.* For North Americans this incentive was especially great: the prevailing system of exchange control established for most of the time a 20 percent margin of advantage for the English. By the Second World War, Argentine economic policy-makers had discarded the notion of industry as a temporary response to a crisis situation and regarded manufacturing as an integral part of the future economic picture. By then, of course, the facts themselves sharply circumscribed the field of economic speculation: it was very difficult to reopen the question of industrial strategy in 1941-1942 as if the process were at its very beginning, for by then local and foreign capital had combined to produce a "modern" industrial plant. The question that must be asked is whether the authors of the Argentine exchange policy were completely conscious of the long-range impact their actions would have. Recently Dr. Enrique Malaccorto, a participant in economic policy-making during those years, responded to this question by saying that

the crisis of '30 demonstrated to the country its tremendous dependence upon external markets. People consequently began to think about the necessity of transforming the country's economy and accelerating the process of industrialization which had already begun with the First World War.

How was that industrialization favored? In reality, in an indirect form through discriminatory exchange rates and customs duties. . . .

There was not, to be sure, a well-defined policy in the sense of saying, "yes, very well, we are going to industrialize the country, for which purpose we are going to take these and those measures." The actions that were taken were directed above all by budgetary considerations; knowing of course that they would have a spin-off effect, an indirect protectionist impact upon industry. [21].

Because of the fact that manufacturing played an increasingly important role in economic recovery, it comes as no surprise that the economic literature stresses that it is precisely during this period that local industry "really" gets its start. Although these commentators concede the prior existence of a certain degree of industrial development, they argue that the growth of manufacturing in its "modern" form was essentially the product of the Depression. While we do not deny the importance of industry to the period under consideration, there is much reason to reject this prevailing view of the thirties as a seminal era. A more careful examination of the facts reveals that the process of Argentine industrial development was far more complex and although such an examination may not totally negate the view cited above, it does at least suggest the need for describing the phenomenon with more caution.

In the first place, available information does not permit one to suppose a particular acceleration in the rate of industrial growth during the thirties.[22] By this we mean not that there was no increase, but rather, that there was no discontinuity, no sharp break with the past. Industry, in global terms, simply continued to grow along lines established many years before (see table 2). What was innovative about this period was the list of products actually manufactured—during the thirties the major growth industries were metallurgical products and textiles, especially the latter. With regard to textiles, development was favored by keen competition between English exporters and manufacturers locally established, either North American, European, or Argentine.

The paramountcy of the thirties to Argentine industrial development is further questioned by data extracted from the Industrial Censuses of 1935 and 1946. In 1935, 78 percent of industrial production was carried out by firms established before 1930, and as late as 1946 the figure had only dropped to 60 percent. The 1946 survey also suggests that, insofar as the establishment of new firms is concerned (excluding considerations of size, about which we offer no judgment), the twenties were no less fruitful than the decade that followed. In 1946, 9,943 firms founded between 1926 and 1930 continued to function, as opposed to 9,962 founded between 1931 and 1935. The survey also shows that the years in which the rates of investment in the industrial sector were greatest between 1900 and 1946 were 1923-1929.

Two additional factors complete the picture. Imports of industrial machinery "between 1920 and 1930 were the highest

TABLE 2

Gross National Product. Share of Rural and Manufacturing
Sectors (1900-1950)

Period	Rural sector	Index[*]	Manufacturing sector	Index[*]
1900-1904	33.3	–	14.0	–
1905-1909	27.8	83.5	14.6	104
1910-1914	25.2	75.6	16.0	114
1915-1919	31.0	93.0	16.0	100
1920-1924	28.3	85.0	17.1	121
1925-1929	25.7	77.0	18.4	131
1930-1934	25.1	75.0	19.3	138
1935-1939	24.3	73.0	21.4	153
1940-1944	24.7	74.0	22.0	157
1945-1949	18.5	56.0	24.5	175

[*]Index = percentage of previous quadrennium.

Source: Adapted from United Nations, Economic Commission for Latin America,
El desarollo económico argentino (Santiago de Chile, 1958).

for any ten-year period in Argentine history, and between 1925-
1930 the maximum for any five-year period." The only comparable period thereafter was 1947-1951.[23] And industrial consumption of electricity, which tripled in 1921-1925 (compared
with 1910-1919) tripled again in 1927-1930. From 1931-1935,
it did not quite duplicate itself.

The data above should encourage us to discard the notion
that Argentine industry experienced a sudden "takeoff" in its
rate of growth in the thirties and to fix our attention instead
on the changes in its internal composition: the wave of foreign
investment introduced fundamental changes in both the range
of products and the level of technology. These changes were
effected through a group of international enterprises, chiefly
North American, which arrived in Argentina in the twenties,
introducing *pari passu* new products and new forms of production and organization, and which were in part responsible for
such growth as took place during the second half of the thirties.

Encouraged by an upward revision of the tariff in 1923,[24]

a clear-cut policy of laissez-faire, and a growing domestic market, a number of foreign firms relocated in Argentina during the twenties. Still more Argentine concerns undertook the elaboration of new products with foreign financial and technical assistance, including the use of foreign patents. Hence by the end of the twenties, many products formerly imported were beginning to be locally produced. And in contrast to 1900-1920, when the bulk of foreign industrial investment was concentrated in food processing (meat-packing and beverages), between 1921 and 1930, 43 major enterprises entered the country led by chemicals (13), metals (7), and electrical products (10).

TABLE 3

Principal Foreign Industrial Concerns Established in Argentina
(1900-1943)

Product	Number of firms for indicated period			Total
	1900-1920	1921-1930	1931-1943	
Food processing, beverages	6	5	2	13
Chemicals and pharmaceuticals				
(a) cosmetics	–	6	5	11
(b) pharmaceuticals	–	7	7	14
Rubber and rubber articles	–	2	3	5
Paints and varnishes	–	–	3	3
Metals	3	7	7	17
Textiles	–	1	7	8
Electrical products	1	10	6	17
Other(s)	3	5	5	13

Sources: Adolfo Dorfman, *Desarrollo industrial argentino* (Buenos Aires, 1944), Luis V. Sommi, *Los capitales yanquis en la Argentina* (Buenos Aires, 1949), and *Los capitales alemanes en la Argentina* (Buenos Aires, 1943).

Under the combined stimulus of further tariff revision (1931) and the system of exchange control, this pattern was simply extended during the next decade, during which 45 major foreign concerns entered the country, again, featuring prominently chemicals (12), metals (7), electrical fixtures (6), and textiles (7) (see table 3). What was distinctive about the thirties was the role played by the Argentine government (and indirectly, by Great Britain) in furthering this development, a point perhaps best illustrated by a brief look at the textile industry. In 1925—that is, before the London treaty—United States textile exporters could claim 9.8 percent of the Argentine market; by 1936, the prevailing system of tariffs and exchange control made their products 20 percent more expensive than British goods, and their share of the market fell to 0.9 percent. Not surprisingly, then, between 1934 and 1936 three great textile concerns of North American origin entered Argentina, and of the five major enterprises of this type that were established in this country between 1934 and 1938, three were North American: the Jantzen Co. (1934), Sudamtex (1935), and Anderson Clayton (1936). Thus what began as a policy to placate British exporters ended by encouraging investment in local manufacturing.

THE "NEW FORMULAS" OF THE THIRTIES: A SYNTHESIS

Between 1933 and 1943 a ministerial team led by Dr. Federico Pinedo devised what later became known as a new economic orientation for Argentina. Initially, the measures of the Pinedo group were shaped to counteract the adverse conditions generated by the world crisis and by British imperial policy. These are the aspects of economic policy-making that have received the most attention, and about which much of the historical controversy has turned. Yet we believe a critical role was played by at least two other factors—both interrelated, both essential to an understanding of what occurred in those years and perhaps even thereafter. These were (1) the conflict between British and North American interests, fighting for domination of the Latin American area, joined in the late thirties by Germany, and (2) the existence from the early twenties in Argentina of industrial enterprises linked to foreign—not necessarily British—capital.

Although one rarely finds *all four* factors explicitly distinguished in the Argentine economic literature, they could not have been ignored by economic policy-makers of that period. First, because they were so closely related, so that to take into account one necessarily required consideration of the others.

Second, because they were of immense importance and at least the first two enjoyed considerable public visibility. To the economic crisis generally could be traced the widespread unemployment and general social malaise, while British imperial policy directly affected the agro-export interests which constituted the basis of the country's political and economic power structure.

Insofar as foreign—especially North American—capital is concerned, it is impossible to imagine that its abundant contribution to local industry and public utilities was ignored, especially if one takes into account that apart from the capital that entered the country at the end of the twenties, the contribution of private international capital to the Argentine industrial sector amounted to 800 million pesos between 1931 and 1937. In 1938 more than half the total capital of Argentine industry was of foreign origin. As economist Adolfo Dorfman has shown, that capital dominated in an almost monopolistic form some of the most important branches of the manufacturing industry: meat-packing, electrical power, cement, automobiles, rubber, artificial silk, and petroleum, as well as electrical motors, radio-telephone sets, and pharmaceutical products. Thus one can be reasonably sure that when the leaders of the period referred to local industry—whether favorably or not—they consciously had in mind an international protagonist different from Great Britain.

In terms of exposition and public debate, the strategy of the economic team of 1933 rested on two types of measures, identified in parliament as "structural" and "anticyclical." The "structural" measures were actually those related to negotiations with Great Britain, where the objective was to assure Argentine cattlemen continued English purchases of chilled beef. For this purpose the English were promised that, insofar as possible, the sterling sums so earned would be spent purchasing their imported goods. In so doing, the government won over, or at least neutralized, the two traditional sources of political and economic power in Argentina. Moreover, it is almost impossible to underestimate the importance that Argentine leaders in the thirties placed, rightly or wrongly, on the preservation of the traditional commercial link with Great Britain. As the elite endlessly declared through its spokesmen in the government, press, universities and other public forums, a contraction in sales to England was an eventuality to be avoided whatever the cost.

The "anticyclical" measures gave special emphasis to the support of local industry, not only to generate employment, but also to attract foreign capital to the manufacturing sector. The latter, however, was never expressly indicated as an objective; rather, it was an indirect consequence of the "exchange wall" to which we have already referred. But by the middle of the thirties, exchange control had become a deliberate instrument of industrialization.

To repeat, the strategy of 1933 and after was composed of two essential and complementary parts: on one hand, the traditional trade relation with Great Britain was maintained through a quota of chilled beef obtained in the Treaty of London. One the other hand, industrial employment was stimulated through the affluence of foreign capital, as well as through a series of public works programs. All these measures not only helped to resolve some of the problems of the Depression, but also made it possible for the government to play off two countervailing sources of power.

As we have indicated before, this was not, in all probability, a strategy conceived in all of its details from the very beginning. However, neither can it be considered something that emerged with no thought whatsoever on the part of leading public men. One must remember that as early as 1930, shortly after establishing the first system of exchange control, the Revolutionary Government of General Uriburu opened talks with North American companies to discuss the direct manufacture of automobiles in the country. As time went on, the idea took on a more explicit shape thanks both to the interest groups concerned and to the economic facts themselves. But in the process, industry frequently became the target of conflicts, since to define the kind of industry that was desired frequently implied a preference for the nationality of the capital involved and the local interest groups to be affected.

It is possible to follow this in much of the literature of economic debate. For example, the manifest tolerance of the great cattlemen and exporters for the "anticyclical" aspects of the new policy (that is support for import-substituting industries) could be purchased only through an unconditional guarantee that the ensuing industrial development would have only a subsidiary character. Pinedo, the central figure in the entire process, never tired of repeating in one form or another, "We do not believe . . . it is possible nor desirable to alter the economic foundations of the country. We do not contemplate establishing autarchy. . . . I continue to believe that the best form of obtaining the articles we need is to sell what we are especially suited [by nature] to produce."[25]

Nonetheless, the changes introduced into economic strategy after 1933 were not achieved without conflicts between leading interest groups. Some advocates of the new course found it necessary to go through remarkable ideological contortions in order to justify their innovations, and then the crudest of pragmatisms was summoned to paper over abrupt departures from traditional practice. Perhaps no better illustration could be provided than that of the subtle "conversion" of Luis Duhau, leading cattleman and President of the Rural Society in the late twenties. In 1927, Duhau was preaching the benefits to the country of its participation in the international division of labor. "With a given quantity of cereals exported to England," he explained, "Argentina can obtain from the same source a given amount of textiles. . . . The indirect cost to us of those textiles is nothing more than what it costs to produce the cereals with which we obtain them. On the other hand, if we wished to manufacture those textiles here, we could only do so at a cost much greater to us than those cereals." Seven years later, the same man, now Minister of Agriculture, proclaimed his discovery that "the historic period of our prodigious development under the direct stimulus of the European economy has come to an end." In the past Argentina could obtain a good part of the manufactures she required "either by producing them directly or by obtaining them from foreign countries through the exchange of agricultural products. The most economical, the most advantageous policy for the country frequently turned out to be the last procedure, that of barter, of exchange. . . . To national industry will fall in the future the task of compensating the Argentine economy for the incalculable losses sustained by the sharp contraction of its foreign trade."[26]

ARGENTINA IN THE SECOND WORLD WAR

The outbreak of the Second World War posed a new set of problems to Argentine policy-makers: it disarticulated world trade, dealt a definitive blow to an already shaky British Empire, and raised serious doubts about Argentina's future in the post-war period. And although a nonbelligerent, Argentina was so closely linked to world trade that the war inevitably affected her foreign commerce, the structure of her production, her labor market, indeed, her society in general. It led to an accentuation of tendencies already at work during the thirties and provided the final dislocation of the ancient structure which had linked Argentina to a wider world economy. From 1939 on, the government returned with ever-greater frequency to those defense measures that turned the country inward, toward its domestic market. Thanks to the fact that many such mechanisms had already been tried during the earlier part of the decade, it was possible for Argentina to pass through the Second World War without experiencing the kind of problems that had afflicted her during the First.[27]

In the first place, the war drastically altered the structure of the country's foreign trade. From the very beginning of the conflict the markets of Central Europe were totally lost; the shipments to the United Kingdom and France were reduced through a lack of inventories and the sea blockade.[28] In search of new markets, Argentina turned to her sister republics of Latin America, with whom she found an outlet for her manufactured goods, and to the United States, to whom she now exported canned meat. In general, however, exports fell in both quantity and value, due both to transportation shortages and a deterioration in the terms of trade.

But this was counterbalanced by the situation of imports. Because of wartime exigencies, the belligerents were forced to curtail drastically their shipments of manufactured goods and fuels. Argentina responded by turning to the United States as an alternative supplier (until 1942), by expanding domestic petroleum production, and by putting the idle capacity of the existing industrial plant to work. Since there had been a respectable level of investment in this area during the previous fifteen years, this proved a relatively easy matter.[29] Here the greatest capacity for response was demonstrated by the consumer goods industries, particularly textiles and foodstuffs, which showed the greatest initial spurt, not only because of high demand, but because both required the least capital (which could not be imported).

The war thus provided a new stimulus to Argentina's fledgling industries. At the same time it generated a favorable balance of payments, for throughout the war she accumulated a significant quantity of gold and sterling reserves, mostly from the United Kingdom, which—although no longer a major supplier of manufactured goods—remained the principal customer of Argentina's agrarian industries.

The war not only affected the structure of Argentina's trade and the course of her economic development, but raised serious doubts about the country's future prospects. The questions everywhere asked were: What would be the fate of the Argentine economy in the post-war period? To which country or group of countries should she commercially tie herself at the close of the conflict? In official and semiofficial publications these questions multiplied and proliferated. Would world trade return to "liberal" principles in the postwar period, as had been the case for the twelve years following the First World War? What exports should Argentina promote: the "traditional" products or the "new" ones produced under wartime conditions? Should the process of industrialization continue in the same fashion in which it had been pursued?

The problem of future commercial relations was indeed serious, not only because of its far-ranging political and diplomatic implications, but also because Argentina's capacity to satisfy many basic economic necessities depended after the war, as before, on the existence of adequate markets for her exports. The experience of the years immediately following the First World War permitted policy-makers to foresee a drop in the prices of primary products, to which prospect was added the dour probability that England would emerge from the conflict virtually ruined. Moreover, the triumph of the United States signified the accession of a power whose economic relationship to Argentina—far from being complementary—was in many ways dangerously competitive. Hence the war required a rethinking of the economic plan drawn up in the thirties. This time, however, the key figures were not only Pinedo, Prebisch, and the staff of the Central Bank, but Colonel Juan Perón, the armed forces, and new centers of power in labor and industry.

THE WAR AND NEW ORIENTATIONS

In 1940 elements of the ruling elite under the leadership of Finance Minister Pinedo took the first steps in elaborating a new economic plan for Argentina. In November of that year President Castillo sent to Congress a "Program of Economic Reactivation" (better known as the Pinedo Plan), which has been the subject of considerable controversy. We believe that its purpose, besides subsidizing the harvest or promoting public works, was to link the Argentine economy to the surging power of the United States and to growing Latin American markets.[30] The plan thus called for Argentina to develop new lines of industrial production based essentially on the availability of local raw materials and cheap labor and upon the existence of a larger market which would facilitate economies of scale. These new industries were oriented not only to the internal market, but particularly to the external one. Those producing predominantly for the local market received only cursory attention.

The new industries that Pinedo wished to promote were the ones he called "natural industries," that is, those activities that transformed locally available raw materials, as opposed to "artificial" enterprises dependent upon imported raw materials, technology, equipment—and, therefore, foreign investment. By advocating this kind of industrialization, Pinedo thought, first, to avoid head-on conflicts with the traditional agro-export sector[31] and, second, to develop trade channels with the United States and Latin American countries. But other elements of the Argentine elite advanced an even more complex strategy. For example, the Argentine delegation to the 1941 Pan American Commercial Conference in Montevideo, recruited from the staff of the Central Bank, argued that with the deterioration of traditional markets for Latin America's raw material exports, foreign investment in local industry was the only solution. In other words, based on Latin America's previous experience, the only alternative was support of those "artificial" industries that derived from direct foreign investment and that in later years would be called "import substituting."[32] This position was re-iterated in the Bank's 1942 report.[33]

Two contrasting attitudes towards industry were apparent around the early 1940s. Pinedo and his associates sought to develop lines of production that would allow Argentina to replicate with the United States—and to some degree, with Latin America, especially Brazil—that economic complementarity that she had once enjoyed with Europe and that the war had placed in mortal danger. This was done by drafting a plan that deliberately avoided a confrontation with interests tied to Argentina's traditional exports. The position articulated by the Central Bank, however, took as its point of departure the prior existence in Argentina of an industry utilizing imported equipment and raw materials and linked in many cases to foreign capital. Yet for their differences, the two strategies were not completely contradictory; in many ways they complemented one another.[34]

The collapse of the *ancien régime* and the rise to prominence, then power, of Colonel Juan D. Perón introduced yet a third formula for Argentina's industrial development. In 1944 the National Council for Post-War Planning, one of the latter's special creations, came out for a strategy that placed particular emphasis on the short-run achievement of full employment and the improvement of real wages. At the same time it supported "existing" manufacturing enterprises and the development of the domestic market rather than the emphasis on finding outlets abroad; as it was often said, already-functioning industries should be supported without sacrificing the "new" export activities. To this was added a new role for the State—that of promoter of the welfare of the working class and mediator between capital and labor. The armed forces, a new participant in the debate on economic policy, converged upon this point, although their objective, particularly that of the Army, was the development of a heavy industry, especially in steel and iron, to meet the requirements of national defense.

CONCLUSIONS

In the preceding pages we have attempted to outline some of the factors that circumscribed the range of economic options open to Argentina during the period spanning the First to the Second World War. In the process we have emphasized two points: first, that the system of exchange controls devised to favor the British had the indirect effect of encouraging direct industrial investment by non-British overseas sources; and second, that such investment joined an already-existing industrial plant created during the boom years of the twenties. Both points suggest an urgent need to revise the conventional view of Argentine economic history, according to which the expansion of industry took place exclusively during the thirties and early forties as a reaction to the Depression and war by a (we can now say understandably) elusive "national bourgeoisie."

In raising the issue of discriminatory manipulation of exchange control, we have been compelled to make an incursion upon the field of economic and political relations between Argentina and the United States on one hand, and between Argentina and Great Britain on the other. These relationships—and the changes they have undergone over the years—frequently furnish the key to the restrictions Argentina has been forced to confront during the twentieth century. The Anglo-Argentine economic connection dated back to the very formation of the nation. For Argentina and her ruling groups, it represented an obvious source of economic advantage: the local economy obtained capital and technological advances while at the same time it gained a large and reliable market for some of its rural products. Some members of the Argentine elite even derived from this connection with the British Empire a sense of poise and pride.

The advantages for Great Britain were hardly less palpable. On one hand, she gained from the importation of relatively cheap chilled beef, which was certainly beneficial to her urban industrial population. In Argentina, she also found a favorable market for manufactured goods made in England. Great Britain also received remittances from previous investments, normally in the form of interest and dividends on government bonds and public services, particularly railroads and tramways. To all this was added the earnings of British shipping lines—for the Argentine utterly lacked a merchant marine to carry her products to her principal foreign market.

Yet strong as were the ties of economic complementarity, the Anglo-Argentine relationship rested upon a considerable measure of political and economic fascination—that is to say, it was held together not only by pounds sterling but by glamour, by a mystique, if one can call it that, at least on the Argentine side. Nothing else fully explains the degree to which, when the economic relationship itself began to sour, the Argentine elites allowed themselves to be backed into a cul-de-sac by the able diplomacy of the Empire; forced into a one-way street, they found but a single route of egress—surrender to the demands of the British Crown.

After the Second World War, the Argentine "special relationship" [35] with Great Britain underwent a sharp decline. During those years Argentina attained a certain diversification of markets for her traditional exports, and unsuccessfully attempted on numerous occasions to establish lines of complementarity with the United States. Moreover, the changing international picture was reflected by transformations in the power structure of Argentine society. The group of ranchers that constituted the linchpin of the relationship with Great Britain lost the power that had so long been its birthright, and the leadership of the country began to be shared by other groups, particularly those related to the industrial sector (both labor and management), which gradually acceded to positions of influence. All these changes in international connections and in the relative power positions of local groups found clear expressions in the different strategies of economic and social development that were being formulated in the years immediately prior to the accession to power of Colonel Juan D. Perón and, to a certain degree, are reflected in some of the latter's government programs, particularly during his first administration (1946-1952).

As we have indicated above, as early as 1940 the Conservative elite, recognizing, perhaps, that the war would deal a mortal blow to the British Empire, began to lay out the lines of a new alliance, this time with the United States, based upon the development of a new economic complementarity. For this purpose Pinedo proposed an industry based upon the maximum utilization of local raw materials, while the technical teams at the Central Bank favored support of the existing "new" industries, many of which depended upon imported capital, technology, and raw materials. Far from choosing between these two options, the post-1943 governments, possessed of far greater political imagination, simply adopted both and fused them with currents of populism, military nationalism, and social welfare.

The important point is that none of the positions discussed above, from Pinedo to Perón, favored the promotion of economic autarchy. All sides in the debate emphatically declared the need to avoid excessive distortions in the configuration of Argentine foreign trade. For some, besides expanding economic ties with continental Europe, it was of paramount importance to develop commercial complementarity with the United States. This idea, initially spelled out in the early 1940s, was often reiterated in the years to come. As one of Perón's finance ministers declared on an official visit to the United States in 1950:

We seek the dollars we need through the most direct route—expansion of our exports to the U. S. market and promotion of U. S. investment in Argentina. . . .

The possibilities of Argentine purchases in the U. S. depend, as I have had occasion to say at a recent press conference, upon the increase in our dollar accounts, whose principal source, given the present world monetary situation, is bound to be constituted by exports to this country. [36]

What finally happened was that in later years the complementarity with the United States was not achieved even by those leaders who most ardently desired it. Instead, local industry was developed, based on the orthodox strategy of import-substitution [37] with the participation of foreign, especially North American, capital. But now, with two more or less equally strong productive sectors in the country—agriculture and industry—new problems arose. Because of a persistent dependence upon European markets to generate the necessary foreign exchange to maintain the strategic flow of imports and service charges (including patent royalties) especially to the United States, Argentina confronted a historic situation of increasing economic complexity, which often congealed into tensions arising out of exchange shortages and the struggle for the distribution of both income and political power.

4.

Foreign Policy

JOSEPH S. TULCHIN

The world depression and the successful revolt against President Hipólito Yrigoyen laid bare the deficiencies of Argentina's liberal model of national growth, one that had provided the framework for public policy since 1880. By ousting Yrigoyen, the rebels symbolically discarded the old model and set the nation adrift in search of a replacement. The essence of the Argentine dilemma from that day to the present has been a lack of consensus on the guidelines for national policy.

In political terms, the stage for the Revolution of 1930 was set in the years immediately following 1916, as a result of the failure of the conservative forces to form a national party to face the Radicals in an ever-widening electoral arena. Without an "organic party," as President Roque Sáenz Peña called it, it was impossible for the conservative provincial oligarchies to maintain their political power through legitimate constitutional means. They jockeyed for power with the Radicals, but Yrigoyen's landslide victory at the polls in 1928 spelled their doom and they swung over to unconstitutional alternatives. At the same time, Yrigoyen's personalism, the venality of his appointees, and the general ineffectiveness of his second administration disillusioned many of his adherents, Radicals and independents alike, and made General Uriburu's work easier. The period between

1930 and 1943, then, as the authors of chapter 2 make plain, was one in which no group or party could put the pieces of the democratic model back together. Even the Radicals remained an unorganized and ineffective opposition force, unable to mobilize the majority of Argentines willing to vote against the government. In fact, it was easier to wield political power by means of the leverage acquired through control over a particular interest group—cattlemen, exporters, the military, labor, etc.—than by conventional electoral politics.

The liberal model postulated a pluralistic society in a land of opportunity. However false or inadequately achieved these postulates may have been, they did set the terms of dialogue over social issues. It was a cliché in the public forums to insist that class conflict, such as existed in Europe, had no place in Argentina. Even the Socialists, who professed Marxist tenets, took a Fabian approach to social problems, urging more education as the best solution, while Yrigoyen, the great popular leader, made no apology for his paternalistic approach to labor. Once the Depression hit Argentina, the old liberal democratic consensus began to dissolve, and the "social question" could not be ignored.

In economic terms, the restrictions on the international exchange of goods and services following the First World War, which were intensified by the financial turmoil of 1929, would force Argentines to cast about for an alternative to the international division of labor that had been the mark of the nation's growth for half a century. Although the Great War had been a shock to the system, the prosperity of the twenties wiped out the disturbing memory of dancing to a tune played in London or New York. Before 1930, then, most Argentines either welcomed or accepted the nation's dependence upon primary product exports as the engine of growth, and only isolated voices cried out against servitude to British interests. A few economists like Alejandro Bunge were disturbed by the structural imbalances of the economy; a small group of nationalist intellectuals railed against Argentina's lack of autonomy; and a small faction within the Radical party worked within the political system to alter Argentina's world role. As Professor Villanueva has shown in chapter 3, it was the Depression that had the decisive effect on Argentine economic thinking and generated a struggle to end dependence or at least to mitigate its effects.

Finally, in terms of foreign policy, the liberal model was designed to preserve the nexus of relationships that defined Argentina's place in the international economy and facilitated her growth and progress. Specifically, that meant opposition to any kind of hemispheric system that would restrict Argentina's access to her major markets in Europe or freeze her in a subordinate relationship to any nation or group of nations within the hemisphere. So long as these axiomatic objectives were assured, foreign relations might remain the plaything of a small elite of diplomats and leaders.

The South American balance of power was congenial to Argentina's vital interests.[1] So long as none of the major Latin American countries was distracted by an extended period of internal disorder, it was fairly easy to counter moves toward hegemony by any member of the system and thereby restore an equilibrium of power. This system left room enough for a rapprochement here, a crisis there, even a bloody conflict between minor members of the system, such as the Chaco War between Paraguay and Bolivia, and was stable enough by 1930 to allow personal animosities between individuals in leadership positions to determine the tenor of relations between nations, as when Argentine Foreign Minister Carlos Saavedra Lamas and Peruvian Ambassador Felipe Barreda Laos refused to communicate with one another in their official capacities because of a mutual personal dislike.[2] Perhaps the classic case is the manner in which Saavedra Lamas manipulated the Chaco peace proceedings to secure for himself the Nobel Prize for Peace.

The point is that foreign policy issues that did not touch closely upon the question of international trade were not considered vital to the national interest and were left to the discretion of the Executive. Interest articulation and aggregation were virtually nonexistent on these matters; the public was unconcerned, the Congress passive. When major newspapers, such as *La Nación* and *La Prensa,* had coherent views on inessential foreign policy issues at variance with that of the Executive, their opinions had little or no impact on the policy formulation process. Thus, during the 1930s Argentina's relations with neighboring countries, as well as her behavior at international conferences or during the Chaco War, reflected the interests and personality of Carlos Saavedra Lamas or the President, not the opinion of the Argentine nation in any sense. However, this was most definitely not the case in questions related to economic growth and material progress stemming from the export of primary products.[3] Here, policy formulation was vastly more complex, taking into account inputs from all divisions of the Executive, the legislature, and the private interest groups in an orderly and comprehensive manner, not unlike the process in the United States or Great Britain, thus suggesting an established pattern of interest aggregation and articulation based upon a fairly broad consensus concerning the importance of the issues under discussion.

What, then, was Argentina's major international concern during the period 1930-1943? The answer, to put it simply, was economic survival. The world depression ended the conditions that had made possible Argentina's economic development up to that time. Foreign policy after 1930 was an integral part of a continuing effort to construct a new model of national development. The objectives of foreign policy were to facilitate the nation's adjustment to dramatically changed conditions in the world economy and to lessen the deleterious effects of dependence upon a world market no longer willing to absorb Argentina's excess production. The goal was to alter the dependency pattern or, where that was impossible, to buy time for the government to formulate and then execute schemes that would modify the structure of the national economy and reduce the nation's dependence upon a capricious and perversely uncontrollable world market.

To analyze Argentine foreign policy during the period under discussion, we shall put forward four closely related hypotheses:

1. that Argentina sought to work out its economic survival within the framework of a triangular relationship with Great Britain and the United States;

2. that the basic objectives of Argentine foreign policy were the same throughout the period;

3. a. that the terms of the Roca-Runciman Pact were the best the Argentine negotiators could achieve,

b. that the pact was designed to defend the national interest and not merely the interests of a limited group, and

c. that the pact did in fact protect Argentina from the vicissitudes of the world economy and buy time for the government to begin to put into effect a policy of economic diversification; and,

4. that the policy of neutrality in the European struggle that led to the Second World War was a popular policy in the sense that it represented a broad consensus of political and economic interest groups and satisfied the needs of national security.

Radical historians have made brave claims for Yrigoyen's nationalistic stance in foreign affairs. On the other hand, some Marxist and revisionist critics of Radicalism have insisted that he was an unwitting tool of the landed oligarchy and the British imperialists. If we make a distinction between vital and secondary policy issues, we can see that the evidence for Yrigoyen's independence in foreign affairs is based entirely on issues of secondary importance and reflect the idiosyncracies of the Radical caudillo. Further, none of these supposed "initiatives" had a lasting impact on foreign relations; their ephemeral quality is demonstrated by the ease with which successive regimes reversed their direction or ignored them. Such is the case with Yrigoyen's attempt to form an economic bloc of American neutrals during the First World War, his dramatic refusal to participate in a League of Nations based upon an unjust peace, his disdain for diplomatic niceties, or his pointed rudeness to the United States flag during the occupation of Santo Domingo and to President-elect Herbert Hoover when the latter visited Buenos Aires in early 1929. When it came to vital matters, Yrigoyen was faithful to the traditional model.

Yrigoyen feared the growing influence of the United States in Argentina because of the pattern of North American intervention in its Caribbean sphere of influence and the threat it implied to the established links between Argentina and her principal customer, Great Britain. The Great War had shaken the international financial system and made difficult multilateral settlement of trade accounts. The war had also weakened Great Britain, reducing her purchasing power and leaving her vulnerable to United States competition for trade, loans, and investments in Latin America. Repeated efforts during the 1920s to expand Argentine exports to the United States proved fruitless. As a result, at the end of the decade, when the British stepped up efforts to recapture their position in Latin America, their warnings of restrictions against Argentine exports found that nation's leaders already nervous about how to generate the dollars to pay for the increasing imports from the United States and meet the payment on debts incurred in the New York bond market. It was in this context that the D'Abernon mission was greeted warmly and that Yrigoyen personally made grand promises of preferential treatment to British interests. Yrigoyen's objective in this case, as in the London Wheat Conference the following year, was to maintain or increase Argentine exports in the face of the ever-widening repercussions of the Depression that threatened to restrict world trade.[4]

While Yrigoyen was unable to coax the D'Abernon treaty through the Senate, he gave evidence of his Anglophilia through a series of executive actions. The state-owned railways ordered steel rails from a British firm without benefit of public bids, the duty on items coming in from Great Britain containing artificial silk was reduced 50 percent, restrictions were imposed on fruit imported in barrels to retaliate against the United States sanitary embargo on Argentine meat, and the Banco de la Nación arbitrarily rejected applications for loans if the proceeds were to be spent in the United States.

Despite these favors, the British Foreign Office was pessimistic about English chances of recapturing the Argentine market. Diplomatic officers lamented the apparent inability of British industry and commerce to take advantage of the opportunity presented by the D'Abernon mission and United States protectionism, particularly the rigidity of the British economic structure, which made it difficult for exporters to combine with shippers, or shippers to combine with bankers. The organization of the British Government was considered an obstacle as well. It was, one officer said of the campaign to expand exports, like bringing "the horse to the water." "The Department of Overseas Trade should handle it," said another; "If the Treasury gave us more money, we could do a better job ourselves," said a third. Whatever the cause, His Majesty's representatives in the Argentine decried the fact that British salesmen were hobbled by archaic advertising methods, by extreme individualism, and by not offering what Argentines wanted to buy—cheap cars and consumer goods.[5] As if this were not sufficient handicap, British enjoyment of official favor in Argentina was undermined by the government's political difficulties beginning in 1929 and culminating in the Revolution of September 6, 1930.

Since Yrigoyen had been openly anti-American, it seemed only logical to anticipate a *volte-face* in foreign policy from the men who ousted him. Such were the expectations of the American business community in Argentina and of United States Ambassador Robert Woods Bliss, who urged the Department of State to "help our situation in Argentina" by early recognition of the Provisional Government. He submitted as convincing proof of his argument that the new government wanted to restore good relations with the United States, which had been so badly damaged by the "unreasonable attitude of Yrigoyen."[6] The Department of State deprecated efforts by "interested Americans" to win an advantage over Great Britain by the early recognition of the new government and, instead, proposed joint consultation on the matter to the British ambassador in Washington. The Foreign Office very much appreciated this gesture.[7]

When the news of the revolution in Argentina first reached London, the reaction of the press was concern bordering on alarm. The British ambassador specifically warned against eulogizing Yrigoyen because several important groups in Argentina resented the British adulation he had enjoyed since the D'Abernon visit. Within a week, the influential financial periodical *The Economist* could balance the good with the bad resulting from the Revolution, and, by the end of September, the Foreign Office observed philosophically that while Yrigoyen would be missed, they expected the same factors that had made him pro-British would "inspire his successor."[8] Appreciation of these circumstances undoubtedly accounted for the State Department's reserve in treating with the new government. It was a question of weighing pious public promises about cooperation with the United States and the Pan American Union against the widespread "depression and consternation" in

Argentina caused by the Smoot-Hawley Tariff, which represented the culminating moment of a decade of growing United States protectionism.[9]

The fact of the matter was that the Provisional Government's openness to the United States was based entirely on the hope that expanded trade between the two nations would save Argentina from the effects of the Depression and insure her economic independence. The debate over how to cope with the economic slowdown produced a package of solutions comprising three distinct elements, not designed to work together but juxtaposed for political reasons to produce a consensus among competing economic and political groups. First, Argentina had to tighten its belt. Vigorous retrenchment, deflation, and national sacrifice were necessary; the foreign debt must be repaid to restore confidence in Argentina and to "achieve our economic independence."[10] Second, the economy had to operate more efficiently. Specifically, agricultural production had to be increased and quality control imposed, grain storage facilities had to be added immediately, and the entire tax system had to be overhauled. This cult of efficiency had an apolitical quality congenial to the military professionals whose support was indispensable to the new government. Moreover, government-by-technician had the added appeal of contrast with the notoriously venal cronyism of the Radicals.[11] Third, the basic economic solution was to be diversification—diversification of production and, until that could be accomplished, diversification of markets for the nation's cash crops.

Given the conservative orientation of the Uriburu regime, it is significant that the prevailing sentiment was in favor of working out solutions to the nation's economic problems within the context of a free enterprise system.[12] Gradually, however, the devotion to laissez-faire collapsed under the pressing needs to react to Great Britain's menacing drift into protectionism and the dysfunction of the market mechanism. The case of foreign exchange was typical. The government began with voluntary controls in September 1931, when the British pound was devalued. Since the peso did not stabilize, the government joined private bankers to form an exchange committee. By October, the government had to take over control of all exchange

operations and was supervising exports to make sure they did
not upset the delicate accounts of the Banco de la Nación. This
is but one example of how the policies of the Uriburu regime
were formulated in the shadow of developments within the
British Empire, developments that culminated in the Ottawa
Conference of 1932. Of course, there had been disturbing signs
even before the Revolution of 1930. Ambassador James Macleay
had told the British Chamber of Commerce in Buenos Aires in
June 1930 not to take British free trade for granted, that there
was a "possibility of a change in this policy."[13]

At the end of 1931, despite unanimously bullish forecasts for
1932, nervousness bordered on panic. The Argentine ambassador
in London importuned the Foreign Secretary to give his government advance information on the British wheat quota and urged
special consideration for Argentina in view of the English investments there. The Argentine Rural Society urged the President
to make special tariff concessions to Great Britain in order to
save the Argentine meat industry; the Argentine Foreign Ministry
began secretly to sound out all of the nation's trading partners
on the possibilities of reciprocal agreements that would preserve
the status quo in international commerce; and, in a much-
publicized move, the President appointed a blue ribbon commission to study Anglo-Argentine commercial relations.[14]

Argentine anxiety was well founded, but efforts in 1931 and
1932 to relieve it were fruitless. The Foreign Office parried all
diplomatic thrusts with the argument that it could not discuss
the matter seriously until the convening of the Imperial Conference in Ottawa scheduled for July 1932. Here was an uncom-
fortable situation for an exporter of primary products. If
"dependency status" signifies that crucial market decisions
concerning primary product exports are made in the industrial
consuming centers, then it describes the situation in which
Argentina found herself. As we have indicated above, before
1930 most Argentines were resigned to, if not actually contented
with, such a relationship with a generally benign, not to say
beneficient, imperial power. It was precisely this satisfaction
with the established order that prejudiced so many Argentines
against the incursion of United States capital. Now, the relationship was changing. A series of decisions going back to the 1920s

had reduced incrementally the control of the Foreign Office
over international economic policy and had undermined the
bargaining position of Argentina in the British market. Whatever
leverage Argentine exports had enjoyed before the Depression
was eroded by the evolutionary changes in the British economy
and in the consequent increasing influence of the Dominions in
imperial decision-making. In the face of mounting pressure from
these overseas territories, the last great bastion of free trade
seemed destined to follow the United States and Europe into
the vortex of protectionist madness. Confronted with such a
disquieting specter, the Argentines had little choice but to
struggle to maintain their markets and to strive, with inadequate
resources and preparation, to achieve some measure of economic
self-sufficiency.

At first blush, the movement for Commonwealth protection
did not imply the ostracism of Argentina. A vocal lobby con-
sisting of British exporters and the Anglo-Argentine Committee
of investors argued that Argentina and Great Britain were tied
by mutually advantageous bonds. In the words of Sir Malcolm
Robertson, former Ambassador in Buenos Aires,

Argentina must be regarded as an essential part of the British Empire. We
cannot get on without her, nor she without us.[15]

Argentines took note of the British tariff measures but without
appreciating their import. It was as if they believed that any
distinction drawn by the British between "Empire" and "foreign"
somehow had to include Argentina in the former category. The
worst that Argentina could expect was a tariff policy based on
reciprocity. Proudly confident, *La Prensa* warned Great Britain
in February 1932 to eschew discrimination or Argentina would
reduce her food exports to England and sell her surplus products
elsewhere.[16] These were brave words! Within a matter of
months, they would have a hollow ring.

As the preparations for the Ottawa Conference went forward,
intelligence reached Buenos Aires that the Dominions most
certainly did consider Argentina one of the "foreign" countries
and that Great Britain probably would have to demonstrate its
commitment to the Empire by extracting material concessions
from the Argentines. The new Foreign Minister, Carlos Saavedra

Lamas, responded with a flurry of initiatives touting the benefits of commercial reciprocity. He even went so far as to leak to the British-run Buenos Aires *Herald* a report of his talks with American Ambassador Bliss on a reciprocal treaty with the United States. It was a transparent gesture. Bliss told the Foreign Minister that the United States was opposed to such pacts as a matter of policy, and immediately communicated the gist of the interview to his British colleague, who surmised correctly that the matter "shows Argentina's eager desire to pave the way for better trade relations with other countries in the event of her receiving a setback as a result of the Ottawa Conference."[17] Manuel Malbran, Argentine Ambassador in London, on home leave, offered Macleay the "same preferential treatment as might be accorded . . . by any of [the] Dominions or even better." This is what the Foreign Office had been looking for. They had been very pessimistic about the chances of establishing bases for trade talks with Argentina if the Imperial Conference insisted upon discriminating equally against all foreign nations. Now, Macleay concluded:

in the light of this statement it appears to me that our delegation in Ottawa could logically argue that if His Majesty's government in the United Kingdom were to agree to impose a tariff on all imported meat and possibly other foodstuffs and to grant Dominions either complete exemption or substantial reductions in duties in return for an increase in existing preferences in favour of our manufactured goods they could only be expected to do so on the understanding that any foreign country which was willing and able to grant a similar or better preferential treatment to products of the United Kindom would have to be accorded the same exemption or reduction accordingly.

The response from Ottawa was a resounding defeat for the Foreign Office viewpoint and a mortal blow to Argentine trade, allowing no room for doubt:

. . . [the] suggestion that any foreign country can obtain the same advantages as those given to the Dominions runs counter to the whole question of Imperial Preference link of Empire. Any suggestion that the Argentine could participate in Preference would never be entertained by delegations of the Dominions and to put it forward would destroy all prospect of agreement. Tell British Ambassador in Buenos Aires this to avoid false hopes.[18]

The details of the Ottawa accords were not immediately available in Buenos Aires, although Macleay carried out the instructions in the telegram quoted above. In what must be considered wishful thinking or a case of whistling in the graveyard, Minister of Agriculture Antonio de Tomaso reassured the crowd at the annual Palermo stock show that Great Britain would resist the pressure to build high tariff walls. Because of the great quantity of British investments in Argentina, because of the high quality of the food Argentina sent to England, because of the British shipping interests involved, and because of the "indestructible moral bonds uniting these two nations," he said, "we have never doubted that whatever agreements might be made with the Dominions, Argentine produce would continue to enjoy the welcome in that market which it had always received hitherto." The Foreign Office Minute noted dryly, "Doctor de Tomaso is perhaps more optimistic than the facts justify."[19]

Ambassador Malbran was sent back to his post in London to extract formal trade commitments from Great Britain in order to blunt the effects of colonial competition. His efforts were unavailing. To make his task more difficult, the Anglo-Argentine Committee and the Foreign Office adopted the stern line that had triumphed at Ottawa. They warned Argentina that her free access to the British market had ended and that a change in attitude was in order. In internal Minutes, British diplomats permitted themselves expression of outrage at the stubbornness of the Board of Trade, its sloppy negotiating technique, and the Ministry of Agriculture's lack of sportsmanship in refusing to compromise with Argentina. The issues that defied solution, thereby delaying the formal trade talks that Argentina now so desperately desired, were the control over the meat exporting quota, the tariff preferences to be accorded to Great Britain, the exchange guarantees that Argentina would offer British traders, and the limitations on the restrictions to be imposed on Argentine trade.[20] By the end of the year Malbran was ready to quit. He was thoroughly depressed by the impasse to which relations between the countries had come. The Argentine government, backed apparently by many sectors of the public, was not willing to make further concessions. There were limits to national degradation. At this juncture, in February 1933 the Foreign Office forced a confrontation at a Cabinet committee meeting and managed to induce the Ministry of Agriculture and the Board of Trade to accept a limitation on the restrictions to be placed upon Argentine meat imports. At the same time it persuaded Malbran to close his eyes to the diminution of Argentine sovereignty implicit in control of the meat export quota by foreign private corporations. With these two obstacles removed, the way was cleared for formal negotiations, and Vice-President Julio A. Roca, Jr., sailed to London to conduct talks with Sir Walter Runciman, President of the Board of Trade.[21]

The formal trade talks were as painful for Argentina as the preliminary discussions, with the added disadvantage that the public was fully aware that they were taking place. Roca's primary objective was to fix the minimum levels of Argentine exports to Great Britain and furthermore to tie the two countries together in such a way that the British firms in Argentina would be dependent upon the prosperity of the host country for survival (and thus would be hostages against further British protectionism). Minister of Finance Alberto Hueyo opposed Roca on the proposed tariff and exchange concessions to be offered. Hueyo wanted to maintain strict control over exchange as an indispensable aid in the financial reforms already underway, in balancing the budget, and in winning the cooperation of the "hostage" British investors. For his part, de Tomaso considered the meat quota the primary goal, but wanted it drawn in such a way as to give the Argentine government the right to distribute it among the meat packers. His clear intention was to increase, over time, the percentage allotted to Argentine companies rather than to foreign-controlled firms, with a view to strengthening national control over the basic industry.

Within a matter of days the central issue was defined as a straight bargain of a meat quota for an exchange guarantee, but then the talks bogged down on the details of the latter, for Hueyo refused to sanction concessions in this area. Saavedra Lamas sought to strengthen the bargaining position of his representatives by another round of diplomatic initiatives in search of new markets. Even before the mission had left for London, the Foreign Minister concluded a *modus vivendi* with Chile promising all sorts of reductions in trade barriers between the

two nations.[22] His trump card would be an agreement with the
United States, where President Franklin D. Roosevelt, elected in
November 1932, and his Secretary of State, Cordell Hull, were
committed to freer trade policies than their predecessors. The
Foreign Office was sensitive to the danger this implied, and
there is little doubt that the Argentine negotiating position was
strengthened in March 1933 by the Democrats' reciprocal trade
policy.[23] Ambassador Felipe Espil in Washington pressed
insistently for a commitment to trade talks, while in Buenos
Aires there was significant improvement in the exchange situation
of American importers.[24]

But Argentina's American gambit came to naught. Hull quickly
disabused Espil of the idea that there could be bilateral talks
before Congress had approved the President's general policy. All
the trumps now belonged to Runciman. His principal concern
was an orderly market. He felt that the Board of Trade and
the Ministry of Agriculture had made a major concession in
admitting the principle of limiting reductions on Argentine meat
imports. Now, the Argentines would have to knuckle under.
Aside from the brutal calculus of political influence, in which
Argentina and the Foreign Office counted for very little, Runciman continually referred to the extremely unfavorable balance
of British trade with the Platine republic. He pointed out that
whereas British exports to Argentina represented but 4 percent
of the United Kingdom's total sales abroad, Great Britain took
37 percent of the former's exports.[25]

By the beginning of April, the position of the Roca mission
was untenable. The Argentines were prepared to break off
negotiations. Political pressure at home was mounting against
the continuing disgrace of Roca's failure to get what he had gone
after. At last, the Vice-President prevailed over Hueyo and
Saavedra Lamas; a final concession on the exchange issue was
granted and the meat quota was left in the hands of the foreign
packers. The key to the agreement was that the Argentine
exporters, ranchers, farmers, economic experts and government
leaders all wanted an orderly market as much as, if not more
than, Runciman. Besides, as one of the members of the mission
put it, linking the Argentine quota to shipments from the
Dominions was the best security for Argentine trade—and the

terms could have been much worse. The British market, in his opinion, was saturated, and the Board of Trade might have cut meat imports by 100,000 tons without raising domestic prices beyond politically acceptable levels.

Nationalists of the left and right in Argentina then and later assailed the Roca-Runciman Pact as a sellout. They argued that Britain called the tune on the meat trade and, through exchange preferences, perpetuated British imperial domination over the Argentine economy, locking their country into the dependency role of a primary product exporter. These are thorny, polemical questions fraught with ambiguous terms of reference. I think it is fair to say that the meat trade provisions of the Roca Pact were not favorable to Argentina. On the other hand, it is not clear what other markets were available for the exportable surplus of beef and cereals. In the 1930s, trade opportunities were shrinking, not expanding. The Argentines did succeed in convincing the Italians to resume their purchases of meat, but this benefited only the producers of the northern littoral and left virtually unchanged the conditions affecting the vast majority of cattlemen and packers.[26] Further, the actual pattern of trade between the two countries was not unfavorable to Argentina after 1933, and there is clear evidence that the Treaty saved her from further cuts and restrictions.

The argument that the tariff and exchange provisions of the Treaty extended or intensified British imperial control over Argentina simply is not true. There is no question that the British talked familiarly of their special relationship with Argentina and that the Foreign Office took a patronizing attitude towards Argentines. But as early as 1931 both the British and the Argentines came to realize that the combination of exchange controls and inconvertibility of the peso put the Argentine government in a position to bankrupt the British firms locally . established by starving them of exchange, or by refusing to allow the railways to raise their fares, or by making them carry government goods at uneconomical rates (half price), or by encouraging in Buenos Aires alternative methods of public transportation to the tramways, which were losing passengers at a rate of more than 10 percent a year.[27] The investments were a doubtful commercial asset to England and a definite political liability. They represented "old" industries with rapidly declining political influence at home. When British diplomats spoke of treating Argentina as part of the Empire, they did not intend it as a means of extending British control. They believed that in the pervasive climate of protectionism it was the only way to extend to Argentina the tariff privileges and preferences enjoyed by the Dominions.

But the formal and specific features of the Commonwealth links reduced to mere nostalgia all talk of making Argentina one of the Dominions. The nexus of domestic and Dominion pressure groups pushed for a return to formal empire and weakened Britain's ability to retain control over what had unquestionably been part of the informal empire. Simultaneously, British control was vitiated by the Argentine policy of import-substitution industrialization and diversification. Aside from modest—not to say minor—changes in economic structures which this policy facilitated, it had the effect of opening decision-making to new groups whose interests were not linked to Great Britain or the traditional export trade. The decline in British influence after 1933, then, was the result of a shift in the balance of political power within Argentina, and changes in the pattern of international trade, especially within the British Empire, more than any fundamental change in the pattern of the Argentine economy.

The Argentines accepted the Roca-Runciman Pact grudgingly. The Executive presented it to Congress without enthusiasm. Most of the senators and deputies felt like Senator Benjamín Villafañe of Jujuy, who declared that he would vote for the treaty, although he thought it was disadvantageous, because rejecting it now would cause Argentine agriculture further damage.[28] Finance Minister Hueyo resigned because he thought the tariff and exchange concessions were excessive. Of the major newspapers, only La Fronda could muster any enthusiasm for the pact. Most disillusioning of all, signing the treaty did not end Argentina's trade problems. The suplementary tariff talks were difficult, in part because British supporters of protection and imperial preference, led by the Beaverbrook press, hounded the government for further restrictions on trade with foreign countries. For the Argentines, the diplomatic negotiations were a constant series of frustrations and humiliations. Even the most compromised

Anglophile began to have reservations about the new terms of dependency.

The Argentine grievances centered on the increasing "experimental" shipments of beef to England—especially the high-priced chilled beef from the Dominions, in violation of the Roca Pact —and on the unexplained delay in the bilateral investigation of the meat industry. In 1935, a tariff on beef was an added threat. The British complained publicly about the distribution of exchange and the treatment of their investments, but diplomats admitted privately that the Argentines were discriminating in favor of the English and that the treaty was having the desired effect.[29] The problem was that the Foreign Office was powerless to prevent the Dominions from violating the treaty. The Produce Markets Supply Committee of the British Cabinet decided that while negotiations over meat were taking place with the Dominions, Argentina should be approached in an attempt to secure her acceptance of a levy. This, in the Foreign Office view, would be difficult without a *quid pro quo*. The question of experimental shipments would become acute if the Dominions asked for increased shipments of chilled beef. Furthermore, it had become clear

that as regards Dominion exports of chilled beef the Board of Trade consider that we cannot any longer maintain that our engagements in Articles I and II of the Anglo-Argentine Agreement are being observed, and that the Dominions Office are in favour of our asking the Argentine Government to be relieved of these engagements. The latter course seems to be hardly possible, especially when we are already involved in approaching them for their assent to a levy. From the Foreign Office point of view, it might with equal force be urged that our engagements with Argentina should be frankly and fully put before the Dominions as we have no reason to believe has been done.[30]

The Dominions were unmoved. Australia was particularly insistent that, treaty or no treaty, the Dominions must be allowed to ship all the beef and mutton they could to Great Britain. The Australian representative went directly to Ambassador Malbran to warn him "that the responsibility for any break in the market in 1936 due to excessive importations of chilled beef would lie at Argentina's door."[31] Malbran appealed to the Foreign Office for help, but the only advice forthcoming from His Majesty's Secretary of State was to sacrifice their treaty rights for the time being in the hope that the Australians would rest contented with their gains. Appeasement was already Foreign Office policy!

The bargaining position of the Foreign Office was not strong. In matters of finance and commerce, the Dominions had a louder voice and the Board of Trade had superior access to cabinet-level ears. Runciman's political strength even intimidated the Prime Minister. The government's public commitment to stable domestic prices and production strengthened the hand of the Ministry of Agriculture in negotiating with the Argentines or with other branches of the British government. It did not help the Foreign Office at all to be in the position of pointing out to members of the government or representatives of the Dominions that the rights of Argentina were being violated and that the British claims were not fair. The interests of another country and fair play commanded very few votes in the House of Commons. Over and over again the Argentines were sacrificed to the needs of British politics and national interest, not as a result of any deliberate foreign policy, but as the result of a political process in which the Foreign Office counted for very little.

The success of the Roca-Runciman Pact made it virtually impossible to settle the differences between the two countries and ease Argentina's anxiety. By the end of 1935 trade between the two was nearly balanced, and this meant that there was no exchange available to facilitate remittances by British corporations, nor could there be an expansion of exports from the United Kingdom to Argentina without a corresponding increase of Argentine sales to England.[32] These considerations, long the linchpin of "informal empire," no longer exercised their sway over the British decision-makers. The complementarity of interest which had long made bearable Argentine dependence upon the British market no longer held. In short, the English were willing to sacrifice the investments that Argentina held hostage behind the wall of exchange control, and even came to support Argentine efforts to nationalize the railroads.[33] Therefore, the Ottawa policy of 1932 was triumphant. Argentina was sacrificed to the lions of Dominion trade preference.

For a short while, from 1935 to 1937, the improvement in Argentina's trade position obscured these harsh realities. But they became painfully obvious in 1938 when Argentina suffered a trade recession and Britain began to tool up for the coming struggle with the Axis. At that juncture, neither country could provide the other with what it needed most—on the one hand, a market for surplus agricultural products to earn the money to buy machine goods, together with the investment capital to fuel a burgeoning industrialization; and, on the other, absolutely secure sources of vital foodstuffs within a sterling area so that the supplies would not require the movement of specie or foreign exchange, together with a promise of political and military support.

The Argentine government was aware of these developments and was far from contented. Domestically, the solution lay in economic diversification. This could not be accomplished in a matter of four or five years, and the job for foreign policy was to find an alternative market for Argentine products or postpone the inevitable for as long as possible. The logical alternative to British trade was closer relations with the United States. This, too, proved to be a source of bitter frustration to Argentina.

Relations between the United States and Argentina had never been cordial. During the "golden age" of Argentina's economic expansion, the pretensions of the United States to the status of a world power were not seen as a particular threat by the South American nation, but by 1930, the northern republic had left no room for doubt as to its economic superiority. Its capital had penetrated deeply into the Argentine economy, and its trade balance was overwhelmingly favorable. Where Argentine products had a competitive advantage in the American market, United States farmers had managed during the twenties to raise protective barriers against them. Meat was the most sensitive issue. What a prohibitive tariff couldn't keep out, sanitary exclusion did, on the grounds that Argentine beef carried *aftosa,* foot-and-mouth disease.[34] As long as the multilateral system of international trade worked, denying Argentine products access to the American market was an annoyance, an insult to national pride and no more. The Argentines could balance their deficit account with the United States through a surplus account with Great Britain. Once the multilateral system collapsed and world trade was forced into rigidly bilateral channels, the American exclusion became a source of tension between the two nations.

The Uriburu government was unable to entice the United States into negotiations for a reciprocal trade treaty. The Justo administration undertook a diplomatic campaign for such talks and frankly admitted using exchange discrimination as a lever.[35] Ambassador Espil all but wore out his welcome at the Department of State seeking to pin down the American government. Sensitive to the difficulties that such negotiations would entail, the Department put off Espil on the grounds that until the President had laid down general guidelines for trade policy, talks with individual countries would have to be delayed. Actually, State hoped first to conclude a series of treaties with countries like Brazil, whose exports offered no thorny political problems. Espil took his case directly to Roosevelt in July 1933 and won a promise to include Argentina on the list of nations with which the United States intended to negotiate. Still, the State Department postponed announcing the intention to hold talks in order to avoid unnecessary friction with Congress.[36] To appease Saavedra Lamas and save face for Espil, the Department consented to have Argentine experts come to Washington to discuss the possible topics for trade conferences, but at the end of 1936 Hull told Saavedra Lamas that he feared "certain interests [that] might secure legislation in Congress defeating our purpose."[37]

The detailed questions of trade were handled by technicians in several branches of the United States government. The State Department considered exchange control a political question between nations and took the position that exchange discrimination must end before the experts' discussion could be transformed into formal negotiations. The Argentines argued that exchange control was another form of tariff and should be taken up with other matters during the trade talks, although they gave repeated assurances that exchange restrictions would be lifted as soon as trade improved. It took nearly five full years to work out a formula acceptable to both parties. Argentina would make a promise to end exchange discrimination, and that would be followed by a preliminary announcement of treaty talks. The Argentines would formalize their assurances on exchange when the statutory public announcement of formal talks was made.[38] The negotiations broke down, however, when the experts were unable to make enough progress to justify the required Argentine concession on exchange. The sad fate of the experts' discussions told the Argentines more than the State Department's pious lectures on liberalizing world trade.

As in the case of Argentina's frustration in seeking satisfaction from Great Britain, the explanation for failure to work out a deal with the United States lies in the configuration of domestic political forces opposed to admitting Argentine agricultural products into the American market. Roosevelt's promise to Espil was made in good faith, and a treaty with Argentina was consistent with the administration's general trade policy. The State Department's officers in charge of Latin American affairs, led by Sumner Welles, were well disposed toward Espil and considered the provisions of the tariff law unduly harsh on Argentine products. Yet neither Roosevelt nor the Department of State, both sincerely desirous of advancing the government's general trade policy, of satisfying what they considered legitimate Argentine requests, and of aiding the cause of American economic interests in Argentina, was able to achieve the trade treaty or any partial trade concessions.

What went wrong? The principal difficulty was that satisfying Argentina's needs had repercussions for the entire United States farm program. While failure to conclude a treaty with Argentina would not undermine the administration's trade policy, further pressure in support of Argentine interests might destroy the coalition that Roosevelt depended upon to support his farm program.

Roosevelt made the initial, general decision that the United States should include Argentina among the nations with which trade treaties would be negotiated. Hull concurred, despite the fat file on trade difficulties between the two countries. Although Hull told Espil that official talks could not begin until Congress had approved the President's policy, he sent experts in the Department to consult with their colleagues in the Department of Agriculture and the Tariff Commission on possible concessions to Argentina. Their findings, communicated by Secretary of Agriculture Henry Wallace in December 1933, were negative. Wallace spoke of a "net loss to agriculture" and felt that a reciprocal treaty with Argentina "would appear to be warranted only as a part of a broad program of reciprocal agreements involving countries that might be expected, as a result of the agreements, to increase significantly their imports of American agricultural products."[39] The State Department took the matter up in the Inter-Departmental Advisory Board on Reciprocal Treaties, obviously a sympathetic forum. It stressed the principles involved, forcing a compromise that included cuts in the duty on goods that Wallace admitted would not be hurt by Argentine competition.

Particularly significant was a token cut in the duty on flax, which the Argentines considered of primary importance. Wallace did not accept the decision of the Board. Flax growers, he pointed out, generally grew wheat as well, and the plan to reduce the acreage planted in wheat depended for its success on leaving open to the farmers as many alternative activities as possible. Assistant Secretary of State Sayre asked Roosevelt for a decision on the basic policy issue involved. Flax was unimportant to the United States, vital to Argentina; from the economic viewpoint the United States could cut the duty on flax to get important concessions from Argentina; from the political viewpoint, the matter was "open to question."[40] Roosevelt preferred to go "slowly and cautiously," to feel out members of the Congress before pushing the Department of Agriculture into anything Wallace thought unwise. The State Department turned its attention to preparations for other trade pacts.

The success of the Hull trade program further delayed talks with Argentina. The government thought it unwise to announce the inauguration of negotiations with too many agricultural countries at the same time. Meanwhile the experts would proceed with their appointed tasks. From the State Department viewpoint, the key to the talks would be flax, and the problem was how to import it from Argentina, benefit the American farmer, and not upset the Agricultural Allotment Act. Or, as the Economic Adviser put it:

It is particularly desirable to reach a solution of the American problem which will guard the interests of Argentina, at the same time that domestic growers are benefitted, and which will make it unnecessary to bring a conflict between these two considerations to the attention of the Executive Committee on Commercial Policy.[41]

With Espil's help, the Inter-Departmental Committee continued its preparatory work and, by the end of 1934, had fixed the American bargaining position as a 10 percent cut in duty on the "safe" items and a 50 percent cut in the duty on flax.[42] The State Department wrenched this compromise out of Secretary Wallace only by appealing directly to Roosevelt; it virtually insisted on the President's support by calling for his decision in a "basic policy question," a matter of "vital and pressing importance to our whole trade agreements program because the contemplated plan [to increase flax production] seems ... to run counter to the whole purpose upon which the program is based."

Although State carried its point, the confrontation showed the vulnerability of a liberal trade policy when it came into conflict with domestic economic problems. Secretary Wallace admitted that flax was not a major factor in American agriculture, but he was afraid that exposing flax to Argentine competition might arouse some senator from a flax district to look for support among colleagues from agricultural districts and embarrass the administration's efforts to control a more important crop. It was nerve-wracking for the State Department's Economic Adviser to follow every agricultural bill through the House and the Senate and lobby to make sure taxes, subsidies, acreage allotments, and the like specifically excluded flax so that an act of Congress would not summarily destroy two years of painstaking diplomatic efforts. Moreover, the constant bickering with Congress and the Department of Agriculture was costly from a bureaucratic point of view. Inevitably, senior officers at State questioned whether it was worth the effort.

During the extensive, severe droughts of 1935 and 1936, Espil tried to sell some Argentine corn in the United States. It was a modest proposal and the Department of Commerce joined the State Department in urging it on Secretary Wallace. The latter resisted, and as the discussions progressed, the liaison officer in the Department of Commerce became alarmed by the growing tension between Argentina and the officers in the Department of Agriculture; he felt that there was a "real danger" that Agriculture's hostility "may lead to reprisals and restrictions which will cripple our growing trade with Argentina."[43] Herbert Feis, the Economic Adviser, and Hull decided in 1936 that it was useless to press the issue without the active support of the Department of Agriculture. They feared the domestic repercussions of any price declines or possible labor troubles linked to agricultural imports. They continued to support the Argentine proposal, but to no avail.[44]

The flax proposal met the same fate. Senators Knutsen, Shipstead, Frazer, and Nye worked together to protect flax, threatening to oppose the sugar quota if duties on oils were cut. To counter this bloc, the Department of State could only count on the frail support of the paint industry, whose representatives admitted to them that they "have not dared to approach Congress because they feel that the combination of the sugar, flax and edibile oil interests would be too hard to beat."[45] Rather than destroy all chances for an accord with Argentina, the Department of State retreated and told the Argentine government that it would be better to wait until the United States had concluded trade agreements with industrial countries to show the American farmer the advantages of a liberal trade policy.[46] That moment never arrived. The exchange issue continued to plague relations between the two countries because the Argentines could see no reason to compromise what had become the keystone of their commercial policy without comparable concessions by the Americans. Meat was out, corn was out, even flax was out. In retrospect, we can see that Argentine needs could have been satisfied in the United States only by total, sustained commitment of presidential power in the Congress and in the policy formulation process. Weighed against the danger to the entire United States farm program that such intervention would have entailed, the possibility of salvaging the trade program by successes elsewhere, and the other demands on the President's time, such a commitment was politically unrealistic.

The constant frustration of Argentina's foreign policy efforts had important consequences at home. The Roca-Runciman Pact never elicited any enthusiasm in Argentina; its onerous terms and the shoddy treatment of the Argentine negotiators encouraged the government to seek new trading partners. Dissatisfaction with Great Britain intensified Argentine desires to trade with the United States, but the protectionist policies of the latter closed

off that alternative.[47] Out of this resentment and frustration
emerged a widespread Argentine economic nationalism with the
goal of maximizing the nation's control over its destiny. In
international affairs, that meant maximum independence of
action. It is significant that the Argentine government made a
major issue of the provisions of the Roca-Runciman Pact granting control of the meat quota to foreign packers, by calling
for an investigation of the meat industry. Such demands indicated
a desire on the part of the government to break the control of
a foreign monopoly over an Argentine industry.

Furthermore, the government's direct intervention in the
economy provided a variety of instruments for the assertion of
the nation's sovereignty. The growing strength of Argentine
industry, a direct result of the Depression, and fostered by
government policy, buttressed the nation's sense of self. By 1936,
there was a general coolness toward the renegotiation of the
Roca-Runciman Pact.[48] One editorial writer noted that the
British commitment to Empire trade "is antagonistic to our
interest in conserving our political and commercial national
identity"; another said, "This interference of foreign capital in
our destiny is getting every day more unbearable and it will be
necessary for the country to prepare to rid itself as soon as
possible of a submission which is incompatible with its national
sovereignty."[49] By the end of the 1930s, antipathy to the
imperial connection was widespread.

The lesson Argentina learned from its foreign relations during
this period was that no other country would or could protect
the nation's basic interests. Sentiments of loyalty to the informal
empire and a long tradition of responsibility, even several
hundred millions of pounds of investments, did not keep Great
Britain from sacrificing Argentine interests on the altar of
Imperial Preference. Sentiments of Pan-Americanism, the Good
Neighbor Policy, and expanded trade did not help Argentina
secure a foothold in the American market. If the Great Powers
sacrificed political sentiment and idealism to cold calculations
of national interests, why should a dependent nation be less
calculating, less selfish?

As the economic conflict between the Axis and the democracies
gradually assumed the form of an armed struggle, Argentina

adopted a posture of "correct" neutrality, intent on preserving her own political and economic interests at all costs. It is in this context that we must understand the Argentine proposal to the United States in 1940 for a nonbelligerency pact. It was a desperate effort to strengthen the hand of political groups favoring democratic government within Argentina by assuring Argentine economic interests within a framework of cooperation with the Allies, one that would allow Argentina a modicum of sovereign independence of action.[50] When the proposal was rejected, President Ortiz and the advocates of constitutional democracy gave way, and Argentina retreated into a shell of neutrality as the only means by which she could defend her national interests. The fact that some government officials explained or justified neutrality with attacks on the democratic system of government might be distasteful, but it was essentially irrelevant. As the British Ambassador noted in July 1940,

The greatest danger to us therefore seems to lie in economic stagnation resulting from the inability of Britain to absorb this country's essential exports of wheat and meat and the unfortunate necessity under which we labour of denying to Argentina the markets, such as France and Belgium, on which the remainder of these products have hitherto been sold—even in war time.

Argentine foreign policy, he said, would be "Yo Primero" [Me First]. The popular and official attitudes would follow whichever way the European conflict tended and, he concluded,

Nationalism is thus in the ascendant among the youth of this country, and this nationalism is often confused in British circles with authoritarian sympathies, since the vested ruling class rightly fears the ballot box.[51]

Neutrality, then, was a nationalistic policy. It and the concept of nationalism from which it was derived, the mechanism of state control over exports and foreign exchange upon which it was based, and the technicians who carried it out were essentially the same under pro-Allied democrats like Ortiz and his Foreign Minister José María Cantilo, or pro-Axis leaders with fascistic proclivities, like Castillo or Ruiz-Guiñazú. It should not be cause for surprise, then, that the military leaders who took power in 1943 followed a nationalistic line in foreign policy. Their policy was not something alien to the Argentine spirit, invented by the military mind. Colonel Juan Domingo Perón, the emerging leader of the 1943 military junta, therefore followed the lead of a foreign policy which had been evolving throughout the 1930s. What was to become the "Third Position" during the *Peronato*, an expression of strong Argentine nationalism, was thus in many ways a response to the failure of Great Britain and the United States to strengthen their commercial relations with Argentina during a period of profound economic crisis.

5.

Intellectual Currents

MARK FALCOFF

When American novelist and critic Waldo Frank returned to
Argentina in September 1942, after a dozen years' absence, he
was astounded by the spiritual transformation wrought by a
decade of economic dislocation and political stagnation. Almost
overnight, he reported, Argentines seemed to have lost faith in
their country, and, for one like Frank, who first visited the
River Plate during the sunshine years of the late twenties, the
contrast could not have been more marked. What so recently
had been South America's wealthiest, "whitest," most literate
and progressive republic (and therefore, also, its haughtiest), had
apparently become its most self-critical, most agonized, and in
some ways most pessimistic.[1]

The crisis was all the more poignant for having been completely unexpected. The Argentines who grew to maturity during
the First World War and the years immediately following believed
that progress and prosperity were their birthright, and in fact
during their lives they had known little else. Whatever social or
economic ills afflicted a decrepit and shattered Europe, whatever
political buffooneries made their Latin American neighbors the
butt of international jokes, up to 1930 Argentines felt that theirs,
at least, was a New World success story. In the space of six or
seven decades their country had evolved from one of South

America's most backward, underpopulated, and insignificant republics into a model and precept for the others—a record so spectacular as to disarm all but the most uncompromising critics. If Argentine society still betrayed certain imperfections, their eradication, it was profoundly believed, was only a matter of time.

It was this boundless confidence that most impressed the Spanish philosopher José Ortega y Gasset on his visit to the country in 1929. The Argentine people, he wrote, "do not content themselves with being one nation among others: they hunger for an overarching destiny, they demand of themselves a proud future. They would not know a history without triumph, and they are resolved to command." But he warned that "the promises of the pampa, so generous, so spontaneous, many times go unfulfilled," and he sensed that "defeats in America must surely be more atrocious than anywhere else. Man is suddenly mutilated, left high and dry, with no explanation and no treatment for his wounds."[2]

What Ortega foresaw as a tragedy of individual proportions befell an entire society the following year. The harvest dropped to a quarter of its value on the world market; the flow of European capital dried up; *villas miserias,* creole Hoovervilles, sprang up to disfigure the outskirts of Buenos Aires; and the collapse of political democracy ushered in an era of rigged elections and police repression of labor, student, and opposition elements. Not one or a few, but literally thousands of people were left "high and dry, with no explanation." In their search for the causes of the crisis, Argentine intellectuals began to question, for the first time in their lives, the assumptions upon which the "Argentine dream" had been based.

What happened to Argentina? This question ran like a unifying thread through practically all of the essays, much of the historiography, and many of the novels produced during the 1930-1943 period. Not that everybody thought he knew the answer; some writers, in fact, overwhelmed by defeatism, treated the time of troubles as a problem with no possible solution, a "natural" calamity like a hailstorm or flood. When a character in Eduardo Mallea's novel *La bahía de silencio* (1941) referred to Argentina as a case of "inspiration cut short," a country whose "original motive force" had mysteriously broken down, he was evoking a theme that appeared and reappeared in the creative literature of the time. Perhaps its best exposition was Mallea's own essay, *Historia de una pasión argentina* (1937), which deplored the disappearance of an "invisible Argentina"—a country whose Roman virtues of creative labor, authenticity, and idealism had been supplanted by the materialism, ostentation, and shallow vanities of a "visible Argentina." The quest for greatness, which characterized so much of earlier Argentine history, had given way to the scramble for bourgeois comforts. The men who led the republic, Mallea wrote, were now "infinitely more mediocre, more stupid, more trivial, more plebian and more individualistic than the men who led us in our infancy as a nation, and if we were to divine their deepest aspirations, our repugnance would know no bounds." Only in periods of penury and pain, he reminded his fellow Argentines, had their country approached its true potential. Its salvation lay not in a life of ease, but in the struggle for a "difficult Argentina," a nation committed to "create without fiction, live without ostentation, survive without resentment, dispens[ing] with a pantheon of 'greats' who are in reality pharisees and philistines."

Since Mallea could not explain why and how Argentina had exhausted its store of creative energy, he had no suggestions as to how it might be recovered. Hence the superficially optimistic note on which he concludes the book does not ring quite true. Instead, *Historia de una pasión argentina* affords a glimpse of the several states of mind of the Argentine middle class—its confusion, its demoralization, its preference for irrational explanations to unwelcome developments, and its tendency to resist the winds of change by embracing an idealized view of the past.

Mallea's grey tones appear a good deal brighter when placed beside those of Ezequiel Martínez Estrada, who introduced the metaphor of biological decadence in his lengthy essay on Argentine life and character, *Radiografía de la pampa* (1933). Unlike Mallea, Martínez Estrada did not deplore the loss of civic virtue or national direction, because he believed that they had never existed. Rather, the Argentine nation suffered from certain "birth defects" which damned it from the very beginning and rendered idle all attempts at cure.

On one hand, he contended, Argentina was a victim of geography. A country of vast, empty spaces, it was isolated in the midst of an empty continent, far from the centers of world civilization and life. No Argentine could contemplate a world map without shuddering, for his country appeared to be situated "in the remotest corner of the planet." The spiritual consequence was a pervasive loneliness, particularly on the empty pampa, whose towns he described as "places of dispersion," "living archipelagos surrounded by indifference and hostility," devoid of art, culture, or even love of life. In his isolation the Argentine was deprived of those imponderables that "help one to live, that make death a bit less abrupt, and permit one to look at the world with unalloyed happiness." Hence the Argentine's ferocious materialism: lacking what gives true happiness to life, he vainly turned to economic aggrandizement to fill the void in his existence.

But for Martínez Estrada, Argentina was a victim of circumstance as well: whatever tragedies she escaped at the hands of God had been unfailingly provided by man. The Spaniards came to the country not to settle or civilize, but to enrich themselves at the expense of the natives. The only Spanish contributions to Argentina were Spanish vices—lethargy, laziness, routine, and ignorance, and an inferior type of human being, the *mestizo,* to assure their perpetuation. The break with Spain, when it came, was not inspired by ideals of liberty and democracy, as textbooks mendaciously declared, but by the aspiration of the wealthiest and most ambitious creoles of the port of Buenos Aires to make the Spanish system work for themselves instead of their peninsular cousins. Independence had no meaning for the poor, who fought the new state over the division of land, cattle, and commerce for decades until they were finally defeated by the Remington rifle, barbed wire, and the railroad.

The Argentina of the 1930s was merely the same distorted organism grown to full maturity. Its economic life was dominated by latifundia and monoculture directed to outside markets; its colonial economic structure was permanently riveted to the body of the nation by British railroads—which ran from the remotest points of the interior to Buenos Aires, and to practically nowhere else. The nineteenth century cattle boom had raised up one of the world's most opulent capitals, a facade for the misery and degradation that stretched endlessly to its rear. "Every sky-scraper in the capital," Martínez Estrada wrote, rendered the provinces of the interior "poorer, more ignorant, more unproductive." In those areas "entire cities never taste of meat; children are raised on mandioc, oranges, and mate; three quarters of the population is illiterate; the percentage of men exempted from military service for thoracic deficiencies or endemic diseases . . . is simply dreadful." The price the country paid for a splendorous city was wildly inflationary, but even of itself Buenos Aires was a study in the evils of exaggerated urbanism—as vacuous and superficial as it was overpopulated and arrogant.

Argentina's colonial economy had produced a culture totally lacking in authenticity; the "modernizers" of the late nineteenth century had overvalued what Martínez Estrada called "cultural cosmetics," and forcibly pushed the nation into forms that did not suit its shape or spirit. "Europe interests us, and we copy from it. . . . Our own affairs interest us not at all, because we are still angry at what we really are." The country's only distinctive "cultural" trait was its crushing economic materialism. Argentina was a nation where a poor man had no right to his poverty and was despised as the destroyer of other men's dreams; where members of the working class would rather starve than destroy capitalism and hence their own chance to become exploiters in turn. It was a country, he concluded, where to deny the ideal of fortune, "the supreme badge of honor and respect, would be to declare the error of an enterprise already four centuries old, to proclaim, in effect, the sterility of one's own father."

Radiografía de la pampa is as exhaustive a catalogue of Argentina's problems as one could have encountered anywhere in the 1930s; virtually nothing was omitted or glossed over. It touched upon every controversy that agitated journalism, politics, economics, and historiography, often with a brilliance and exactitude that eluded other, more systematic commentators. And yet the underlying tone of the work was one of bitter, angry resignation—a pessimism that deprived it of much of its potential critical power. Some have gone so far as to suggest that it is precisely this quality that endeared the author to the Argentine establishment and won for his book the National Prize for literature in 1933 ($100,000). Whatever Martínez Estrada's intentions, one perceptive Marxist critic has written, "by diluting and dispersing the responsibility for the country's frustration, he could not fail to favor its ruling class." It was left to Martínez Estrada, he explains, "to provide the oligarchy with one of the loftiest excuses to put its conscience at ease. After all, how can one feel oneself responsible when fate determines everything? Why reproach oneself for backwardness . . . that is irremediable?" For those with a vested interest "in perpetuating the country's social and historical contradictions, it is useful to sustain that the entire matter is one of ontological—and therefore, of inalterable—contradictions, thereby convincing dissenters that things should not change—because they cannot."[3]

A more direct attempt to indict the Argentine elite for the nation's ills was made by one of its own members, Manuel Gálvez, in *Hombres en soledad* (1935), a novel that depicted the decadence of a once-great Argentine family whose fortunes had taken a turn for the worse since the advent of political democracy in 1916. The central figure is an unsuccessful lawyer and frustrated writer, Gervasio Claraval, who has married one of the daughters of patriarch Don Ezequiel Toledo.

Although he owes his social position and his scant legal clientele to his wife's family, as a sensitive and cultured man Claraval is repelled by his in-laws' vulgarity and cynicism. For him the Toledos embody all that is wrong with Argentina: unearned economic privilege, subservience to foreign capital, contempt for art and literature, and a tendency to compute social and human worth in terms of "a box at the Colón Opera, a luxury automobile, a summer house at Mar del Plata, and a yacht at Tigre." But above all Claraval/Gálvez condemns the oligarchy for that collusion with foreign capital that has made Argentina a "colonial trading post" for British and North American imperialism. By betraying Argentina's economic interests, he explains, the elite has also deprived the country of a distinctive culture and personality. This, for instance, accounts for his own inability to succeed as a writer.

But the matter does not quite end there. Although he feels no sympathy for the Conservatives, Claraval considers the Radicals utter incompetents and applauds their downfall in the Revolution

of September 1930, which occurs midway in the book. At one
point he even explains that as products of "classical culture,"
Argentines would fare best under enlightened despotism.
("Today," he says, "democracy is a weepy, romantic, declama-
tory thing . . . the remnant of the vicious degenerate that was
Rousseau.") But the greatest paradox of all is that in spite of
his vaunted nationalism, Claraval lives only to return to Europe,
an obsession that reaches almost pathological proportions. The
book is replete with speeches on the superior "spirituality" of
the European environment and of the contrasting flatness and
vacuity of Buenos Aires. At one point he blurts out that "God
made a mistake. Instead of letting us be born in a land of
tradition . . . he sent us to these empty pampas, lacking in
sensibility, personality, and culture." Gálvez develops this theme
ad nauseam; fully half of the characters in the novel suffer from
the same *mal d'Europe,* which drives them to alcohol, love
affairs, suicide, or the Catholic Church. Claraval's only hope is
that the Toledos will be able to influence General Uriburu to
name him secretary of a European legation; when this fails to
materialize, the book ends on a note of frank despair. Thus,
what begins as a specific indictment of a class and a system ends
as an admission of inevitable defeat, a motif not very different
from that of Martínez Estrada, with whom Gálvez otherwise
differed markedly in style and ideology.

One highly popular alternative to the constant self-flagellation
of Mallea, Martínez Estrada, and Gálvez was offered by Gustavo
Martínez Zuviría (Hugo Wast) in two entertaining if somewhat
trashy antisemitic novels, *El Kahal* and *Oro* (both 1935).[*] Inspired by *The Protocols of the Elders of Zion,* they relate the
apparent discovery by an Argentine scientist of a method of
turning lead to gold, and the consequent panic of World Jewry,
whose power, it is explained in a "historical" introduction, rests
upon a global monopoly of the precious metal.

Wast actually seemed less interested in developing this fantastic
story line than in blaming Jews at home and abroad for what
he found distasteful in modern Argentine society—labor agitation,
the threat of universal suffrage, the emancipation of women,

---

[*]Although published as two separate novels, *El Kahal* and *Oro* are actually one
continuous work and are treated here as such.

liberalism, modern apartment buildings, and Hollywood films. He also launched into an impassioned defense of the beleaguered oligarchy by establishing a clear distinction between "good" and "bad" landowners. Fernando Adalid, the pasteboard example of the former, insists that "we have created the best Argentine *estancias*. We have founded cities that bear our names. We have not travelled. Can it be said that we have idly enjoyed ourselves?" Yet these kindly philanthropists, "constructors of a nation," were ungratefully referred to as *latifundistas* in the Chamber of Deputies and in comic strips. "And taxes were rained upon us! We sustained losses. There might still be time to save half our fortune, sacrificing the other half. We preferred to mortgage our holdings, trusting in the future. We have fought for twenty years; we have created enormous riches, and today we recognize that we have been defeated." The victors were "those who have not worked, those who have lived at the expense of the rest"—the Jewish bankers and Jewish-controlled meat trusts.

To make this ridiculous caricature a bit more believable, we are introduced by way of contrast to one of Adalid's brothers, the "bad" *estanciero* who has sold his lands at an early age and has for years led a libertine existence in Europe, loaning money at usurious rates and making only occasional visits to the country. Fernando Adalid explains that his brother "by instinct, has adopted the policy of the Jews. He doesn't work the land or raise cattle or construct railroads. If from time to time he forecloses on a debtor's property he resells it when prices improve. His force is liquid assets . . . the instrument with which wars and crises are made." Not only does Adalid's brother adopt the tactics of the Jews; early in the book we learn that he actively collaborates with them. Hence the land question in Argentina is really a "racial" question, and social protest is a Jewish device to destroy "Argentine" capital and distract attention from growing Hebrew domination of the nation's economy.

It may seem as if this silly work has received more space here than it deserves; yet *El Kahal* and *Oro* were widely read and believed, and by 1942 had gone through nine editions (53,000 copies), making it one of the major best-sellers of the period. The secret of its success consisted in the assurance Wast offered that all was really well with Argentina—that the problem was really an "alien" infection that could be purged from the system. Whatever else one can say about his grotesque sociology, it "explained" certain economic and social changes that Argentina was undergoing at the time. Above all, Wast's certainties afforded relief from writers who were victims of their own confusion and despair.

Many Argentine historians, as intellectuals (and often) as public men, shared the disenchantment of creative writers. But in place of metaphysical or existential explanations, they searched for the "wrong turns" of Argentine history, the missed options of the past excluded from official texts and syllabi. Thus the crisis of 1930 not only undermined Argentina's self-image, but produced a sharp break in her historiographical traditions— dividing establishment "liberals" from opposition "revisionists."

Liberal historiography, which originated in the late nineteenth century, glorified (and justified) the overthrow of the dictator Juan Manuel de Rosas in 1852, the subsequent elimination of provincial resistance to a strong central government, and the opening of Argentina to European capital and immigration, in terms of the creation of a prosperous export economy and the establishment of stable republican (if not precisely representative) political institutions. By the appearances of 1910, or even 1928, the liberal "modernizers" of the previous century seemed marvelously right, and their historians had said so. But in the perspective of the 1930s, both they and their apologists seemed tragically mistaken, for the Depression had shattered the myth "of uninterrupted progress toward perfect democracy . . . the rhetoric of the promised land based on the size of our national territory and its herds, and the myth of growing prosperity with which our politicians attempted to explain away their lack of foresight and their indolence."[4] The revisionists proposed to write a new Argentine history that would explain the nation's "defeat," and they began by reopening the case of Juan Manuel de Rosas.

The literature on Argentina's great nineteenth-century *caudillo,* which occupies so prominent a place in the historiography of the period, had its counterpart in many other Latin American republics, where the conservatives of the immediate post-independence period (Alamán in Mexico, Portales in Chile, Francia in Paraguay, García Moreno in Ecuador, Oribe in Uruguay) were rehabilitated for their opposition to the economic and political liberalism that inspired the break from Spain. Instead of reactionary spokesmen for a dark Hispanic past (as orthodox historiography had long maintained), to the revisionists these men were far-seeing patriots whose economic and cultural nationalism, if followed rather than abandoned, would have prevented later maladies. In the case of Rosas, Argentine revisionists could build their case upon a truly fascinating and in many ways attractive personality—rancher, Indian fighter, popular leader of the masses of the city and countryside, Governor of the Province of Buenos Aires (1829-1832) and then, entrusted with "the totality of state power," chief of the Argentine Confederation from 1835 to his overthrow nearly two decades later.

The first major attempt at his rehabilitation came in 1930 with the publication of Carlos Ibarguren's biography, *Juan Manuel de Rosas, su vida, su tiempo, su drama.* Actually the date is somewhat misleading, for the book bears all the marks of the previous decade, when Ibarguren—having made a poor showing as a presidential candidate in 1922—figured prominently in the Conservative intellectual movement against the Argentine Radicals. What attracted him to the Rosas period was its apparent lack of social conflict and its freedom from "un-Argentine" ideologies. The caudillo himself, for Ibarguren, was eminently a man of order: enemy of parliaments, intellectuals, the press, cities, Freemasonry, and above all, anarchy and revolutions; friend of hierarchy, property, and religion. In other words, Rosas' personality and political system for Ibarguren represented nineteenth-century models of what Argentina needed in the twentieth.

Far more characteristic of the interpretations of the 1930s were the works produced under the impact of the economic crisis and the Roca-Runciman Pact (1933). For example, in Julio and Rodolfo Irazusta's *La Argentina y el imperialismo británico* (1934), the dictator's refusal to grant extraterritorial concessions to Great Britain and France under the pressure of two naval blockades transformed him into the one national leader who had resisted the pressures of foreign imperialism—and won.

José María Rosa, Jr. went even further; in *Defensa y pérdida de nuestra independencia económica* (1943) Rosas was not only the leader of an incipient "national bourgeoisie," but an agrarian reformer! By the time of his overthrow, Rosa asserted, Argentina had developed "a powerful national economy whose industrial [artesanal?] production had reached a notable level." The development of a powerful industrial state was prevented only when Rosas was overthrown by Argentine liberal expatriates in league with foreign powers anxious to replace creole manufactures with their own.

It was left to Manuel Gálvez to conjure up the image of a truly "popular" Rosas, and in his *Vida de Don Juan Manuel de Rosas* (1940) he successfully fused the economic nationalist and man of order with the great national leader. Gálvez depicted his hero as a democratic Caesar who treated rich and poor alike, who lived modestly, who frequently ventured out alone from his estate at San Benito de Palermo to visit the poorer districts of the city incognito; who, faithful to his wife during her lifetime, discreetly adopted a mistress from the popular classes after her death; who "mystically" divined what the masses were thinking and acted accordingly; the "good" estanciero who never missed the baptism of a child on his estates, nor failed to provide for the widows and orphans of his tenants. In short, Gálvez's Rosas was a conservative with a popular touch—always in contact with the masses, sincerely and selflessly concerned with their desires and welfare. In this, Gálvez seemed to suggest, consisted a critical difference between Rosas and later conservatives, who possessed economic privilege but shunned its corresponding responsibilities.

Having restored "the Restorer of the Laws" to his proper place, the revisionists then re-examined the conditions under which Argentina became a major area of British investment in the last half of the nineteenth century. What they found hardly seemed to justify the celebration of earlier historians. Instead, the story of Argentina after Rosas became a dour tale of national decline, and nobody told it better than Raúl Scalabrini Ortiz, who abandoned a promising literary career in the mid-thirties to become his country's most important revisionist economic historian. In his *Historia de los ferrocarriles argentinos* (1940) he attempted to show that although British concerns owned and operated 70 percent of Argentina's railroads, English capital had been unnecessary to their construction in the first place. The British, he explained, had acquired ownership of their lines either by taking over already thriving Argentine concerns, or constructing new ones on the basis of concessions that were little short of spectacular giveaways tendered by corrupt native governments. In the best muckraking tradition, Scalabrini turned British and pro-British sources against their authors to show that the English never actually paid for the lines they "bought"; thus the entire history of British railroad enterprise in Argentina—and by implication, of all British investment—was one vast financial fraud.

More important still, in British hands, Scalabrini wrote, the railroads became "an instrument of colonial domination." Taking advantage of the free-trade legislation enacted after the fall of Rosas, the English inundated the remote provinces of the interior with cheap finished goods, destroying the livelihood of thousands of helpless creole artisans. Through the manipulation of freight rates, the new owners then reshaped Argentina's entire economic geography, making it "impossible to manufacture cigarettes in the tobacco regions, spin and weave in the wool centers, mill wood in the lumber centers." The result was that "Argentine" railroads, except for the relatively insignificant state lines, were "as far from Argentina's reach as if they were in India." In other words, he concluded, the lines were only Argentine to the extent to which they obstructed Argentine economic development.

Scalabrini did not deny that the British had facilitated a certain kind of "modernization," but it was a process that served their own purposes to the detriment of the long-term interests of the Argentines. A few beef barons benefited, of course, but their six-month stays on the French Riviera had cost the nation her independence and reduced the majority of her inhabitants to economic ruin. Under Rosas, he wrote, "so-called progress ground to a halt, but so did the penetration of the invisible forces of foreign capital and diplomacy," preventing "the consummation in a few short years of the total alienation of the country," and maintaining the preconditions for later independent economic growth. It was Argentina's tragedy that the men who succeeded the dictator were utterly detemined to discard this precious legacy by inviting British capital to do what creoles should and could have done for themselves.

It is ironic that the most eloquent reply to the outpouring of pro-Rosas books and pamphlets during the thirties and early forties came not from "establishment" historians at all, but from Marxists like Rodolfo Puiggrós and Aníbal Ponce. Since the appearance of José Ingenieros's *Evolución de las ideas argentinas* (1918-1920), left-liberal writers had treated the age of Rosas as if it corresponded to the feudal period of European history. Marxists found this scheme doubly attractive: one one hand, it assured an unambiguous place for Argentina in the mainstream of Western development; on the other, it seemed to ratify the belief—firmly held by the Argentine Communist party from 1918 to 1935—that, having had its bourgeois revolution in the mid-nineteenth century along with all other respectable states, Argentina was ripe for a dictatorship of the proletariat. To regard Rosas as something *sui generis* would place the whole question of "historical epochs" in the murkiest of doubt. Hence, in *La herencia que Rosas dejó al país* (1940) and in *Rosas el pequeño* (1943), Puiggrós found it necessary to assert that the dictator "rejected foreign capital not in order to favor a progressive and independent development of the national economy, but rather to maintain stagnant the archaic modes of production and class relations inherited from the colony." Far from defending the fatherland, he concluded, Rosas "reduced it to a miserable existence that could only lead it to be, sooner or later, a country dependent upon the great imperialist powers."

The plausibility of this argument was flawed by Puiggrós's rather inconsistent claim that foreign capital had in fact played a "progressive role" in Argentina; that the only problem arose from its late arrival, "after capitalism had become imperialist." With this Puiggrós did not satisfactorily explain why the creation of an export economy based on the extraction of raw materials would have had a more "progressive" effect on Argentine society had it come fifty to eighty years earlier. Nor did he seem to appreciate Scalabrini's point about the extremely selective (and therefore distorting) role of foreign investment. In any event, Puiggrós's interpretation never won back the considerable terrain lost to the *rosistas,* because, for all its undoubted revolutionary intentions, in the end it amounted to little more than an indirect if somewhat original justification of Argentina's dependent economy. It was not that the *rosista* revisionists were necessarily right, but that by 1940 the only significant group of Argentines willing to publicly applaud the "progressive" role of British capital were spokesmen for privileged groups who obviously had little else in common with Puiggrós or men like him.

It should be clear by now that the strongest intellectual current of the period was a strident and often resentful nationalism. This, too, represented something of a departure from earlier years, when Argentina boasted of being, in the lapidary phrase of José Vasconcelos, "a branch office of Europe."* As an ideology, nationalism was already evident in the late twenties, but its greatest impact came in the following decade. By 1939 it had found expression in a wide variety of political organizations, some of which openly emulated European fascist movements even to the point of recruiting their own party militias. It is tempting to associate this phenomenon with the intensified efforts of the German and Italian embassies in Buenos Aires to promote a climate of opinion hostile to Great Britain and the United States—tempting, because it is partly true. But it would be quite wrong to overlook the purely Argentine developments that more fully explain why nationalism rather than Marxism became the most "dynamic" ideological response to the crisis of 1930.

Any survey of the subject, however cursory, must begin with an artificial but useful division between two styles or traditions of Argentine nationalism, each voicing the grievances of a different social and economic group. The older tendency, which for want of a better term will be referred to here as "aristocratic" or right-wing nationalism, originated as a militant Conservative response to the re-election of Yrigoyen in 1928 and the prospect of an apparently perpetual succession of Radical

---

*It is true that even before the First World War important Argentine publicists, notably Ricardo Rojas, had raised serious objections to foreign domination of Argentina's economy and culture. However, these critiques tended to be issue-oriented and somewhat fragmented, rarely approaching anything that could be called an ideology.

governments. As advanced in *La Nueva República,* a daily founded in 1927 by Julio and Rodolfo Irazusta, this nationalism was reactive and reactionary, and although initially influenced by Maurras, Maeztu, and other European traditionalist ideologues, it rapidly developed a distinctly creole flavor.

The aristocratic nationalists spoke for important sectors of the Argentine landowning classes, the church, the army, and the "old" (i.e., non-immigrant-descended) middle class who professed to see in broader suffrage an open sluice gate for the tides of social revolution. In their peculiarly baroque style they mourned the breakdown of pre-existing "hierarchies," the subversion of political "order," the allegedly free hand that popular democracy afforded subversive "slavic and semitic" elements—all the while ignoring the thoroughly unrevolutionary nature of the Radical administrations of the time.

The right-wing nationalists shared much the same sense of loss as many historical revisionists. The Argentina of nationalist nostalgia was free of immigrants, radical ideologies, "relativism of values," and therefore political and social unrest. It was a society, as one of them wrote, in which "we were all cousins and did not need to ask anyone to spell his last name in order for us to catch it."[5] It was also primarily rural, for the aristocratic nationalists profoundly regretted Argentina's "excessive" urbanization. In the countryside, they claimed, *patrón* and *peón* had labored side by side in peace and harmony for generations until "outsiders," that is, immigrants, came to teach the latter dissatisfaction and sedition, upsetting the equilibrium of a nearly perfect society.

Recognizing that any restoration of pre-1852 Argentina was out of the question, aristocratic nationalists nonetheless thought that its essence might be recaptured were they to replace liberal democracy with an authoritarian regime based on corporative rather than individual representation. The masses of laborers, in this scheme, would collectively have no greater power, in spite of their overwhelming numbers, than the clergy, the landowners, the military, or any other element of what they liked to call the *fuerzas vivas.* But the emphasis was decidedly on "authoritarian" rather than "representation." As Carlos Ibarguren put it, only "governments of force" were capable of maintaining "social order, hierarchy, and discipline," thus avoiding the "menace of Soviet Communism." Such a regime could only be brought about by the "last aristocracy," the Argentine army.[6]

The concern for purely political solutions was characteristic of Argentine nationalism of the twenties. Apart from a few gestures in the direction of restoring the Church to its "rightful" place and purging the cultural milieu of non-Hispanic influences, its advocates limited themselves to devising formulas which would justify their seizure of power and the implantation of an authoritarian system of government. On economic questions their position was not at all clear. Many favored continuing the time-tested relationship with Great Britain, and the nationalist daily *Bandera Argentina* even applauded the Roca-Runciman Pact! Some, like historian Vicente Sierra, were unabashed agrarians who staunchly opposed the growth of Argentine industry on the grounds that a "country of proletarians" would be more susceptible to Communist blandishments.[7] Others, like the Irazustas in *La Argentina y el imperialismo británico* called for a limited program of industrialization in order to provide the country with greater defense in depth when negotiating with England over cattle prices or terms of trade.

Of all the right-wing nationalists of the late twenties, only Leopoldo Lugones, poet and anarchist-turned-man-of-order, managed to fully integrate the political notions of nationalism with demands for economic independence and social justice. His *La grande Argentina* (1930) reiterated the call for authoritarianism and corporative representation but also advocated industrial protectionism, strict limitation and control of foreign investments, and state exploitation of petroleum and other vital raw materials. Even more important, Lugones displayed great sensitivity to the plight of the humble masses of the interior— the forgotten majority of Argentines—and his economic program called for redressing regional imbalances, so long tipped in favor of the provinces of the littoral. Of all the nationalist theoreticians, Lugones was closest to General Uriburu, and it is probable that a reform something like the one outlined above was what the latter had in mind before he was outmaneuvered by General Justo and cynical establishment politicians in 1931 and 1932. Uriburu's failure forced the aristocratic nationalists to re-evaluate their position; some accepted posts in the Justo administration on the grounds that "order" had indeed been restored, if not exactly along the lines they had anticipated. But others were so repelled by the return to the "old" politics of jobbery, corruption, and subservience to foreign interests that they broke completely with the regime they had helped to install. Lugones himself committed suicide in 1938.

Shortly after Justo's "election" in 1931 and the conclusion of the controversial Roca-Runciman agreements, a second, "popular" or left-wing variety of Argentine nationalism emerged to express the frustrations of an effectively disenfranchised middle class. Its most coherent expression was provided by a group of young Radical intellectuals who founded the *Fuerza de Orientación Radical de la Joven Argentina* (FORJA) in 1935 under the leadership of Luis Dellepiane, Arturo Jauretche, and Raúl Scalabrini Ortiz. FORJA's message was a compound of economic nationalism and populism, neatly summarized in its battle cry, "Fatherland, bread and power to the people! " (*Patria, pan y poder al pueblo*) In hundreds of street-meetings and lectures, in pamphlets, books and short-lived periodicals (*Forjando, Víspera, Reconquista*) it popularized the image of Argentina as a sort of gigantic ranch whose productive capacities were being ruthlessly exploited and whose industrial potential was being stunted by Great Britain, operating through a subservient Argentine elite. The discovery of an unholy alliance between "country-selling" (*vendepatria*) oligarchs and foreign imperialists led the Forjistas to reject the notion, so near and dear to right-wing hearts, that the country's problem was subversion from below. Quite the contrary; the cause of national ills was the continued political hegemony of the Argentine upper class, whose vital economic interests as exporters of raw materials lay outside the country. In other words, Argentina suffered not a crisis of authority but one of legitimacy; the nation could ill protect itself from British imperialism as long as its affairs were managed by men from aristocratic families, prototypically portrayed as lawyers for foreign firms or their willing pawns in national politics. The national patrimony could only be recovered by a popularly based government such as that of Hipólito Yrigoyen, whose overthrow, incidentally, was credited *post hoc* to a supposed unwillingness to bend to the pressures of foreign capital. By developing an explicitly Jacobin dimension to Argentine nationalism, FORJA thus offered the embittered middle class the gratifying possibility of pursuing its private goals (social mobility, economic opportunity, political influence) within the framework of a crusade for national sovereignty.

Like many middle-class "revolutionary" parties in Latin America at the time, FORJA sought not so much to radically alter the structure of society as to make an ongoing system work for its own sector rather than for the traditional elite. The fact that it failed to wean most middle-class Argentines away from their perennial allegiance to the Radical party should not cause its influence to be underestimated. While Argentina's middle class was not exclusively bureaucratic, the question of political patronage was not, and had never been, a negligible one. Yrigoyen had fashioned a spectacular career—and later a legend—by vastly expanding opportunities for his followers in this area, and the Conservatives' parsimony and favoritism during the thirties remained one of their weakest points of defense. Even those Argentines—and they were many—who attained a measure of success in either the professions or business could hearken sympathetically to FORJA's preachments. What the latter seemed to be saying was that the productive, useful (and patriotic) Argentines were being unfairly deprived of their rightful place in the directing organisms of the state. In other words, FORJA built its appeals on the growing discontinuity between Argentine economic and political development. This was a theme that would be heard again, in an appealing orchestration by Juan Perón.

For all the vituperation heaped upon them, the Argentine Conservatives themselves produced some of the strongest arguments in favor of new departures in the economic field. Influential figures clamored for a vigorous program of industrialization, and if theirs were still minority voices within the elite, they were at least ones that were clearly heard. The principal exponents of Conservative economic nationalism were Luis Colombo, President of the Argentine Industrial Union, Alejandro Bunge, editor and publisher of the highly respected (and respectable) *Revista de Economía Argentina,* and Dr. Benjamín Villafañe, Senator for the province of Jujuy.

Both Villafañe, who represented the older industries of the Argentine interior (wine, cotton, sugar) and Bunge, who spoke for the more modern enterprises centered about Buenos Aires (textiles, cement, construction, cigarettes, beer and soap) sought a compromise rather than a confrontation with dominant agro-export interests. Bunge studiously avoided attacking either the British or the Argentine grazing establishment, but in his *Una nueva Argentina* (1940) he made it clear that the end of the country's "pastoral era" was long overdue. British capital and investment had played an indispensable role in the nation's development, he freely conceded, and without the cattle industry Argentina would still be a backwater of South America. But times had changed. Argentina was bearing the burden of a foreign debt whose service came to more than half a billion pesos yearly, and an annual repatriation of profits that amounted to ten billions more. In a period in which exports were growing, perhaps this might be permissible, but in the context of a stagnant or diminishing world market, it clearly was not.

In a larger sense, Bunge continued, changing world economic conditions, especially since the First World War, made a reliance on the international division of labor unreliable and unrealistic. By failing to appreciate this fact and make the proper adjustments, Argentina had made no qualitative economic progress since 1908. True, since that time she had experienced periods of economic prosperity, but these were due to developments outside the country rather than within it. Conversely, the crisis of 1930 had left Argentina defenseless against European policies of retrenchment and imperial protection; she was forced to accept whatever prices industrial countries might offer for her raw materials. For Bunge the only solution was a planned program of industrialization, diversification of production, and the development of the domestic market. "We must decide," he wrote, "that this is the last generation of importers and estancieros . . . With leadership and sacrifice, Argentina possesses the capability not only of attaining economic independence, but even autarchy."

What distinguished Bunge from popular nationalists like Scalabrini Ortiz was his determination to fix the blame for Argentina's industrial backwardness not on the Argentine cattle barons or the British, but on "irresponsible politicians" (presumably Radicals and Socialists) whose allegedly demagogic appeals to workers fomented "slackening, disloyalty in all areas . . . arrogance and class hatred . . . inefficiency and disorder" in factories and workshops. Villafañe agreed in even stronger terms. Demagogues, he wrote in *Cosas de nuestra tierra* (1939), had not only promoted chaos in Argentine industry but had undermined its very economic foundations. By encouraging strikes and achieving "unreasonable" wage increases for workers, Radical and Socialist politicians forced a rise in the price of Argentine goods, which made it impossible for them to compete with products from "countries near and far, where labor costs are less and the working day longer."

Both men viewed universal suffrage as the chief obstacle to the growth of Argentine industry, a curious view—to say the least—considering how elections were managed in Argentina at the time they were writing. In *La ley suicida* (1936), *Chusmocracia* (1939), and other diatribes, Villafañe looked back on the period 1916-1930 as "the blind mob in power . . . regression to barbarism, elimination of merit in government leadership, the death of science, of the arts, of culture in all its manifestations." Bunge was more cautious but just as categorical. Democracy did not necessarily mean, he wrote, "a pernicious electoralism with frequent campaigns throughout the country, nor indefinite toleration of mediocre representatives frequently out of touch with national problems and necessities." But Bunge was more prescient than most Conservatives in at least one respect. In *Una nueva Argentina* he acknowledged that reforms in housing, health, education—especially in the more backward provinces—were long overdue. If the Argentine establishment continued to shun its responsibilities in those areas, he warned, they could expect the advent of a demagogic movement that would destroy all it held dear.

Until 1930 Argentina was regarded as one of the few Hispanic countries where liberalism had taken root and flourished; yet during the severest crisis of her history, she failed to produce a significant current of liberal reformist thought. Any explanation would have to begin with the peculiarities of the Argentine variety of liberalism, for European political doctrines have a way of undergoing curious mutations south of the equator; labels are often misleading. Specifically, the "liberalism" introduced into Argentina in the middle of the nineteenth century, which—miraculously unchanged—remained the ruling political philosophy for more than eight decades, rarely betrayed democratic or egalitarian tendencies, much less commitment to social reform. Rather, it was regarded as an *organizing principle* for state administration and economic development. Rosas's successors understood it to mean republican institutions, free trade, laissez-faire, and religious toleration. The first inspired the establishment of a "modern" state (civilian, lay, rational, and federal) whose facade masked continuing features of traditional Spanish absolutism. A congress was created and a constitution proclaimed, but the power of the executive was all but unlimited, and regional autonomy remained a legal fiction. Elections were neither free nor universal until 1916 (and not always afterward), and most Argentine liberals right up to the First World War regarded suffrage as something best restricted to the rich and well-born. Even in the thirties, they ritually affirmed the tenets of popular sovereignty while tacitly insisting that the masses were incapable of immediately exercising their rights. Instead, for an indefinite period "select minorities" would best be the repositories of political power.[8] As for economic policy, laissez-faire had doubtless attracted the capital and technology (and won the markets) which had made Argentina the most advanced Latin American nation. But it had also created entrenched economic interests that showed few signs of permitting a transition to more modern forms of social and economic organization. As late as 1934 land ownership, great wealth, and social position were all but synonymous, the larger the tract the better. Whatever positive role one might have attributed to economic liberalism in the nineteenth century, by the second third of the twentieth it seemed to many an obstacle to further progress.

It was the conservative and elitist nature of Argentine liberalism (or perhaps merely its identification with the "regime") that led the Radicals to proclaim themselves as "anti-liberal," although their alternative hardly consisted of more than a change of personalities. Their rivals, the remarkable group of men who led the Argentine Socialist party, worked within this liberal tradition but sought to infuse it with social content. During the period under consideration, two books by Senator Alfredo Palacios, *El dolor argentino* (1938) and *Pueblos desamparados* (1944), grimly documented the malnutrition, disease, and illiteracy that afflicted less fortunate Argentines, particularly those in the northern provinces, and in *La burguesía terrateniente argentina* (1930) Jacinto Oddone revealed how little landed property had actually changed hands since the late colonial period. In the Chamber of Deputies, Congressman Nicolás Repetto attacked the government's policies on meat prices, transportation, electoral fraud, and civil liberties and, together with Palacios, drafted and secured passage of a wide range of labor laws (most of which went unenforced before 1943).

The record of the Socialist party was impressive, but its philosophy of reform was fully adequate only to its special constituency, the working class of Buenos Aires. Largely immigrant or immigrant-descended, bourgeois in aspirations if not in fact, this class was almost as dependent upon a flourishing export economy as were the estancieros. Its goal, like that of the Radicals, was not to destroy the system but to maximize its gains within it, not precisely an outlook upon which to base an effective program of social transformation. Hence whether the issue was the "poor provinces" or the condition of the urban worker, the Socialists proposed not structural change, but a more equitable distribution of the nation's earnings from the sale of its foodstuffs to Europe. It was, in short, an opposition that the more conservative liberals could live with.

The ideological impact of the Argentine Communists was considerably less than that of the Socialists because of an apparent inability to adapt Marxism to the peculiarities of Argentine development. The Communists regarded their country as a full-blown capitalist society ripe for proletarian revolution, and those who spoke of liberation from British imperialism and the development of native industry as the necessary antecedent (as did the minuscule Trotskyist groups that later supported Perón) were summarily dismissed as Social Fascists. When the Third International called upon its member parties to promote the formation of Popular Fronts in 1935, the Argentine Communists muted their criticism of the regime and until 1939 (and after 1941) concentrated their attack on its nationalist opponents both left and right.

The Communists took over the defense of nineteenth-century liberalism at the very moment when many Argentine liberals themselves were abandoning it as a cause irretrievably lost. By 1937—that is, midway through the period under discussion—liberalism of any variety seemed on the wane throughout the world. Laissez-faire had been abandoned in varying degrees by Great Britain, France, and the United States; authoritarian traditionalism in Eastern Europe and fascism in Germany and Italy seemed to have revitalized once-decrepit nations; and the Spanish Republic, perhaps the most liberal government on the continent, was already deeply embattled with the forces of "romantic" reaction. Even had they ignored contemporary international events—which they were not wont to do—Argentine liberals could have found ample reason at home for feeling that history had overtaken them. As Saúl Taborda wrote in *La crisis espiritual y el ideario argentino* (1934), one of the few certainties left to his fellow-countrymen was that "the nineteenth century has run its course. . . . The parliamentary system with its corresponding political parties represents the pastoral period of our institutional history. It was fine then . . . but does not suit the realities of the present day."

Roberto Guisti, one of Argentina's most important men of letters, sadly concurred. "We are today where we were twenty years ago," he wrote in 1940. Liberalism had not solved "a single fundamental national problem. Alarming demographic indices, the economic and physical degradation of much of the population, latifundia, the surrender of land to grasping foreign consortia, the enfeoffment to gigantic monopolies, the lack of a merchant marine, a myopic, petty sort of politics, an educational system that is all facade and no content, growing unemployment—thus a minimum list of the host of problems" which Argentines should have confronted to avoid "the extremely bleak future" that now awaited them.[9]

There were of course liberals who doggedly continued to argue to the end of the period that a change of national course was neither possible nor desirable. But they were usually men with an all too obvious interest in the established order. Such was the case of Federico Pinedo, finance minister in the Justo and Ortiz governments, who in the press and public forums led a spirited defense of the policies of the past. Those who objected to the presence of foreign capital or to Argentina's subordinate role in the international division of labor, he scolded in *La Argentina en la vorágine* (1943), "overestimate our relative international status"; collaboration with foreign interests had made Argentina what she was, and "in the terrible world in which we live, with our thirteen million inhabitants and our lack of essential resources, it is as necessary today as it was in the time of our grandfathers." The problem was that for Pinedo there was no problem, at a time when practically everybody else felt otherwise.

Only in considering the disenchantment with liberalism and its consequences can the Argentine attitude toward the Second World War be fully understood. Even before the fall of France, Franco's victory in Spain convinced many that the values that inspired the republic had lost their vitality—that the forces of reaction were the wave of the future. One need not belabor the point (now richly documented) that there was an abundance of Axis sympathizers in Argentina; the right-wing nationalists recognized the fascist cause as their own and said so openly. It is seldom noted, however, that neutralist sentiment fed not only on ideological affinities or opportunism, but also on a desire to settle accounts with a system that in Argentina was regarded as synonymous with economic and social privilege.

The left-wing nationalists of FORJA, for example, viewed the interests of Great Britain and those of the Argentine oligarchy as virtually identical and believed that the fall of one would mean the collapse of the other. It was an ingenuous notion, to be sure, but one often encouraged by the Argentine Conservatives themselves. During the North Atlantic summer months of 1940 a steady stream of estancieros and Conservative politicians made the pilgrimage to the British Chamber of Commerce to affirm "our vital interest in the cause which the British Empire upholds and defends," for "with the loss of the British cause, we too should lose forever."[10] Nor could there be any doubt as to what was meant by "our vital interest." As cattleman Carlos Alberto Pueyrredón explained, the defense of Britain amounted to a defense of the Argentine beef industry. To this end, Argentina should not "yield to the temptation of seizing the opportunity provided by the war to industrialize *à outrance.*" By all means, he said, we should defend our small industries, "but it behooves us to refrain from importing machinery, materials and workers for certain manufactures protected by customs duties." After all, "we cannot sell without buying from those who buy from us."[11]

One need not have been a practicing Argentine nationalist to resent the confusion of national and class interest, and those who objected to the way men like Pueyrredón had run the country for thirteen years naturally viewed their overseas partners with distaste when not with antipathy. Even those Argentines who supported the Allies for humanitarian reasons often felt compelled to apologize for their preference by insisting that they were opting for the lesser of two evils.

The bad news from Allied war fronts during the first three years of the conflict, combined with growing political unrest, created a climate of uneasiness in the highest circles of Argentine society. Perhaps the clearest sign of malaise was the breach in Conservative ranks introduced by President Castillo's refusal to break relations with the Axis. While former presidents Justo and Ortiz and former foreign minister Carlos Saavedra Lamas vehemently argued in favor of loyalty to the nation's traditional trading partners, the "accidental president" from Catamarca not only refused to yield to Anglo-American pressures but actually initiated conversations with opponents of the government.

This bold attempt to capitalize on the political regroupment taking place in Argentina failed in its objective,* but aggravated the mood of cynicism and defeatism in the ranks of the traditional elite. The atmosphere of intrigue surrounding the comings and goings at the Casa Rosada, the midnight meetings at the Campo de Mayo garrison, even Castillo's sudden embrace of

---

*It was Castillo's peculiar genius that he, almost alone among Conservatives, recognized that a realignment was taking place at all. Most Argentines became aware of the fact only after the elections of 1946 when General Juan Perón—to the surprise of many—defeated a coalition of virtually all the traditional parties, from Conservative to Communist, with the support of nationalists of both the left and the right and that of a labor movement which was largely of his own creation.

"nationalist" rhetoric, were a sure sign that the old regime in Argentina was coming to an end. It was not merely that its defenders faced more disaffection than their fathers or grandfathers had been forced to confront, but that their critics no longer argued within the same frame of reference. Differences of opinion no longer turned about who would run Argentina, but what kind of a country it would be.

The themes that dominated Argentine thought throughout the period—the nation's economic relationship to the outside world, the need for industrialization, the role of foreign investment, the authenticity of national culture and the repatriation of the national patrimony, the condition of the provincial populations and the readjustment of regional imbalances—if translated into concrete policy, offered few prospects of stability and continuity, and the Conservatives knew it. As Senator Antonio Santamarina confessed to a friend in late 1940, "We are sitting on top of a volcano."[12] Ten years of attacks from below had not dislodged him or his associates from power but had seriously undermined their self-confidence, and, as the French historian Pierre Gaxotte pointed out many years ago, an elite that has lost faith in its own mission is an elite that is lost. In this sense, if in no other, the doubts and dissatisfactions of the Argentine intellectuals had done much to bring "the infamous decade" to an abrupt and inglorious close.

6.

Popular Culture

GUSTAVO SOSA-PUJATO (translated from the Spanish by Mark Falcoff)

One of the most important developments in Argentina during the 1930s was the appearance of a mass culture of national content. Until 1930, there were actually two "Argentine" cultures co-existing side by side—one "creole," that is, grounded in the country's ancient Hispano-Indian heritage, and another arising from the massive entry of Italian and Spanish settlers in the late nineteenth century, hence, "immigrant." From about 1890 to the 1920s, these two sociocultural currents developed alongside one another, sometimes peacefully, sometimes in conflict. But at no time did they show signs of fusing into one. The reasons were purely historical: for much of the time the great mass of immigrants had not fully assimilated into national life, and the reaction of the native was to resentfully shut himself up in the subculture of the *arrabal*.* But the inevitable social intercourse between the two groups, combined with a perception, however gradual, of common social grievances, eventually reduced the differences.[1] Hence, by the 1930s what had once seemed two irreconcilable modes of expression were becoming one. A new sensibility, although lacking in specific political content, was

---

*arrabal: an urban slum, unlike those of the United States, located on the out-skirts of the city rather than in its older sections. Actually the arrabal was a sort of twilight zone between city and countryside to which were relegated those rural people not annexed to ·the great *estancias* in the late nineteenth century. [Tr.]

amply reflected in popular art and literature, in the nascent mass media (radio, films) and the creation of a new set of national myths.

This new mass culture rested fundamentally upon Argentina's native—that is, Hispanocreole—tradition, but recast the timeless themes of pampa and the arrabal in a modern idiom. A new element reflected the melancholy, the resentment, the frustrated strivings of the masses crowded into urban areas. These two sources placed a distinctively Argentine (as opposed to Latin American) stamp upon what eventually emerged as the characteristic popular expression of the period.

To fully understand the significance of the change, it must be borne in mind that the official culture of the day was aristocratic both in style and substance. It neglected or distorted the actual content of Argentine life.[2] Subservient to European models, it articulated the sentiments of a small upper class and its allies among the intelligentsia—both disinclined to consider our country a region separate and apart from the Old World. But even the popular culture that emerged during the thirties failed to comprehend adequately the nature of Argentina's national experience. Neither Raúl Scalabrini Ortiz in political thought nor Leopoldo Lugones and Manuel Gálvez in literature, for example, fully liberated their vision from the limitations of the aristocratic "official" culture they sought to supersede.

Even today the importance of the culture of the thirties is not fully appreciated. It has inspired few monographic studies of consequence, although it is extraordinarily rich in social and cultural data not normally found in the documents conventionally utilized by social researchers. The revisionist historian Juan José Hernández Arregui, one of the few to attempt an organization of the materials, does in fact discover social content in certain popular expressions, but his analysis is very limited and his approach is basically political.[3] Unfortunately, from such a restricted perspective (which we might call "Peronist realism"), it is impossible to encompass all the complexities of the subject. Nor has Argentine sociology—overwhelmed as it is by the weight of an excessive "scientism"—concerned itself with the analysis of cultural phenomena except in the most marginal sense. Finally, the small amount of research dealing with our popular culture, carried out largely by nonspecialists, does not leave us with a sense of adequate coverage.

This chapter will discuss the most representative vehicles of popular expression during the thirties—the tango, the myth of Carlos Gardel, the motion pictures—each in its own way voicing different aspects of a nascent national culture. Certain motion pictures and tangos have been selected as illustrations because they offer the most direct, "raw" indices of Argentine society at the time. In contrast to the official culture (based on abstract concepts and imported models), the popular expressions of the thirties arose out of concrete social and historical circumstances. It is of course true that at the start their importance was limited, but their later manifestations were both more sophisticated and more exact. At any rate, these popular art forms represent an authentic witness, not a colonial mirror; with all their faults they contain the elements of a truly distinctive national culture.

Throughout the thirties the tango was by far the most important form of musical expression. Then, as now, far from being a mere element of folklore or one more means of diversion, the tango was "a constant and important cultural phenomenon, an indispensable element in the life of our people."[4] The Argentine of the thirties derived from tangos not merely entertainment, but a reflection of his social and spiritual situation, a projection of his innermost feelings, or the sarcastic evocation of his frustrations. In the verse and music of this uniquely Argentine musical form he found his intimate thoughts cast in the idiom of daily speech.

The origins of the tango are unknown. Experts alternatively attribute it to African or Hispanocreole sources; dates are uncertain; authors often mythical. We can say with some precision that it first appeared on the banks of the River Plate or in the outlying reaches of the capital as an expression of marginal social groups living in the twilight areas between city and countryside. It was sung in the brothels of the port and constituted a fundamental element of the subculture of the *compadrito:** the dance possessed erotic content and was regarded

---

compadrito: one of those uniquely Argentine types whose label defies translation. The compadrito was something of a free-lance tough who lived by his knife, offering his services to whoever would contract for them. A sort of unofficial alliance often existed between compadritos and the political bosses of various wards of Buenos Aires. [Tr.]

as a form of virile sexual provocation. At the same time it is very possible that the steps of the dance originated in those of the creole duel. This "anti-social" basis led the embryonic tango to be a form of musical expression forbidden by the Argentine establishment, and it was only after its resounding success in Europe that it was gradually accepted in the country of its origins—first as a diversion for the gilded youth of Buenos Aires (attracted by its erotic implications) and later as music appropriate to popular cafes, cabarets, and downtown bars. It was also utilized at political meetings to publicize candidates or parties.[5]

But only by the mid-twenties did the tango come to possess a definite language of its own and become a form of expression of enormous popular significance. Its older, "early" form, light and vivacious, became heavy and serious; its content became more complex. No longer merely a vehicle for erotic encounter or sexual provocation, it became a means of articulating in words and music the resentment and the demoralization of the urban masses. During the thirties the radio, phonograph, and motion picture vastly extended its possible range, and this access to mass communication acquired an almost revolutionary significance, for diffusion of the tango amounted to the ratification not merely of an art form but an entire range of popular values. For want of a better term these values are often referred to as *tanguidad,* defined by Julio Mafud in his *Sociología del tango* (1966) as "an entire style of life—a metaphysic and psychology that support a set of Argentine and Platine characteristics. A master of the tango craft is not someone who merely sings or dances to the musical form, but rather one who—without necessarily doing either—lives and embodies the spirit which lies behind it."

To succeed as the author of tango lyrics a writer had to be able to condense and compress basic elements of popular thought and feeling. For example, the most representative and stylistically accomplished practioners of the art, Celedonio Flores, Enrique Cadícamo, and Enrique Santos Discépolo, angrily rejected the present in favor of melancholy recollections of times past. In their work the present was viewed as something uncertain, pervaded by economic difficulties and impossible amours. But in the suburbs of memory, there survived the human values worthy of consideration: the cult of courage, manly friendship, devotion to one's mother—and what we call *viveza criolla* (loosely translated "native shrewdness"). In the tangos of the thirties the past became an obsession; the less satisfactory present, a necessary evil.

The verses related capsule stories of daily life in popular language—at times not very imaginative, but always functional and direct in its description of the milieu and the frustration of the man in the street. Hence the verses of Celedonio Flores for the popular tango, *La Cumparsita:*

PORQUE CANTO ASÍ

Porque ví el desfile de las inclemencias
Con mis pobres ojos llorosos y abiertos
Y en la triste pieza de mis buenos viejos
Cantó la pobreza su canción de invierno.

Y yo me hice en tangos;
Me fui modelando en odio, en tristeza,
En las amarguras que da la pobreza . . .
En llantos de madres . . .
En las rebeldías del que es fuerte y tiene
Que cruzar los brazos cuando el hambre viene.

Y yo me hice en tangos
Porque es bravo, fuerte; tiene olor a vida
Tiene gusto a muerte.

Porque quise mucho, porque me engañaron,
Y pasé la vida engarzando ensueños,
Porque soy un árbol que nunca dio flores,
Porque soy un perro que no tiene dueño,
Porque tengo odios que nunca los digo,
Porque cuando quiero me desangro en besos,
Porque quise mucho y no me han querido,
Por eso canto tan triste . . . por eso.

WHY I SING THIS WAY

Because I saw misfortunes file by, one by one,
With my poor eyes tear-weary and sleepless
And in the sad room of my Old Man and Old Lady
Poverty sang her winter song,

I became what I am through tangos,
I was modeled in hatred and sadness,
In the bitterness that comes from being poor
In the tears of mothers . . .
In the anger of men who are strong
But have to sit helpless in the face of hunger.

And I became what I am through tangos
Because the tango is tough and strong,
And smells of life
And tastes of death.

Because I loved much and had my heart broken
And spent my life spinning dreams
Because I'm a tree that never bore flowers
Because I'm a dog without a master
Because I have hatreds I never mention
Because when I love I give myself away
            in kisses
Because I loved much but wasn't loved
            in return
That's why I sing so sadly, that's why.

Here Flores utilized the melodramatic tone of the popular
folk tale—a lament that treats reality as a painful fact. It is virile
while admitting defeat; it asks not for relief, but accepts frustration as an inevitable component of the tragedy of life.

This fatalistic sense, which the tango exploited through lamen-
tation and sarcasm, reflected an essential characteristic of the
popular class. Chained to the boring routine of repetitive labor
in urban centers, it took refuge in defeatism and in the worship
of the values of a mythical past. Having lost the resources of its

ancestors of the pampa and the *suburbio** to manifest liberty
and courage, it took out its wounded feelings in the tango. But
it is important to interpret that emotional projection correctly.
For Hernández Arregui it means "the weariness of a humiliated
people seeking consolation in the fantasy of the gaucho's knife,
in maternal devotion, or in an appeal to one's lover"[6] —a rather
simplistic view based on too literal a reading of certain tango
lyrics. Instead, it is in the *assumptions*—what lies between the
lines, as it were—that one must search for the fundamental
meaning and message.Thus viewed, the popular commitment to
the past signified not merely a reaction to the culture of the
establishment, but something more creative—a massive attempt
at the construction, in affective terms, of authentic values based
on the nation's popular traditions.

It is Enrique Cadícamo who best adumbrates the melancholy
of days gone by through the evocation of the bohemian milieu
of the early tango, the chaotic (and picturesque) atmosphere of
the waterfront bordellos, the duels-to-the-death between *guapos,***
the headstrong women of the suburbio, the silent, sober friendship between men—a whole range of sentimental tones depicting
in an idealized fashion a way of life at once vital and extinct.
During the thirties, the arrabales, transformed into *barrios,****
nostalgically preserved their ancient splendor in these lyrics of
Cadícamo:

> *Yo soy del barrio de Tres Esquinas*
> *Viejo baluarte del arrabal*
> *Donde florecen como glicinas*
> *Las lindas pibas de delantal.*
> *Donde en la noche tibia y serena,*
> *Su antiguo aroma vuelca el malvón*
> *—Y bajo el cielo de luna llena,*
> *Duermen las chatas del corralón . . .*[7]

Suburbio: used interchangeably with arrabal. [Tr.]
**Guapo:* used interchangeably with compadrito [Tr.]
***Barrios:* the districts of Buenos Aires (or any Argentine city) lying outside the center.
  With the growth of the metropolis, the shabby arrabales were absorbed and became
  more integral parts of the capital. [Tr.]

> I'm from the borough of Three Corners,
> The old bulwark of the ward,
> Where the pretty schoolgirls flourish
> Like garden plants in a row.
> Where on warm, quiet nights,
> The air smells of geraniums,
> And the cottages of the lane
> Sleep under the sky of a full moon.

From a spicy (and forbidden) dance, practiced by a small minority at the turn of the century, the tango became a complex and creative manifestation of mass sentiment in the thirties. The process coincides, logically enough, with the development of radio and motion pictures, producing a collective sensibility that united creole nostalgia with certain features of Argentine immigrant culture. The result was a truly national musical genre.

Although Enrique Santos Discépolo—or Discepolín, as his friends and public affectionately called him—was a composer and lyricist of tangos,[8] he requires separate treatment in view of the overwhelmingly important place his work occupies in the cultural panorama of the period. For in Discépolo popular expression attains both profundity and a capacity for reflection. His tangos best distill the bitter essence of the disillusionment, the frustration of Depression-decade Argentina. The brutal "philosophy" which emerges from them is neither casual nor counterfeit, but carefully fashioned (it took him about a year to compose each one), and expressed without formal complexities. His style—dry, ironic, and utterly free of illusions—utilizes the spontaneous syntax of popular speech to produce a dramatic interpretation of social situations.

It is impossible in a few lines to analyze the entire corpus of Discépolo's work, which in its multiple aspects represents a singular and valuable social, psychological, and cultural testimony of the period. Hence we will limit ourselves to transcribing almost integrally three of his most representative tangos: "¿Qué vachaché? ", written in 1926, "Yira . . . yira . . ." (1930), and "Cambalache" (1935). The first actually foreshadows the coming decay of established values by showing as early as the mid-twenties

an Argentina torn by ruthless competition, lacerated by economic
want, devoid of any ethics, in which only the most elementary
elements of subsistence are readily available. Hence the protagonist of Discépolo's first tango cries out:

> *Lo que hace falta es empacar mucha moneda,*
> *vender el alma, rifar el corazón;*
> *tirar la poca decencia que te queda,*
> *plata, plata, plata . . . y plata otra vez . . .*
>
> *Así es posible que morfés todos los días,*
> *tengas amigos, casa, nombre . . . ¡lo que quieras vos!*
> *la panza es reina, y el dinero Dios!*

What you've got to do is make your pile,
Sell your soul, auction off your heart;
Get rid of the little decency they've left you,
Money, money, money . . . and more money . . .

That way you'll have three squares a day,
Friends, house, respect—hell, whatever you want!
Your belly's king, and money is God!

In the Discepolan universe there is no place for naive illusions
or hidden hopes. His philosophy is condemnatory and any sign
of hope is dismissed with sarcasm:

> *¿Pero no ves, gilito embanderado*
> *que la razón la tiene el de más guita?*
> *¿Que a la honradez la venden al contado,*
> *y a la moral la dan por moneditas?*
> *¿Que no hay ninguna verdad que se resista*
> *frente a dos pesos moneda nacional?*
> *Vos resultás haciendo el moralista*
> *un disfrazao . . . sin carnaval . . .*
>
> *¡Tiráte al río! No embromes con tu conciencia,*
> *sos un secante que no haces ni reír*
> *¡Dáme puchero, guardáte la decencia,*
> *plata, plata y plata . . . yo quiero vivir!*

¿Qué culpa tengo si has piyao la vida en serio
pasas de otario, morfás aire, y no tenés colchón?
¿Qué vachaché? Hoy ya murió el criterio . . .
Vale Jesús, lo mismo que el ladrón!

Don't you see, you poor fool,
That whoever's got the most dough is right?
That honor's sold for cash, and morals for pennies?
That no truth can withstand two bucks?
When you try to moralize you only seem
Like a circus clown without his tent.

Go to hell! Don't bother me with your conscience.
You're a fool that can't even make me laugh.
Give me bread on the table—you keep your decency,
Money, money, money . . . I want to live!

Is it my fault if you've played life by the rules,
And so, like a dope, you have to eat air,
And haven't a bed to lie in?
"What'll I do? " Honor just died today,
And Christ's worth no more than the thief!

Discépolo was capable of painting in vigorous strokes the popular personalities of his tangos; in their majority they are ridiculous types, failures or fools—anonymous individuals, commonplace types from everyday life in Buenos Aires who question with acrimony and bitterness the world in which they are compelled to live. Their personal histories tend to be chronicles of disillusionment narrated with veracity and without concessions to sentiment. In the final analysis, fiction or argument barely existed in Discépolo's tangos; he preferred to extract the themes of his own personal experience or events observed around him. His vision of Argentine society was acute, detailed—and highly critical.

"Yira . . . yira . . . " dispenses with the irony of his first works, and becomes instead an anguished cry or hopeless lament:

Cuando la suerte qu'es grela
fayando y fayando
te largue parao.
Cuando estés bien en la vía
sin rumbo, desesperao . . .

Cuando no tengas ni fe,
ni yerba de ayer
secándose al sol.

Cuando rajes los tamangos,
buscando ese mango
que te haga morfar.
La indiferencia del mundo
—que es sordo y es mudo—
recién sentirás . . .

When Lady-Luck, just a damn-sel,
deceiving and failing,
throws you on the beach;
when you remain in low water
without a North, or a hope . . .

When you no longer have faith,
or yesterday's tea,
drying out in the sun . . .

When you have worn out your soles,
in search of that buck, for
to go and take a bite,
the people's perfect indifference,
you'll have to perceive.

Here not only the most ambitious dreams but even the most
elementary human needs encounter insuperable obstacles—even
the possibility of loving and being loved in return is denied.
Discépolo's characters are reduced to so narrow and impoverished
an existence as to be unable to develop their personalities.

Verás que todo es mentira,
verás que nada es amor
que al mundo nada le importa.
yira . . . yira . . .

Aunque te quiebre la vida,
aunque te muerda un dolor
no esperés nunca una ayuda
ni una mano, ni un favor.

Cuando estén secas las pilas
de todos los timbres
que vos apretás
buscando un pecho fraterno
para morir abrazando . . .

Cuando te dejan tirao
después de cinchar,
lo mismo que a mí
cuando manyés que a tu lado
se prueban la ropa
que vas a dejar . . .
Te acordarás de este otario,
que un día cansado
se puso a ladrar . . .

You'll see that all is a big lie
you'll see that no one cares a little,
Geehra, geehra . . .

Even life kills you, no matter,
no matter pain breaks your heart;
don't wait for any protection,
for some hand, or
for some help.

When all the doors of the houses
where you go, stay closed,
in spite of your knocks;
searching for the breast of a brother,
to die embracing someone;

When you're left along the way
while others saddle up;
When you see that they're
trying on the clothes
they know you'll leave;
You'll think of this guy
who one day decided
to bay at the moon.

The woman appears in Discépolo's tangos as an indispensable element of human frustration. She invariably ends up prostituting herself or degrading the ideals of masculine character, and since she utterly lacks values of her own, she can only vindicate her humanity through maternity. In essence, Discepolan women are mothers or prostitutes, and this condition renders impossible the union of man and woman on a solid and lasting basis.

With all paths of escape closed, the world of Discépolo is claustrophobic and asphyxiating. His characters, who have met with defeat frequently, often opt for self-elimination. This may reflect the fact that in this period the country experienced the highest suicide rate in its history. Discépolo's tangos constitute one of the few testimonies of this symptom of social ills. The last words of Leopoldo Lugones prior to taking his own life, "There is nothing but filth, filth, and more filth!", find their corresponding echo in the lyrics of the tango "Cambalache":

Vivimos revolcaos en un merengue,
y en un mismo lodo todos manoseaos.

Hoy resulta que es lo mismo
ser derecho que traidor . . .
Ignorante, sabio, chorro,
generoso o estafador . . .
Todo es igual . . . nada es mejor

Lo mismo un burro
que un gran profesor.
No hay aplazos, ni escalafón,
Los inmorales nos han igualao . . .

Si uno vive en la impostura
y otro roba en su ambición,
da lo mismo que si es cura,
colchonero, rey de bastos,
caradura o polizón . . .

¡Qué falta de respeto, qué atropello a la razón!
¡Qualquiera es un señor! ¡Qualquiera es un ladrón!

We live bogged down in the muck
All pawing through the same filth.

Today everything's the same:
patriot and traitor . . .
Moron, sage, and thief,
Philanthropist and swindler . . .

Everything's the same—nothing's better.
An illiterate equals a learned professor.
There are no dunces nor promotions
The immoral and us—we're all alike.

If one man cheats
And another robs, to satisfy his ambition,
Makes no difference if he's a priest,
Mattress-maker, King of Clubs,
Parasite or peon . . .

What a lack of respect! What a twisted belief!
Anyone's a gentleman! Anyone's a thief!

In all of its aspects the world of Discépolo creates a sort of popular critical consciousness. To be sure, it is a consciousness expressed in emotional terms, but it unquestionably expresses an intelligent and uncompromising appreciation of the social situation. But apart from its social content, the work of Discépolo anticipates "an authentic cosmology—an interpretation of existence based on subjective perceptions, intuitions, and spontaneous and reflective appreciations of the universe and its component parts" (Mafud)—an entire tanguistic "metaphysic" which in the thirties became a part of popular language.

One of the most spontaneous and creative manifestations of mass culture in the thirties was the elaboration of new myths to embody collective aspirations. The myth of Carlos Gardel—the most enduring and most genuinely popular—was born in the middle of the decade following the singer's death in an airplane crash in Colombia. Up to that moment Gardel had been an unchallenged popular idol, but following his premature disappearance at the very peak of his career, his figure began to transcend its personal and professional context to enter the realm of national legend.

Let us briefly consider the origins of the myth. As an artist and a man Gardel possessed a series of qualities that made him amply representative. In the first place, he had invented all of the singable forms of the tango and excelled at each of them. When we consider that the tango is essentially oral (its written forms having secondary importance), Gardel's profoundly idiomatic tone had a decisive significance. At the same time, his violent and untimely death played a considerable role in stimulating the public's imagination and sympathy.

Moreover, Gardel's public personality had much to do with gaining him a wide following. This point is essential to the myth. In contrast to Discépolo's characters, Gardel was a success. He had money, fame, friends; his photographs always showed him smiling and happy, elegantly dressed, rubbing shoulders with fashionable society. He had attained a status of equality with the wealthy classes and international recognition by the powerful of many countries. But at the same time—at least, so the legend ran—he continued to be the same simple, unpretentious fellow, faithful to his friends and to his mother. That is to say, he rises to the top without losing the common touch, and this aspect of Gardel finds expression in a series of anecdotes. Gardel becomes, then, the symbol of what the people would like to be but know they never can be.

But the Gardelian myth is something more than that. It expresses a new, mass sensibility with national and popular roots. In choosing Gardel as an archetype, the masses gave form and content to their dreams while contributing some new elements to their culture.

These new values have been subject to considerable misinterpretation. For instance, the left-liberal essayist Juan José Sebreli regards Gardel as "symbolic of the fantasies of social misfits who hate the rich because they cannot be rich themselves. He represents the man that has arrived and avenges all those who could not—he who has risen from an obscure tenement in Abasto* to the dazzling social functions of the international big bourgeoisie. Nonetheless, his myth implies no social scores to be settled; it clashes with none of the fundamental structures of society."[9] This is somewhat wide of the mark. Doubtless the masses found in Gardel psychological compensation for their own failures, but what Sebreli fails to grasp is that in mythologizing Gardel they were actually ratifying an entire scale of cultural values. If Gardel is, among other things, the symbol of aspiration for economic well-being, he also (in his legendary success) retains intact the values of the "little people."

Several other popular myths emerged during the decade, although none had the force, originality, and broad-based appeal of that of Gardel. The myth of Hipólito Yrigoyen[10] comes next in importance, dating from the death of our first popularly-elected president in 1933. In death Yrigoyen became—in Manuel Gálvez' best-selling biography (1936), in word-of-mouth anecdotes, and in tangos—what he had been in far smaller measure in life: the symbol of the political and social aspirations of Argentina's large and heterogeneous middle class.

The Argentine film of the 1930s and early 1940s constitutes one of the most valuable sources for studying the theme that concerns us here, for its rapid emergence as a medium of mass expression was in its time an utterly unique phenomenon in Latin America. To offer some idea of its social and cultural importance, we shall briefly sketch the main lines of its development and then discuss in greater detail some films that cast considerable light upon the period.

Two different periods distinguish the evolution of the popular

*Abasto: one of the poorest working-class districts of Buenos Aires. [Tr.]

cinema in Argentina. The first, from 1933 to 1937, corresponds
to a period of gestation, during which the film draws upon
purely folkloric sources. The second, which runs from 1938 to
1942, reflects more complex cultural roots and coincides with
a period of overall national industrial development.

The film of the first phase finds its thematic material in tango
verses and in the creole *sainete,* or theatrical sketch. Eschewing
stylistic or conceptual refinements, it exploits the ingenuous
sentimentalism, the crude humor, the musical improvisations and
the caricatured personalities that habitually satisfied the simple
tastes of the proletarian public—which, by the way, constituted
almost exclusively the audience for the earliest Argentine films—
from whose ranks also emerged the actors, directors, and
producers. In much the same way as the imaginative literature
of the period belongs to and reflects the spiritual preoccupations
of the middle and upper classes, the cinema emerges from the
very bosom of the common people. For this very reason it was
blithely ignored or scorned as a medium by loftier social strata,
so much so in fact that the only attempt to create an "artistic"
or intellectual cinema (by upper-class writer Enrique Larreta)
resulted in resounding failure.

Shaped to and circumscribed by the needs for expression of
the proletarian mass, the new medium projected a genuinely
popular vision of the world. It gained rapid popularity by
transliterating tango verse into celluloid images—exalting the
homely knowledge of the humble, ingeniously poking fun at the
nation's political and social elite.

José Ferreyra, the most important of the pioneers, created
the tango-melodrama, a genre that spontaneously captured the
popular imagination. This type of film almost always told the
story of a hero or heroine perpetually pursued by misfortune.
Only in the protective maternal embrace, or, to a lesser degree,
in disinterested friendship, does the hero obtain partial relief
from his almost continuous misfortunes. In his melodrama
Ferreyra managed to replicate in an idealized form the shabby
landscape of the urban slum, where his stories were always set
and where they were actually exhibited to overflow audiences.

Summarizing production trends for 1935, critic and film
historian Domingo Di Núbila writes, "Our film industry, although

still lacking a consciousness of social purpose, began at all events to exercise a sociological influence. The popular sources of its themes, the human types, their language—with all their formal defects—helped to give an idea of the character and sensibility of the Argentine people."[11] It was precisely in this period that Argentine films began to find their way beyond national borders, winning additional audiences in other Latin American countries and even in the United States.

In this aspect a decisive factor was the series of films shot by Gardel in American and French studios, productions that helped to diffuse on an international level a picturesque image of the country and its human types, familiarizing Latin American audiences with the peculiarities of *porteño** speech and character, and with a series of popular personalities that would later achieve massive and spontaneous popularity with the hemispheric public.[12]

But it was only with the appearance of Manuel Romero that our cinema was converted into a massive means of popular expression. A former author of successful tangos and sainetes, and creator of the porteño musical review, Romero in his humorous pictures played upon tragic and even mawkishly sentimental themes, reviving the best traditions of creole humor —whose characteristic features were a scorn for honest labor, contempt for progress, and a rejection of the utilitarian values of the bourgeoisie. His comic personalities—tramps or slick con-men—always possessed an alloy of decency that placed them in opposition to (and preserved them from) the society into which they had been cast. They lived in their own world, one built upon sentimental values such as friendship and love, and their only possible end was one of unforeseen disaster. These characters were never family men: they did not hold regular jobs—indeed, they did not seem particularly suited to regular employment. In some ways they resembled the *pícaro* (rascal) of classic Spanish literature, but they differed from him in their emotive and sentimental character. This latter quality, however, did not prevent them from possessing a large measure of viveza

---

*porteño: a person of the port—in this case, a native of Buenos Aires or, as an adjective, pertaining to the Argentine capital. [Tr.]

criolla (a typically River Platine quality that Romero understood better than anyone else), thanks to which they negotiated the greatest of difficulties, purposely violating social conventions and enjoying a laugh at the expense of the mighty. The popular classes could thus sublimate many of their desires and frustrations in the imaginary revenge of these comic characters. Moreover, taking Gardel as a model, Romero created the archetype of another cinematic hero: the tango singer who struggles at the cost of great personal sacrifice to ultimately give expression to the innermost sentiments of his people.

The first popular cinema contains no explicit references to social problems, but its dramatic and comic heroes live in permanent opposition to the existing social order. This is particularly evident in certain grotesque situations where Romero's comic personalities afford a corrosive vision of a society ridiculously solemn and morally hypocritical.

Like the tangos of Discépolo, the cinematic opus of Mario Soffici is a prime source through which to study popular culture during the thirties. Soffici's films indicate a consciousness of form utterly absent from the work of Ferreyra, Romero, and other early film makers, but his esthetic concerns are not the product of foreign influences, nor a commitment to formalism as such, but rather emerge from the creator's actual necessity to fully express the country's diverse and original aspects. Hence his first important picture, *Viento Norte* (1937), based on Lucio Mansilla's tales of the desert campaign,* develops a national epic which fully captures authentic scenes of the Argentine past. His next work directly attacks social themes of the period, and he reaches his highest expression in the tango melodrama. It would be no exaggeration to say that Soffici tried his hand at virtually all film genres and succeeded in placing his distinctive stamp upon each of them.

What concerns us here, however, is that portion of his work which is specifically critical of Argentine society. This cycle of films, all made in the final years of the decade, gave birth to

---

Excursión a los indios ranqueles (1870), a classic narrative of Mansilla's dealings with the pampa Indians immediately prior to their extinction in the so-called Desert Campaign of General Julio A. Roca (1879-1880). [Tr.]

two distinctly Argentine film genres: the cinema of social region-
alism (*costumbrismo social*), exemplified by *Kilómetro 111*,
El viejo doctor, and *Héroes sin fama;* and the social-folkloric
tragedy, brilliantly represented by *Prisoneros de la tierra*. These
films directly attack national problems of the period, but the
selection of their themes was totally spontaneous, free of any
preconceived political or social theories. Cast in the same type
of popular language as that utilized by Ferreyra or Romero,
they could exploit sentimental and humorous affinities of the
audience, but more refined both formally and thematically, they
succeeded in giving an extremely penetrating vision of Argentina
at the time they were made.

The first film of Soffici's social cycle, *Kilómetro 111* (1937),
is based on Carlos Olivari's play, *La tercera invasión inglesa*
(1936), a semidocumentary, fictional treatment of the British
railroad monopoly. The latter, having initially agreed to transport
rocks, Portland cement, and other road-building materials, either
invents endless excuses in order to avoid fulfilling the contract,
or causes the trains to arrive only after lengthy—and unexplained
—delays. The object, of course, is to prevent completion of a
road whose existence would undermine their transport monopoly.
Set in a picturesque town in the Argentine interior, the film
also documents the tragedy of the region's impoverished farmers.
who are compelled to sell their harvest to a local usurer who is
working in collusion with the railroad. In a desperate attempt
to avoid the increasingly intolerable economic exploitation, the
farmers attempt to send their wheat to Buenos Aires on their
own, but they run up against insuperable obstacles. For instance,
the local bank presents absurd excuses to deny them a short-
term loan. In spite of this, they finally manage to achieve their
objective, thanks to the generous aid of the station-master, who
adjust the rates to make it possible for the farmers to utilize
the line. In this way they obtain a direct link to the capital,
eliminate the usurious middleman, and obtain a fair return for
their product. But the victory of the farmers is also a defeat for
their friend the station-master, who is promptly cashiered by
his employers.

Soffici presents the conflict in the simple and emotive terms
required by the film-going public, but he is conscious of the

deeper issues involved. "We were well aware of the social consequences of a railroad network designed without taking into consideration the needs of the small farmers," he told the present writer, "and by denouncing its evils through the film, we hoped to contribute to changing the situation. That is, we hoped to see the railroads nationalized. But of course," he added, "our goal was essentially artistic rather than sociological, political, or historical. Like many others, we had been struck by the injustices of the situation, and it merely happened that the dilemma made good film drama."[13] In spite of Soffici's avowed intentions, these and other films of the thirties could hardly be called apolitical, inasmuch as they dealt with real and current problems of national concern, and they openly denounced social evils and unequivocally placed the blame where it belonged.

The theme of *El viejo doctor* (1939) was inspired by a personal experience of the director. When a relative fell ill he became aware of the enormous difficulties involved in obtaining hospital care and pharmaceuticals for a person of modest means[14] at the very time that there was a proliferation of modern clinics in Buenos Aires. The hero of the film is an old idealistic doctor in the best creole tradition—paternalistic and generous—who finds himself overwhelmed and disgusted by the lack of ethical principles in the practice of modern medicine, which ignores the indigent patient of public hospitals to attend to the trivial or imaginary ailments of the rich in luxurious (and highly lucrative) private clinics. Apart from documenting this grave deficiency, the film ranges a bit farther afield; in the failure of the old idealistic doctor—who attempts to change the situation but fails—Soffici calls into question the utility of benevolent paternalism of an earlier period; he does not criticize the old-fashioned gentleman directly, but allows one to infer that in the harshly competitive society of the day, the alternatives of generosity and well-intentioned paternalism are dysfunctional and consequently doomed to failure.

Héroes sin fama (1939) closes Soffici's social trilogy. The film was to have been originally entitled *Empanadas, taba y vino* in reference to the classic instruments of the political committee, the venal forms of populist demagogery utilized by the nation's elite.* The action takes place in a small town in the interior, and amid ingenuous and sentimental touches, Soffici unmasks political corruption and depicts the struggles of independent journalism, affording us one of the few cinematic portrayals of civic life in the provinces during this period.

Drawing on various short stories by Horacio Quiroga, Soffici filmed *Prisoneros de la tierra* (also 1939) in the midst of the forests of Misiones province. A sharply etched tale of human exploitation in the yerba mate plantations, *Prisoneros . . .* is a social-folkloric drama of deeply Latin American content in its dramatic conception, its theme, and its style. The laborers of the plantation, the *mensús,* are compensated for their crushing tasks in chits redeemable only at the plantation store. There their purchases are limited—at five times their real worth—to stale food, deteriorated clothing, and alcoholic beverages. The purchase of the latter is especially encouraged to promote drunkenness and consequently passivity on the part of the workers. The hero of the film is a young mensú who rebels against the situation and is brutally punished but manages to overcome the restraints placed upon him and vindicates his humanity in a violent, individual, and ultimately fruitless fashion —by whipping to death the German landowner who had originally degraded him.

With these stories vividly dramatizing the problems of the popular class in various regions of the country, Soffici, like Discépolo, contributed to the development of a mass critical consciousness. But he did something more as well—he fashioned the tools by which the cinema could comprehend national problems.

Between 1938 and 1942 the Argentine film industry produced an average of around 50 pictures a year of authentic national style and content. Its success was ratified by audiences throughout Latin America, in Spain, and in the United States. In a fashion totally unthinkable a few years before, the Argentine industry became a highly productive enterprise affording well-paying jobs to thousands of actors and technicians and excellent

---

*It was the practice of provincial political bosses to treat their humble constituents to an outdoor picnic of meat pies and wine on the eve of elections in gratitude for their voting "correctly." [Tr.]

profits to producers and investors. A decline in motion picture production in the industrial countries as a result of the Second World War favored our own cinema in a great measure, since it permitted expansion into the Spanish-speaking market, until then dominated by dubbed or subtitled American films.

But what concerns us here, of course, is above all the particular content of these films. Their sources of inspiration were no longer limited to the tango theme. Now they often searched in past struggles for independence to state the problems of the present. This new orientation was due in a great part to entry into the industry of a school of professional scenarists deeply concerned with Argentine problems and capable of translating their views into well-wrought film scripts. Many, like Homero Manzi and Carlos Olivari, members or sympathizers of FORJA, had embraced nationalist ideas and worked out the arguments of their scripts on the basis of actual political and social research. At any rate, the vision of Argentina that appears in these films is invariably critical.

Moreover, the introduction of a large middle-class audience for films coincides with a thematic renovation of the Argentine industry, whose traditional genres—the tango melodrama and the human interest comedy—acquired a more sophisticated tone. But it is two new genres—social realism and the epic—that develop the critical and revisionist perspectives that imbue our cinema with a truly national significance.

In the field of social realism, Francisco Mujica, one of the first film directors of petty bourgeois origin, played a preponderant role. The majority of his films are invaluable documents on the social customs of the period, and in the case of *El mejor papá del mundo* (1941), an explicit indictment of the shady economic deals of international trusts working hand-in-glove with the local oligarchy—both to the detriment of national interests. The film centers about a romance between a university student and the daughter of a small cotton farmer in Entre Ríos province, while referring in a parallel fashion to the harassment to which the girl's father is subjected by an international financial interest seeking to destroy independent farmers in order to monopolize the cotton industry. The young student, upon learning the facts of the case, decides to denounce these interests publicly, for which purpose he seeks the aid of his father, a prestigious lawyer of the oligarchy. The latter accepts the assignment, but in spite of his apparent efforts the farmers are defeated by the clever maneuvers of the foreign company, which succeeds in ruining them economically. Later it is discovered that the student's father is in fact a lawyer for the trust.

The film depicts in a thoroughly unvarnished manner the evils of economic imperialism, while at the same time exposing the servility of the oligarchy and the Argentine government. At various points we see the lawyer bribing various highly placed state officials, who go so far as to revoke laws to facilitate the trust's activities. But the film is fundamentally concerned with a popular theme, in which the romance of the youthful protagonists, the disenchantment of the student with the man he had always believed "the best father in the world," and the constant humorous sallies acquire an artistic significance as great as the picture's political content.

In 1942 the appearance of *La guerra gaucha* aroused the greatest public response in the history of Argentine film-making. Based on the stories of Leopoldo Lugones, the film depicts on a heroic scale the epic of the liberation struggles of the gauchos of Salta province on the country's northern frontier. Its story relates the dramatic adventures of two creole captains, co-provincials of General Güemes,* who must oppose the powerful Spanish royalist army with a small group of poorly armed and undernourished men. They achieve their goal by imagination, resort to guerrilla tactics, and all types of native tricks, sustained only—and in this sense the film makes its point completely clear—by a limitless faith in the destiny of the fatherland. At the same time, *La guerra gaucha* traces the conversion of a young Argentine officer serving in the Spanish army. In the beginning of the film he believes himself to be fighting for order and against barbarism, but upon falling prisoner of the gauchos, he becomes enamored of a beautiful patriot girl who compels him to read the letters of General Belgrano.** Through these documents he comes

---

*General Martín Güemes (1785-1821): Salta Landowner and politician; prominent leader in the independence movement of the Argentine Northwest. [Tr.]

**General Manuel Belgrano was one of the leaders of the Argentine independence movement, 1810-1816. [Tr.]

to understand the ideals of the insurgents and eventually to make them his own. But the true protagonist of the film is the anonymous gaucho, selfless and courageous, who spontaneously sacrifices his life in the struggle for national independence. This *chef d'oeuvre* of the Argentine cinema, directed by Lucas Demare, electrified the public in its initial showings. The dramatic battle scenes, the flowery language of the gauchos, and the evocation of creole values all made it a true cinematic reconstruction of our living past.

One of the principal creators of *La guerra gaucha,* Homero Manzi, was a poet, tango composer—and political activist. Although a university man, he rejected his formalistic training to become one of the leading voices of popular culture. In his film scripts he explored the fundamental aspects of the Argentine character. In *Fortín alto* (1941), *La guerra gaucha,* and *Pampa bárbara* (1945), he penetrated the culture of the gaucho and the pampa; in *El viejo hucha* (1942), he recast the creole sainete, combining a social and folkloric approach to the life of Italian immigrants. Manzi also successfully evoked the mood of every day life at the turn of the century, revived the tango melodrama, and established the bases of cinematic biography (with his *Su mejor alumno,* a life of Sarmiento),[*] but basically all his activities bear the stamp of the culture of the thirties; together with Soffici and Discépolo, Manzi was one of the most lucid interpreters of a desire to forge a culturally independent Argentina.

Apart from the nationalist overtones implicit in the epic and in the social cinema, the newly revived tango melodrama continued to reflect an important part of popular psychology. *La canción de los barrios* (1941) of Luis César Amadori—a director who would later become a favorite of the Perón regime —is a typical product of the cinema that satisfied the needs of a wider public. Its protagonist is a young man who abandons his father's business to dedicate himself to the tango and a bohemian existence. After some amorous disappointments (which provide pretexts for tangoistic interpolations), he returns to his father's factory as a humble worker. There his abilities propel

---

[*]D. F. Sarmiento, President of the Argentine Republic (1868-1874), Prominent writer and educational reformer. [Tr.]

him to leadership of the shop trade union. The inevitable romance occurs with the daughter of an old foreman who has been unjustly discharged; this leads the young man to rebel against his father, becoming spokesman for his companions' demands that the cashiered laborer be rehired, and that the wretched wages of all workers be increased in the bargain. The owner gives in to all demands, leaving management of the factory in the hands of his son. The film closes on an idyllic note—the marriage of the new factory manager to his working-class sweetheart, consummating a sort of "romantic" alliance between capital and labor.

After 1943 the Argentine film entered into an acute process of decline. The number of productions decreased, but, more serious still, the original themes all but disappeared. Films with reiterative and stereotyped arguments became standard fare, and in a short time the Latin American market was lost. The causes of this decline are rather complex. On one hand, the North American distributors never reconciled themselves to the competition of Argentine films, which at one point made it difficult to place their own products in the Spanish-speaking market. As a measure of self-defense, the United States reduced its allotments of raw film stock to Argentina, while at the same time making available a much superior quantity to Mexico, which at that time possessed an undeveloped and deficient industry. The Americans also invested large amounts of capital in the nascent Mexican cinema, which in short order dislodged the Argentine product from the South and Central American markets.

On the other hand, we must acknowledge that inefficiency and negligence on the Argentine part—particularly on the part of producers—contributed much to the collapse of the industry. The estrangement from genuinely popular sources of inspiration and the loss of critical sense and guidance that distinguished the work of Soffici, Manzi, Mujica, and many others is basically what led to a decline of the Argentine film.

The so-called "white telephone comedy," notoriously reminiscent of its Hollywood archetype, is one of the characteristic genres of our industry after 1942. In it the ideals of the bourgeoisie supplant those of the masses, and the protagonist becomes an idealized upper class packaged for mass consumption.

Because of its ingenious sense of humor and its genuine dramatic qualities, *El muerto faltó a la cita* (1944) is one of the few fine films of this type. The story concerns a young millionaire play-boy who hits a bicyclist while driving intoxicated on the way home from an all-night bachelor party. Upon realizing what he has done, he hides the body and flees from the scene. Later, overcome by remorse, he surrenders himself to the police, but the body cannot be found—as if the whole affair were nothing but a bad dream. However, in short order he receives a visit from a stranger who represents himself as the brother of the slain cyclist; the visitor explains that he has hidden the body, and on the basis of this claim installs himself in the young man's home prepared to live at his expense. A fortuitous circumstance eventually reveals that the cyclist and the stranger are really the same person, and the film closes with a comic scene in which the young man humiliates the would-be blackmailer. The plot illustrates a radical turnabout in the moral of the new films: in the primitive "popular" cinema the blackmailer would have been treated as a poor devil compelled to engage in such operations to eke out an existence, and the frivolous young bourgeois roundly condemned. Here the formula is reversed to appeal to the petty bourgeois sensibilities of a new and more prosperous film-going public.

Gradually, however, Argentine films lost their original quali-ties and became either hybrids or bad replicas of foreign models. In any event, the period of apogee left a record of cultural self-determination that, regrettably, has not been repeated.

The revolution in popular expression of the thirties and early forties—like so many other contemporaneous developments—proved far richer in promise than in ultimate achievement. Argentina is still very far from having found her own authentic popular voice. Yet the balance of this period is far from negative. Because popular values found a means of mass diffusion—through the radio, the cinema, and the tango—Argentine culture was never quite the same again. The framework, the focus had been altered; things would have to be restated in a new context. The underlying assumption was that Argentina as a nation was no longer an extension of Europe, but an unformed people still forging its own identity.

Without an appreciation of this fact, it is difficult to understand what followed. To be sure, no historical period can be regarded as the mere sum total of all that preceded it; hence, we will not claim a purely filial relationship between what we have described in this essay and the popular culture of the Perón era (1943-1955). Actually *Peronista* culture was as vague and contradictory as the movement itself. It represented a peculiar convergence of new and old, bourgeois and popular—even foreign and national elements.[15] On one hand, it tempered the critical edge of Argentine expression, as exemplified by the fact that its films abandoned their condemnations of the existing social system.* On the other hand, we cannot regard the culture of the late forties and early fifties as purely regressive. For example, the masses continued during those years to elaborate myths to serve as repositories of their deepest aspirations. In this case, instead of Gardel, the chief objects of popular devotion were Eva Perón and General Perón himself. An adequate study of this phenomenon remains outside the scope of this essay—which is particularly unfortunate. For today nothing places in jeopardy the entire self-image of traditional Argentina so much as the myth of Perón.

---

*In a way this was logical, because Perón professed to be changing that system and thus rendering exposés and condemnations "unnecessary."

7.

The Provinces

RONALD H. DOLKART

In his memoirs General Pedro Ferré attributes the following phrase to Juan Manuel de Rosas—an affirmation often belied by his acts: "We must make the provinces feel the crush of poverty, and this we shall do by allowing the importation from abroad of the very products they themselves produce." The truth is that this and no other is the policy we have been practicing for the past fifty years.[1]

THE SETTING

The federalization of the city of Buenos Aires in 1880 marks a clear dividing point in the history of the Argentine provinces, the individual territorial units that made up the Spanish La Plata region. Before this act, which transformed the port city into a federal district and established the framework of a modern republic, provincial politics had generally been the focus of Argentine history. Regional caudillos were the possessors of power; gauchos and other local, indigenous types were the bases of militias; primitive economic development was spread fairly evenly across the country, as the result of self-sufficiency or a limited trade in certain locally produced commodities. Argentina was not then a nation, but a rather loosely joined confederation in which each province had a great deal of local autonomy. The tendency toward the Hispanic parochialism of the *patria chica* (one's own region) and the resultant suspicion of centralism remained strong. Yet the realities of power and the forces of modernization gradually and then rapidly undermined the ability of the provinces to maintain their semi-independence.

The expanding world economy of the nineteenth century demanded increasing quantities of the agricultural products for which Argentina had a comparative advantage. Not only was the development of the rich pastoral activities concentrated in the historic province of Buenos Aires, but the port city of the same name became the center of the export trade and contact with Europe. And thus an irreversible process was set in motion, the ever-greater centralization of economic development in the city and province of Buenos Aires, and the gradual decline in the importance of the other provinces, except to serve as "colonies" of the evolving leader.[2] The initiation of vast commerce and industry only added to the resources of Buenos Aires.[3] And, of course, political power and social prestige were a natural result of economic predominance.

The tendency for domination of the Plata area and beyond by Buenos Aires had been clear ever since the colonial period and became a source of conflict during the governorships of Juan Manuel de Rosas (1829-1832; 1835-1852), when the other provinces were subordinated politically to the port city. The local caudillos fought gallantly against the loss of their autonomy and indeed seemed to triumph with the establishment of the principles of federalism in the Constitution of 1853 and the final federalization of Buenos Aires city in 1880. The victory was Phyrric: they had worn themselves out in the military-political struggle only to see the city and province of Buenos Aires, freed of the need to argue further about constitutional questions, "take off" on a line of unparalleled development, bringing with it a concentration of modernizing forces necessary for supremacy. The Constitution was a hollow shell of legalism. The "Provincial Question"—the ever-declining position of the territorial units outside of Buenos Aires and their resultant frustration—was thus born. Yet in the decades of rapid progress, from 1880 to 1930, the issue was dormant, only to emerge, however tentatively at first, in the crisis period of the 1930s.

Geographical realities had in large part contributed to the lack of national cohesion and the dominance of one section of the republic.[4] The original thrust of Hispanic colonization had occurred from two directions: from Peru and Chile a series of towns was founded along the eastern Andean mountain foothills during the latter half of the sixteenth century; and from Asunción, during much the same period, settlements were established in the littoral along the Plata-Paraná river systems. The remaining area of the provinces then developed in a typical Spanish pattern of principal towns (*municipios*) that controlled all the intervening rural territory. Regional political systems arose around the cities, with local governors having a great deal of autonomy. The formation of the Viceroyalty of La Plata in 1776 with Buenos Aires as its capital marked the attempt by Madrid to bring southern South America under its direct control, but the movement for independence destroyed central government, and local caudillos arose in the major towns once again and asserted their power over the old domains.

By the end of the nineteenth century (and lasting until the administrative reorganization of the Perón period) there were fourteen provinces and a number of *gobernaciones,* or territories controlled directly by the federal government because of their very small populations (see fig. 1 and table 1). These divisions can generally be grouped into six regions, each with its own rather distinctive economic and cultural characteristics.[5]

The Patagonian highlands, although comprising 25 percent of Argentina's territory, have remained the most remote area. This region south of the Río Colorado has been colonized only in the course of the twentieth century, mainly for the purpose of raising sheep, and has remained under the administration of the federal authorities, scarcely considered a part of modern Argentina.

The Northwest is a continuation of the Bolivian *altiplano;* although important during the colonial period, it did not participate in the modernizing process because in recent times it produced no commodities for which there existed a great demand. Tucumán has been a notable exception, a curiously semitropical valley suitable for sugar cane. Yet this area has maintained a strong sense of regional identification, known throughout Argentina for its unique folklore: therefore, its revival has been an indication of the central government's concern for the "historic" Argentina.

Fig. 1. Argentine territorial divisions as of 1943.

TABLE 1

Argentine Political Divisions During the 1930s[*]

Regional designation	Provinces	Gobernaciones (territories)
A. Pampa	1. Federal Capital (City of Buenos Aires)	
	2. Buenos Aires	
B. Littoral	3. Santa Fe	1. Misiones
	4. Corrientes	
	5. Entre Ríos	
C. Central	6. Córdoba	2. La Pampa
	7. San Luis	
	8. Santiago del Estero	
D. Andean	9. Catamarca	3. Neuquén
	10. La Rioja	
	11. San Juan	
	12. Mendoza	
E. Northwest	13. Tucumán	4. Los Andes
	14. Salta	5. Chaco
	15. Jujuy	6. Formosa
F. Patagonia		7. Río Negro
		8. Chubut
		9. Santa Cruz
		10. Tierra del Fuego
		11. Comodoro Rivadivia (Military Zone)

[*]Subsequent changes:
Los Andes was divided between Salta and Catamarca in 1943.
La Pampa and Chaco were raised to provincial status in 1951 and Misiones in 1953.
Comodoro Rivadavia was divided between Chubut and Santa Cruz in 1955.

The Andean foothill provinces are marked by aridity, for the low rainfall has resulted in a specialized type of irrigated agriculture, the "oases" formed by the streams flowing down from the mountains. A series of important cities, such as Mendoza, act as commercial centers for typical Mediterranean products, particularly wine. This is a reasonably well-developed part of the republic, but heavily dependent on the agricultural policy of the government.

The Central designation is as much historic as geographical—for it is a region with a unique sense of its own past, a consciousness often bordering on a "superiority" complex. The ancient city of Córdoba is the guardian of this contemptuous attitude towards the rest of the country and, along with the other provinces of the Center, remained a bastion of conservatism. Inevitably drawn into the orbit of the industrial metropolis to the east, a large outflow of population has contributed to the frustrations of this region.

The Littoral refers to the provinces lying up the Paraná-Uruguay river systems. These were traditional foci of discontent, because their products, grains and cattle, were similar to those of Buenos Aires, but their ability to export competitively was rigidly controlled by the port city. Thus, the cultural identification of the Littoral people rests on the firm foundations of a desire to maintain their distinctiveness from their powerful neighbor, Buenos Aires.

Finally, the Pampa remains the heartland of Argentina, the combination of the province and city of Buenos Aires, the center of agriculture—principally meat for export—of industry, and of commerce. Most of the resources of the republic are to be found here, and with them the Pampa overwhelms the other provinces.

The development of a modernized Argentina has often tended to reinforce provincialism, rather than having the predicted opposite result, because the change has been so unbalanced. The transportation pattern developed out of a vast program of railway construction during the late nineteenth and early twentieth centuries, when the railroad became the chief channel of communication. However, the lines were almost always built from the interior to the ports, with very few cross-cutting connections (see figure 2). Thus the provinces became "colonies" supplying products for the urban markets and for overseas trade and receiving manufactured goods from the urban centers. While the new transportation network had a significant economic impact for a privileged few, it did little to break down the isolation of various regions, where communities remained relatively primitive and underdeveloped.

The population complex of Argentina has changed dramatically from a rural to an urban pattern, with one of the highest concentrations of city dwellers in all Latin America. Soon after the turn of the century over half the population lived in a few

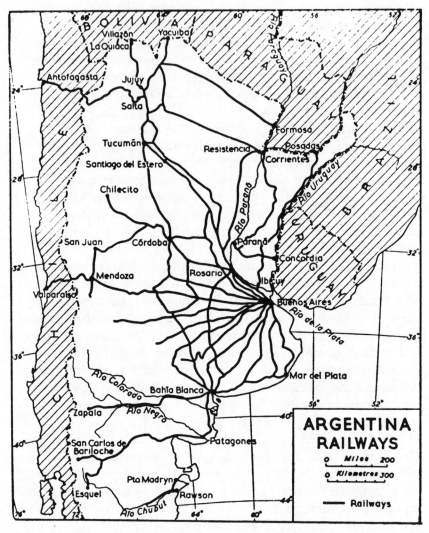

Fig. 2. Major trunk lines of the Argentine rail system.

principal cities, and the ratio of urban to rural has grown ever since. The European immigrants who poured into Argentina helped increase the population in almost all regions of the country; nevertheless, about three-quarters of them went to the Federal Capital and the provinces of Buenos Aires and Santa Fe, the most urbanized parts of the republic. While the developed regions were transformed into vital, middle class, urban societies along Western European lines, the interior provinces remained essentially communities of indigenous, mestizo, peasant peoples, living in isolated rural settlements.

Most of the provinces were organized on the historic basis of a capital city, which served as a center of administration and commerce, joined to outlying areas with a very low population density, made up either of families subsisting on small farms or of workers and tenants on large agricultural estates. The way of life remained strictly traditional and conservative. Each state had its own "oligarchy" of principal landowning families in firm control of the political system, a small middle class made up of shopkeepers and professionals, such as teachers and lawyers, and a large mass of the peasantry, who were well off by most Latin American standards, since the richness of the land provided them with adequate food, but who lived without most of the services of a modern society, in glaring contrast to their urban country-men. The federal government and the large banks, monopolizing most of the available credit, saw little reason to invest in the interior, with the exception of a few zones producing marketable or exportable commodities. Local budgets thus remained minis-cule and appropriations of the national authorities were directed toward the development of Buenos Aires, where immediate results could be seen. Only in the field of education did there exist some sense of federal responsibility; schools were estab-lished throughout the nation, although the rural illiteracy rate remained relatively high.

During its first century of independence Argentina was seen as having made miraculous strides toward becoming a modern, progressive country, but only in the context of a typical nine-teenth-century liberal viewpoint: change for the better was identified strictly in terms of a rising gross national product and showcase cities. Provincial decay was attributed to a lack of natural and human resources, and very few commentators seemed concerned with this problem. The malaise that affected Argentina after the Revolution of 1930, however, would produce a revival of that most traditional of Argentine problems, the condition of the provinces.

THE PROVINCIAL PROBLEM

To most observers the "Provincial Problem" seemed to have been eliminated after the Constitution of 1853 set up a federal system (which became fully operative with the federalization of Buenos Aires in 1880) because the states had gotten exactly what they wanted. According to the basic charter, authority is divided between the national government and the provinces, with the former having only those powers expressly delegated by the Constitution or implied under its provisions.[6] In theory the major subdivisions of the Argentine government have a great deal of latitude, although precisely what this entails is not spelled out in the Constitution itself. Above all the provinces are to be self-governing, with substantial control over local affairs under a "republican" form of their own choosing. Yet one clause of the Constitution has always threatened the autonomy of the provinces: Congress and the President are empowered to "intervene" in order to "guarantee the republican form of government . . . or reestablish such authority."[7]

This prerogative has been used often to ensure the political supremacy of the party that holds the presidency, because although the Constitution provides that Congress shall approve the intervention of the President, as a regular practice the executive names his own man as "interventor," or acting governor, while the legislature is in recess, and then presents it at a later date with a *fait accompli*. The threat of intervention by the President of the Republic, therefore, hangs over every provincial governor, and the reality of continuing in office lies in the nature of a state administration's relationship to the federal authorities: if a provincial government tries to pursue an independent line, it will be dissolved. As the political divisions of Argentina became more polarized in the course of the twentieth century, the practice of intervention increased; the independence of the provinces has become a myth. Although Argentine commentators have generally viewed the problem as essentially political—that is, the need to make the Constitution work more effectively—the underlying economic reality of preponderant wealth held by Buenos Aires has, more than any other factor, undercut the autonomy of the provinces. "In my judgement," one Argentine jurist has written, "when we refer today to the problems of federalism, we do not state the division of 'National State versus Provincial States' or 'Central Power versus Provincial Powers,' but rather 'central power synonymous with the Federal Capital versus powers and rights of the provincial entities.'"[8]

Nevertheless, concern for the declining position for much of the area outside of Buenos Aires remained limited as a result of the vast upsurge of national wealth that occurred in the last decades of the nineteenth and the early years of the twentieth centuries. The export-oriented economy of Argentina was closely integrated to that of Great Britain, providing meat, wheat, and other staples for the English market and receiving manufactures and capital in return. The average annual export trade, for example, climbed from 139 million pesos in 1880 to 2 billion pesos by the end of the decade of the twenties. Most of the provinces shared to some extent in this wealth, and the change must have seemed dramatic for them, but as Argentine prosperity grew so rapidly in the half-century before the great world depression, it was the city and province of Buenos Aires that benefited most and increased its share of the national wealth. The population mirrored this change most dramatically: while the total Argentine population grew from 1.8 million in 1869 to 8 million in 1914 (and doubled by the next census in 1947), the share of this growth concentrated in Buenos Aires rose from 28 percent to 46 percent (and remained fairly stable for the next half century). The basis of economic progress was land, and in this pampa region were to be found the great concentrations of cattle and wheat production. The communications and transportation networks of Buenos Aires far exceeded those of the rest of the nation, having about one-third of the railway mileage in this vast country. When industry became the most significant growth sector of the economy in the course of the twentieth century, it too tended to concentrate around the port, especially in an industrial belt just outside the city limits, founded initially on the trade of the *frigoríficos* (meat-packing plants), but developing rapidly into other large-scale manufacturing that was substituted for goods traditionally imported. This concentration included over half the industrial production of the nation and soon came to overtake agriculture in importance.

By the turn of the century, the most capable and public-spirited members of the liberal oligarchy lived in Buenos Aires and provided it with enlightened and progressive government. The basis of their power was land. The land tenure system and the concentration of ownership were reflected in the social structure: as Argentine exports were integrated into the multi-lateral trade patterns of the last half of the nineteenth century, the *estancieros* (estate-owners, or, as some would have it, cattle barons) became an oligarchy capable of monopolizing political power on a national level. The provinces were left in the hands of their local elites, usually older, nonimmigrant, Hispanic families who had held title to large plots of land since the colonial period. The organization of a strong national government put an end to the power of the provincial caudillos when they refused to cooperate, but their place was taken by an establish-ment aware of the benefits to itself in cooperating with the national regime. The provincial oligarchs firmly entrenched themselves by producing staples that could be sold in the major cities of Argentina or abroad. Beyond the cattle, wheat, corn, and mixed farming belts of the pampa lay centers of yerba mate in the Mesopotamia (Entre Ríos and Corrientes), cotton in the Chaco, sugar cane in Tucumán, vineyards in the Andean foothills, and fruits in the valley of the Río Negro, as well as livestock in other parts of the country.[10]

All these regions were integrated into a national market system, and the landowners saw their interests in terms of keeping the rural peasantry docile and themselves well-connected to the politicians in the capital. Thus what had been a historic pattern of constant revolts against and resistance to the hegemony of Buenos Aires became a system of complicity with the national government to maintain the status quo. While the social system of the developed parts of the nation opened up to absorb the immigrants and the middle class, the provincial organizations closed tightly and permitted no real competition. The Saénz Peña Law, guaranteeing free, secret elections, was a mockery in the provinces, where open, acknowledged fraud and coercion assured the vote to the party in power. In addition, the most influential members of the provincial oligarchies took part themselves in the national government, either by being elected senators or receiving appointed positions of cabinet or subcabinet level. The presidency and many of the major government offices were often in the hands of famed *provincianos.* As early as the 1880s, President Julio A. Roca, himself a *tucumano* linked by marriage to the highest aristocracy of Córdoba, appointed Federico Ibarguren of Salta to organize the national system of courts. Ibarguren's son has told in his autobiography how this led the family, which had deep historic roots in the Argentine Northwest, to establish close ties with Buenos Aires, dividing their time between management of their estate and their responsibilities in the national capital.[11]

Intellectuals, whose numbers grew rapidly as a result of the increasing prosperity of the republic, followed a pattern much like that of the provincial oligarchies; many of them came from the provinces also and were attracted to the cultural centers of Buenos Aires. The dichotomy between urban and rural value systems dates from the middle years of the nineteenth century, when the "Europeanists," as represented by Domingo Faustino Sarmiento in his *Facundo,* declared that the "barbarism" of the interior must be ended. Defenders of the regional cultures arose, perhaps best exemplified by José Hernández in *Martín Fierro,* but only after the battle had been lost and Buenos Aires had emerged dominant from the political struggles of the period. Three successive generations of Argentine writers continued to reflect this division of opinion—that of 1880, of 1910, and of 1930. The first group quite naturally hymned the magnificent accomplishments of a progressive nation and the greatness of Buenos Aires. The interior and the gaucho became an object for nostalgia and humor for some cultivated writers of the port city, but most of the *pensadores* were interested in national problems. The generation of 1910 brought to the fore the issues of nationalism and what was called *Argentinidad,* and obviously within that context the question of the provinces could not be ignored. The split now became eminently political, with a division between Socialists and Radicals on the one hand, and Conservatives and Nationalists on the other. Both groups evidenced a concern with the provinces, but from differing perspectives.

The Socialists viewed the problem, predictably, as an economic issue—that a viable Argentina could not emerge while citizens of the interior lived in poverty and misery, and that the federal government had the responsibility for providing solutions through programs of social action. From the Radical perspective, a strong current of attention was directed toward the provinces by Ricardo Rojas and Joaquín V. González, who, like most of the other writers of this generation, were provincianos. Their view was that a materialistic Argentina must be humanized, and that the immigrants must be made part of an older, Indo-Hispanic national culture and taught the values of an indigenous past. The Conservatives presented their argument in terms of a crisis of values, that Argentine traditions had been perverted through excessive "Europeanization," and that the nation would be best served by the reassertion of more authentic (that is, more paternalistic and premodern) social attitudes. A clear emphasis on historical scholarship is manifest in the writings of Leopoldo Lugones and Manuel Gálvez, who chose as their hero the dictator of the early nineteenth century, Juan Manuel de Rosas, and the militant and militaristic spirit of the gauchos surrounding him and the other caudillos: their feeling was that a corrupt Argentina must be turned back to the *criollo* values of loyalty and patriotism and that the governments of the provinces must be strengthened for this purpose. These writers then galvanized public attention on a serious crisis of significant concern to intellectuals of the succeeding generation of 1930.

THE THIRTIES

The period after 1880 was therefore one of significant and far-reaching negative change for the provinces, which stagnated or declined as the pampa heartland around Buenos Aires developed and modernized. The decade of the thirties served to underscore dramatically the deteriorating conditions for those living outside the charmed geographic circle, undoubtedly because the rapid recovery from the effects of the Depression, once again, was concentrated in Buenos Aires. Thus an awareness of the depth of the Argentine disequilibrium now surfaced and made it appear as a major cause of socioeconomic dysfunction. Agricultural and pastoral activities, which had been the mainstay of the Argentine economy in the era of free trade with Europe, began to give way to an accelerated process of industrialization, as traditional trade patterns were disrupted and the country found it necessary to manufacture many of the products it formerly imported. This significant industrial "explosion" was centered in an area just south of the Federal Capital and rapidly moved from small-scale production to larger corporations (defined as those employing more than 250 workers): between 1935 and 1939, approximately 31 percent of all salaried employees in Argentina were occupied in businesses classified as "big," a figure that compares not unfavorably with 55 percent in the United States at this time.[12] The total of manufacturing establishments concentrated in the Buenos Aires area is estimated to be almost 60 percent.

This economic development resulted in significant social and geographic mobility. Prosperity had attracted massive immigration from Europe, forming a middle class made up of urban merchants, government workers, and professionals, as well as land and factory owners, on the one hand, and a small proletariat, mainly artisans, on the other. Then net immigration from abroad as a factor of population growth dropped off precipitously with the beginning of the great world depression. In contrast with the period after 1880, when millions had entered Argentina, the thirties was a decade in which the nation received fewer arrivals from other countries than at any period before or since.[13] The reasons for this turnabout included the passage of restrictive legislation to control immigration, the lack of economic opportunity, and European, as well as Argentine, political difficulties.

However, a new phenomenon of Argentine population movement was beginning: the migration from the interior to the urban areas and particularly to Gran Buenos Aires. As a result, the provinces were now faced with the most serious of all threats—a loss of population. However, population migration defies easy analysis, as a brilliant study has shown.[14] Generalities abound to "explain" the growing numbers leaving the countryside for the factories, with various estimates about the flow of migrants each year after 1914, but reliable data have been almost entirely lacking. Any consideration of demographic changes in Argentina must take into account the differences between foreign immigrant population movements and those of internal migrants, as well as issues of life expectancy and sex-age distribution. Only a sophisticated analysis, then, can give us the needed insights into the socioeconomic impact of demographic patterns, and of necessity any consideration is restricted by the irregularity of and the length between Argentine censuses, in this case particularly from 1914 to 1947.

With the emphasis on population movements rather than mere growth rate, it is notable that, while all provinces have gained population from an increment of births over deaths and limited foreign immigration, the Northwest, Patagonia, and some of the Andean states have suffered constant losses of native-born men and women, who have generally moved toward the Atlantic coast. More specifically, the constant losers have been the poorer provinces of Santiago del Estero, La Rioja, Salta, and San Luis, and more recently Jujuy, Tucumán, Catamarca, Corrientes, Córdoba and La Pampa (although it must be noted that while native Argentines were attracted to the opportunities of developing areas, the citizens of neighboring countries, such as Bolivia, Paraguay, and Chile, where the standard of living was much lower than in Argentina, were attracted to the unskilled agricultural jobs in the provinces). The principal recipients of these movements were Mendoza, Santa Fe, and Buenos Aires (city and province): however, the Federal Capital itself was soon overcrowded and the major growth spilled over into what is called Gran Buenos Aires: the suburban areas, including such industrial centers as Avellaneda.

Contrasts in the tempo of migration can be noted over the periods between censuses, related above all to the technological factor of readily usable and inexpensive means of transportation, principally the railway. Between the initial censuses of 1869, 1895, and 1914, Argentina began its economic development, and agricultural labor was attracted to centers of opportunity, but for the most part movement was limited to changing residence between neighboring provinces. For example, workers went from Buenos Aires to Santa Fe, following the opening up of the wheat frontier as the railroad was constructed into the interior. Such migrants, however, amounted to only a few thousand a year and the statistics made no clear distinction between native-born criollos and European immigrants.

The years between the censuses of 1914 and 1947, of major concern here, witnessed the increased attraction of labor from the interior to the industrial belt of Gran Buenos Aires, with particular emphasis on the decade after 1935. The early years of the Depression forced many workers to the cities when demand for their services as migrant harvesters and cowhands declined on the great estancias, and manufacturing benefited from this surplus labor. In addition, movement took place into the frontier areas, such as the Chaco, which held promise for the landless. Then, after 1947, the trend of the previous period was clearly reinforced, with families moving into the urban industrial centers, as Argentina became a manufacturing nation.

Depopulation sprang from the reality of adverse economic circumstances and declining social stability. The concentration of wealth in the pampa became an irreversible trend, but precisely within the context of an economic disaster after 1930, the situation of the provinces became manifest. Formerly the interior seemed to have given up the struggle to combat the dominance of Buenos Aires and acquiesced in sharing at least some of the wealth of a growing export economy. A shrinking national income, however, seemed to hit hard at the provinces and then, when a rather early recovery began through import-substitution manufacturing later in the decade, it was concentrated in the restricted area of Buenos Aires. The geographically imbalanced modernization seemed to hold out no possibilities of rectification, and it became a growing source of concern.

The oft-cited tri-zonal classification of Argentine inequality of development, created by economist Alejandro E. Bunge (see figure 3) was based on published statistics for 1938. The heartland area of the first zone centering on the pampa contained only 20 percent of the surface territory of Argentina, but a rapidly growing 67 percent of the population, and in almost every category of development, such as agriculture, telephones, and capital invested in manufacturing, more than three-quarters of the republic's total. The second zone comprised a fan-shaped region bordering on the first and ranging about one thousand miles from the federal Capital: this 40 percent of the nation averaged only between 10 and 30 percent of the productive resources. Finally, the third zone, at the most distant points from Buenos Aires, also had 40 percent of the territory, but less than 10 percent of the people or the national wealth.

Fig. 3. The three zones designated by Alejandro Bunge in 1938.
(From his *Una nueva Argentina* [Buenos Aires, 1940], p. 225.)

Other statistics as well demonstrate the great divergence of
resources among the provinces during the thirties, with Buenos
Aires, Córdoba, Mendoza, and Santa Fe, the most developed,
always in the leading rank, and the first-named far outstripping
all the rest (see tables 2 and 3). A standard indicator of the
changing economic structure of Argentina can be found in a list-
ing of the number of industrial establishments: Gran Buenos Aires
and the other manufacturing cities in the pampa region had
almost 50,000 of the 86,000 factories in the republic. Santa Fe
was next with 10,000 units, and there was a rapid decline from
that point.[16] A look at the economically active population (i.e.,
the percentage of persons between the ages of 15 and 59) shows
a concentration in the four major provinces, with figures ranking
from 60 to 72 percent, and then a falloff to the low fiftieth
percentile for the poorer interior states, which have a much
larger number of individuals concentrated in the lower and higher
age brackets, those least capable of migration.

TABLE 2

Economic Capacity per Inhabitant* by Province

Base (Gran Buenos Aires) = 1,000

Jurisdiction	General Index	Population	Capacity per inhabitant
The Republic as a whole	2,626.6	13,174,980	731.2
Gran Buenos Aires	1,000.0	3,666,585	1,000.0
Federal Capital	706.8	2,463,269	1,052.1
Buenos Aires Province	581.0	2,348,960	906.9
Catamarca	3.8	147,153	94.6
Córdoba	232.5	1,253,200	680.2
Corrientes	29.7	508,261	214.2
Entre Ríos	88.1	723,253	446.6
Jujuy	13.4	110,634	441.1
La Rioja	3.6	109,160	121.0
Mendoza	84.7	504,877	615.0
Salta	22.5	207,699	397.1
San Juan	18.7	211,785	323.8
San Luis	9.5	193,456	180.1
Santa Fe	309.4	1,522,776	745.1
Santiago del Estero	12.5	472,975	96.8
Tucumán	57.8	530,237	399.7

*"Economic capacity" comprises four factors: total value of production; amount of industrial capital; total value of industrial production; number of automobiles in circulation. For further information on the methods used to arrive at these figures, see source: Alejandro Bunge, *Una nueva Argentina* (Buenos Aires, 1940), pp. 212-219.

An important variable, often considered as a sign of development, is infant mortality, for a high birth/death rate shows a lack of nutrition, medical services, and state care for mothers. The median infant mortality rate for Argentina in the period of interest to us is about 85 per thousand births, but the figure soars to 100 as an average (and as high as 176) for the poor provinces of the Northwest and the Andes. Other indices of disparity are less useful for Argentina—for example, illiteracy or per capita income—because federal effort built an effective national school system in all the provinces, and because the real cost-of-living figures are unreliable.

TABLE 3

Fiscal Resources of the Federal Capital and the Provinces[*]
(in thousands of Argentine pesos)

	1910	1920	1930	1935	1939
Federal Capital	36,604	57,228	95,863	107,677	124,864
Buenos Aires	36,965	61,508	119,685	125,373	171,445
Santa Fe	11,882	19,666	42,522	43,816	49,394
Córdoba	7,889	14,956	30,357	28,972	32,794
Mendoza	4,498	7,731	22,359	25,061	26,376
Tucumán	4,773	9,211	13,215	13,239	15,675
Entre Ríos	5,831	11,745	15,403	13,802	14,856
San Juan	1,671	2,421	12,174	11,962	10,000
Corrientes	2,835	4,977	5,719	5,823	10,807
Santiago del Estero	3,210	3,410	4,518	5,849	7,423
Salta	1,083	1,758	3,758	2,885	7,000
Jujuy	1,014	1,041	3,315	3,114	3,420
San Luis	900	1,041	2,267	2,890	3,154
Catamarca	474	608	1,041	1,232	1,352
La Rioja	470	674	1,400	974	1,329

[*]Figures are not strictly comparable because some provinces and some time periods vary as to whether statistics are based on tax revenues or budget proposals. Series should, therefore, be taken as a general comparison of the relative governmental resources of each unit. *Gobernaciones,* of course, were directly subsidized by the federal government.

Source: Alejandro E. Bunge, *Una nueva Argentina* (Buenos Aires, 1940), pp. 409-412.

Another vital sign of wealth versus poverty can be found in the amount of revenue spent by each state (although many services were provided directly by the federal government). One need only consider that the province of Buenos Aires had a budget of 181 million pesos in 1937, the Federal Capital 118 million, followed by Santa Fe with 49 million, Córdoba with 33 million, Mendoza with 27 million—and then the slide begins. The next highest state revenue was in Tucumán, with only 16 million pesos in its coffers, and the figures then plunge downward to La Rioja, with only a miserly million pesos a year to finance all its operations. In addition, despite the depression of the thirties, budgets of the wealthier provinces had been growing rapidly, as the result of spending on public works to provide employment, but no such social programs could be carried out in the interior, so that the migrants had even more inducement to leave.

The popular reactions to the provincial demographic and socioeconomic problems sketched here are difficult to estimate, except in an impressionistic manner, since we must rely on a few strident voices. As indicated earlier, a long tradition of provincial unrest and protest existed in Argentina. For some decades, the agro-export boom silenced or muted many misgivings. Once again, however, the issue appeared in intellectual circles, around the time of the centennial celebration, with a skeptical and introspective spirit. An indicator of concern with the provinces can be found in *El diario de Gabriel Quiroga* (1910), by Manuel Gálvez, a native of Santa Fe, and in *El país de la selva, Las provincias* and other books by Ricardo Rojas, whose origins were in both Santiago del Estero and Tucumán. Yet this younger generation of protesters found no popular response for their essays and novels, for Argentine nationalism tended to emphasize the country's expanding wealth as a whole rather than to question its inequitable distribution.

Certain newspapers and journals did see the problem in a more practical light, pointing out that the declining provinces were a drag on the country and that their potential needed to be considered. The decade of the thirties brought such criticism into sharper focus, thanks to the widespread opposition to the "internationalist" economic policies of the *Concordancia* on the part not only of Radicals, but various nationalist and left-wing groups, as well as a growing circle of well-trained economists. Bunge and the contributors to his *Revista de Economía Argentina* —by far the most influential economic periodical of the time— continually argued that there was a vast imbalance within the Argentine nation, one that might be roughly calculated on the basis of the economic productivity of the developed region at a maximum reference point of 100, while the less developed areas ranged between 9 and 15 percent of that figure.[17]

The apparent question was clear: why did Buenos Aires buy products from Europe that could be produced, with some government assistance perhaps, in the interior? These ideas of a "reincorporation" of the provinces were most forcefully voiced by the nationalists of the right, whose newspaper, *La Fronda,* took up the question of provincial grievances: "The governing regime which rules in the above-mentioned provinces is no different from that which controlled [the country] in the last few years. . . . Nevertheless, all the official provincial parties have lost votes. . . . The provinces are too wise to the politics of the Casa Rosada."[18] Although the controversy, then, was seen as basically socioeconomic—fashioning techniques to increase the productivity of the interior and make it an attractive place to live—the only means to accomplish this goal was political activity, a field generally overshadowed by national issues.

Exclusively provincial party organizations had been encouraged by the Argentine political system in order to represent local networks of *caciquismo** and oligarchy. Although the federal government sought to maintain its position of supremacy over the provinces through national parties, in reality these were nothing but confederations of provincial organizations. If the President could not come to an understanding with state party leaders, or if the opposition won a provincial election, then he was forced to intervene.[19] After 1880 such an arrangement worked effectively because it rested upon the narrow base of landowning interests dominating the individual provinces and because the provincial elites concerned shared an interest in maintaining the equally exclusive "regime," as it became formalized in the Partido Autonomista Nacional. The formation of the Radical Civic Union in the 1890s, drawing on wide middle-class support, created a viable opposition, and laws providing for universal manhood suffrage and the secret ballot opened the way to power after 1912. The Radicals formed strong provincial organizations of their own, but, again, each was semi-independent, generally under the control of strong caudillos, such as José Néstor Lencinas in Mendoza or the Cantoni brothers in San Juan. Thus began a love-hate relationship between the Radical leader, Hipólito Yrigoyen, and the provincial governors, most of whom were Radicals themselves, but fiercely loyal to their provinces. Like all Argentine presidents, Yrigoyen ruled from Buenos Aires, and as such inevitably found himself drawn into the age-old con-

---

caciquismo: the practice of government through elaborate patron-client relationships.

flict between the port city and the provinces—a conflict still
further aggravated by the President's own stiflingly personalistic
political style. The split between Yrigoyen and his successor,
Marcelo T. de Alvear, also divided the provincial Radical parties
into warring factions.

The Revolution of 1930 brought into power a military government, and intervention followed in all the provinces, usually
under an officer of the armed forces. The initial attempt to
return to political normality occurred with the call for elections
in the province of Buenos Aires, but the victory on April 5, 1931,
of the old-line Radical ticket showed that this party had the
only effective organization and grass-roots support, and the
results were annulled. The Conservatives, the principal civilian
allies of the "Revolution" and the major opposition to the
yrigoyenistas, rushed to form an establishment of their own. For
the rest of the decade the federal government was dominated
by the Concordancia, a coalition made up of the Independent
Socialist group, the Antipersonalist wing of the Radical party,
and, as its basis, the newly formed Partido Demócrata Nacional
(PDN). The PDN itself was made up of the older Conservative
parties of each province—the Autonomistas of Corrientes, the
Concentración Popular of Entre Ríos, the Demócrata of Córdoba,
the Provincial of Jujuy, the Unión Provincial of Salta, the
Conservador of Buenos Aires, and the Liberales of San Juan,
San Luis, Mendoza, and Tucumán.[20] These groups were resolutely
controlled by the estanciero elites who employed various underworld elements to ensure their victory at the ballot boxes.

Every local election was marked by incidents of violence, with
a systematic campaign of terror against the opposition, and
electoral fraud reached unprecedented proportions: *libretas de
enrolamiento,* the papers presented by every Argentine eligible
to vote, were taken from rural laborers and used by Conservative
agents as they saw fit, while Radical party poll watchers were
repeatedly excluded from observing. Thus a majority vote was
created for parties commanding almost no popular following, and
La Prensa of Buenos Aires, certainly no propaganda voice for
the Radicals, could only despair: "Not since the electoral reforms
of 1912 can there be found . . . conditions as deplorable as those
at present in regard to the exercise of suffrage by our citizens."[21]

Although in weakened condition and in opposition to a well-entrenched establishment, the Radicals now became the true party of provincial protest and reorganized themselves accordingly. The initial tactic they adopted was abstention from participation in what they characterized as a dictatorship under President and General Agustín P. Justo. After the middle of the decade, however, they revised their strategy and decided to work on capturing control of the provinces with programs of reform, public works, and social security. Although continually harassed and split between "personalist" and "antipersonalist" groups, the Radicals continued to make progress, electing governors and many more deputies and senators by 1940. This process made state politics the center of controversy during the thirties, and the "provincial question" once again became a primary issue.

One other party should be noted as a provincial group that secured its local base as a platform for national politics, much like the United States progressives in an earlier period. The Progressive Democratic party (PDP), led by Lisandro de la Torre, was dedicated to the interests of the small tenant farmers of the interior, who were most numerous in the wheat-growing state of Santa Fe. The PDP achieved power there in the twenties and rewrote the provincial constitution, giving viable autonomy to municipal governments, but the reforms did not last long. During the following decade, de la Torre tried to translate this home rule point of view into a national crusade against the "imperialist"—British and American—dominance of the Argentine meat market. Neither the public nor the institutions of the country, however, responded, and de la Torre committed suicide, a disillusioned crusader. The attempt of a provincial political protest group to gain some national power was a failure against the entrenched interests of the established parties.

If the provinces had difficulty articulating and developing concrete programs and remedies to canalize frustration with economic stagnation and political repression, they met with considerable success in the promotion of a revival of interest in provincial cultures. The characteristic Europeanization of Argentine culture, derived from the Anglo-French models emulated by the upper class and the Italo-Spanish life-styles brought over by the immigrants, came to an end as a continuing process. What a few writers had been discussing for years now became a more popular point of view, as the result of disenchantment with Victorian optimism and the consequent search for indigenous roots. A typical thirties nostalgia for a rural past and its rough and ready ways overtook the country, within the context, of course, of a cultivated and urban environment.

On an intellectual level, this transformation might be indicated by three prominent writers of the period. First (and somewhat before the thirties), there was Ricardo Güiraldes' *Don Segundo Sombra,* an enchanting idealization of the gaucho figure, the uniquely Argentine *provinciano,* who showed the city-bred youth lessons to be learned from an association with the countryside. Continuing this theme, the short stories and poems of Jorge Luis Borges represented the cultured Argentine's feeling for the frontier he had never known. And finally, Ezequiel Martínez Estrada led the campaign of vituperation against the city of Buenos Aires (*La cabeza de Goliat,* 1943) with its sterile formalism, which he contrasted with the telluric virtues of the indigenous rural folk.

More important, from the standpoint of a popular introduction to the provinces, was the rapid upsurge of such activities as tourism, folk music, and festivals. The motor car and the effort toward extending a road system by means of federal grants throughout the republic encouraged the middle class to forego its long-cherished journey to Paris (which they could not afford anyway during the years of the Depression) in favor of a tour of their own country. Visits to the interior made it imperative to know something about the history and culture of regions so long ignored.[22] The instruments of popular culture, the cinema and the radio, dwelt on romantic stories of rural love and violence, but perhaps no vogue was as important as folklore, the music of the *zambas* and the *carnavalitos,* sent out over the airwaves. The songs of the Pampa, the Northwest, and the Littoral, most of them written by modern composers, were melodic and rhythmic. More and more often, family and group activity took the form of an outing in the country for a *fogón* (cookout) at some *chacra* (small farm house), serving a typical *asado* (roast meat and sausages *a la gauchesca*) and concluding with group singing of folk songs. Political meetings were especially suitable for such festivities, and were often described in the news media.[23] *Criollismo* then took on a new emphasis and meaning, an emotional attachment to the localisms of a great nation, and focused interest on the lost provinces.

THE CASE OF BUENOS AIRES AND CÓRDOBA

The disparity between provinces and the issues arising from this condition might best be expressed by means of a brief comparative case study. The provinces selected for this treatment are Buenos Aires and Córdoba: the former an obvious choice because of its overwhelming importance, its position as "first among equals," its runaway development, and its firm connection with the ruling establishment during the thirties. The latter provides an excellent contrast, thanks to its historic importance, its declining economy, its feeling of frustration, and its political opposition to the authorities in power.

A basic comparison between the two provinces shows Buenos Aires with a surface area of 307,571 square kilometers and a population at that time of about 4,272,000 (of whom some 60 percent lived in the industrial settlements surrounding the capital city), while Córdoba covered 168,766 square kilometers and had a population of 1,498,000. In terms of size these two provinces were the largest in area (leaving aside the extensive gobernaciones of Patagonia), and along with Santa Fe the greatest in population. A review of most social indicators, such as urbanization, education, health, and occupational structure would establish Córdoba's ranking close behind Buenos Aires in most categories. However, when relative stages of economic development are considered, Córdoba would be revealed as having advanced about half as far as Buenos Aires, and by the 1930s was just about holding its own in terms of population, while the pampa province was expanding rapidly.[24] What makes the connection between the two provinces significant lies in their historic relationship since colonial times: they were the major rivals for dominance in the Plata region, but by the time of independence, power and wealth were flowing inexorably toward the port city, and the center of the country was becoming its vassal. Córdoba could only point with frustration to its glorious past as a basis for natural leadership in the nation, not a leadership based on material progress, but rather on a kind of historical-spiritual superiority, or as one author has put it, in a chapter entitled "When Córdoba Was the Moral Capital of the Republic": "In place of modern commerce . . . the modest businesses of the past [still] prosper in old stores, where the commercial success of an enterprise has no relation to superficial appearances."[25] The emphasis on scholarship, religion, and tradition made Córdoba a center of cultural conservatism in contradistinction to the cosmopolitan atmosphere of Buenos Aires. Nevertheless, during the thirties, when Buenos Aires became the stronghold of oligarchic politics supporting the PDN and the Concordancia, Córdoba opted for a protest movement supporting the Radical Party.

This political split was indicative of the different socioeconomic situations of the two provinces, symbolic of the crisis of Argentina after the Revolution of 1930. On the one hand, Buenos Aires recovered rapidly from the Depression under a national government policy favorable to traditional agricultural exports and import-substitution manufacturing; on the other, Córdoba sank further into isolation, and its tenant farmers left for the opportunities of the cities. Buenos Aires then represented dynamic manufacturing and, by 1935, possessed about one-quarter of the factory capacity of the entire republic, particularly concentrated in large-scale, technological production. The Radicals who had governed the province through the twenties had proposed numerous schemes of social security to improve the lot of the working class, but they had never made much headway in the industrial belt, which remained firmly in the hands of local caudillos—the political bosses in Avellaneda and other municipalities. After the 1930 Revolution, these Conservative ward bosses allied themselves with the PDN and took over control of the state government by means of fraudulent elections, a technique they perfected to the highest degree. While the Conservatives favored industry as a developmental factor, they feared the possibilities of politicization of the rapidly growing proletariat.

What the Conservatives needed above all was a charismatic leader to capture control of the workers' movement, and such a figure was to appear in the person of Manuel A. Fresco, elected governor of the province in 1936. Nothing concerned Fresco more than labor policy, and it is in this area that he was to have his greatest impact and influence. He represented that faction of rightist thought which viewed the increasing industrialization of Argentina as a problem of compelling importance. Fresco's concern with labor relations reflected his realization that the nation was now definitively changing its productive orientation, and that the workers must be controlled by a paternalistic government sensitive to their needs, or they would vote Radical or Socialist.

This statist-authoritarian supervision of proletarian movements would set a pattern in Argentina. The governor spared no effort to portray himself as a champion of the oppressed, and he backed this claim with an impressive record of legislative and administrative accomplishments. The Labor Code of 1937 and the reorganization of the Labor Department incorporated the views of the Fresco government on means of bringing about a functional equilibrium between capital and labor through an activist interventionism by the state. The governmental machinery supervised some 243 worker-management contracts, covering about 115,000 employees, 35 unions, and 4,342 companies. In addition, Fresco pushed through some 400 laws, many of them relating to social legislation in such diverse areas as penal reform, education, conservation, health, land reform and minimum wages and hours.[26]

Buenos Aires, however, had a special reason for and advantage in implementing such advanced socioeconomic policies, namely, the peculiar relationship between this province and the federal government. Not only was it powerful in terms of size and location, but the urban and economic extension of the Federal Capital into the surrounding province made it imperative for the national authorities to maintain the best possible relations with the leaders in the provincial capital, La Plata. After all, the greatest threat to any Argentine government might come from discontented workers in the suburbs. Hence the President wanted a friendly governor in the province, one who would exercise control over, and find solutions for, popular dissatisfaction. Fresco was an obvious ally and therefore enjoyed the backing and resources of President Justo. The latter's successor, Robert M. Ortiz, who had an understanding with the Radicals about ending the use of fraudulent elections, disliked Fresco's opposition to his democratic stance and ousted him through intervention in 1940.

Córdoba presented a distinct historic opposition to Buenos Aires and the federal authorities, and such feelings took the form of political support for the Radicals. This state suffered harshly from the maldistribution of funds in the republic: its tax base was small and its ability to sell bonds almost negligible. Although Córdoba felt it had resources, environment, and labor for industry, very little investment was made in this economic sector. The September Revolution brought immediate intervention in the province; President Uriburu appointed his cousin, Carlos Ibarguren, as acting executive. Ibarguren fostered the new Conservative tactic of government intervention in the socio-economic sphere through the Executive Economic Board, acting mainly in the areas of price control and labor relations.[27]

But the interventor was faced with a situation that was to agitate Argentina, and especially Córdoba, during most of the next decade: the willingness of the Radical party to strike back violently at attempted Conservative domination, particularly when the federal authorities were involved. In fact, the provincial Radicals apparently planned an uprising soon after the Uriburu takeover; the plot, if there actually was one, was uncovered and the leaders thrown into prison. The *Partido Demócrata* of Córdoba, allied to the PDN, was able to take over the province, but clashes continued to occur, as in late September 1933, when some 200 persons were wounded and one state deputy killed, because of the continued strength of the opposition.[28]

Within the context of the period it might be assumed that Córdoba would be one of the most reactionary adherents of the Concordancia; on the contrary, although traditionally conservative, its brand of conservatism was different from that found in Buenos Aires and the national government. Whereas the pampa region was dominated by large landowners, who wanted policies that would enhance their enormous profits, Córdoba was dominated by medium-sized farms, whose owners were religious and moralistic.[29] The Demócratas, therefore, refused to engage in the same type of electioneering fraud as the Conservatives in other provinces, preferring to set a more legalistic tone, and therefore permitting a great deal more meaningful Radical political activity.

Córdoba was selected for a major test of Radical strength by the middle of the thirties, when one of the few capable remaining leaders of this party, Amadeo Sabattini, was nominated for the governorship.[30] The national authorities, furious and fearful, sent in paid agitators, many of them supporters of Fresco in Buenos Aires. Nevertheless, Sabattini won the election and prepared to put into operation his own form of social legislation, but he was far less successful than Fresco in Buenos Aires. And the reasons why are quite revealing. Obviously, the resources of this rather poor province would not stretch very far, and the federal government was not interested in providing funds to Sabattini; the tradition of municipal government was very strong in Córdoba, and therefore more effort had to be put into constructing new jails or hospitals in local communities than into pursuing an overall plan of development, as Fresco did in Buenos Aires; and, finally, the constant campaign of vituperation and violence against Sabattini was intense. Nationalist groups roamed the streets and infiltrated the university, which had to be closed. The police made massive arrests, to no avail.[31] Sabattini did attempt some reforms and changes, in the fields of labor relations, health, and particularly education. Yet he, like most of the Radicals of the thirties, had become eminently "liberal" in an archaic sense, and completely bourgeois in orientation. Hence Sabattini represented a rather sterile alternative to the PDN and the Concordancia.

Ironically, as the case of Buenos Aires and Córdoba shows, during the thirties, where opposing political programs were put into operation on the provincial level, the fundamental concerns were the same. Whether liberal or conservative, the question was the "worker," agricultural or industrial, who had to be integrated into the national life and given a stake in the country. This question, of course, was an overriding one in Europe and the United States as well during the Depression and caused the deep division between left and right that characterized the entire period, world-wide. But rapid industrialization made urban class divisions a problem that appeared rather late in Argentina and that was fought out in the beginning on the provincial level.

As the comparison of Fresco and Sabattini demonstrates, the the Radical-liberals seemed a nineteenth-century anachronism, whereas they had seemed advanced only a decade earlier, and the Conservative-activists, advocating a kind of "oligarchic populism," generated a more dynamic response to the crisis of the day. Provincial politics was indeed preparing the ground for change in Argentina as a whole.

CONCLUSION

The almost thirteen-year period from the Revolution of 1930 to the Revolution of 1943 has been dismissed by the majority of Argentine historians as an "infamous decade," and yet, as we have seen, it was not a time of drift. Argentina was undergoing substantial political, economic, and social movement toward an emerging industrial state. We can regard these years as a time of transition from a traditional to a modernizing nation. Perhaps the most important aspect of such a process of development was the emergence of a new national consciousness about certain unresolved issues. Certainly this was the case with the provincial problem; these territorial divisions seemed now, more than ever, victims of the injustices of an archaic, nineteenth-century liberal system.

As in many transitional periods, however, the pull toward the future was accompanied by a tendency to look back to the past. The provinces thought in terms of reasserting their ancient federal autonomy: the belief was strong that over the years the states forming the republic had given up the rights of self-rule promised to them in the Constitution, and Argentina had in effect become a unitary government. But the future decreed that such problems would no longer be looked at within a nineteenth-century framework of federalism versus centralism: rather, the focus would change to the concern of a twentieth-century society divided between "haves" and "have-nots."

The emergence of Peronism in the following decade took up the challenge of a continuing crisis resulting from provincial decay in precisely these terms: the *descamisados* and the *campesinos,* the "people," against the urban bourgeoisie and the landowning oligarchy. Obviously local governments could not be trusted to represent any interests but those of the estancieros, and so, almost immediately after the 1943 Revolution, the nationalist military forces that controlled the country intervened in all the provinces. These regions were held in a condition of direct dependence on the federal authorities until the election of 1946, when governors and state legislatures were constitutionally re-established. Subsequently, all the provinces remained firmly in the hands of the Peronists, except Corrientes, where the expected decree of intervention came on September 4, 1947. Throughout the Perón period, even some supposedly loyal governors were replaced, and intervention, legally considered a temporary measure, tended to last for years. In addition, Peronist governors and interventors were expected to follow uniform policies in order to ensure that national decisions would never be countered on the local level.

The Constitution of 1949 marked the crystallization of Peronist doctrine in law. Ostensibly it included most of the statements on federal-state relations in an almost word-for-word transcription from the older document. However, the provinces were all forced to rewrite their own basic charters at this time to conform with the national code—a certain move away from provincial diversity. In place of constitutional autonomy, Perón offered material benefits: he never missed an opportunity to make a show of his concern for the provinces, to tour them, to discuss their local issues and, most important, to provide much greater funding for public works and development. The provincial lower classes, like the urban descamisados, had every reason to be grateful to *el líder,* and when two of the gobernaciones were raised to the status of provinces, they chose the names of Presidente Perón (Chaco) and Eva Perón (La Pampa).*

Perón's control of the provinces thus became total and complete, and the issue of Argentine local autonomy gave way to a "New Federalism." Perón realistically pointed out that the traditional division of powers in Argentina had never been what the Constitution promised, and that he was going to bring about the only kind of change that counted, an improvement of conditions, a better standard of living throughout the republic. In many ways he succeeded; the evidence of development in the

*These provinces resumed their original names after the Revolution of 1955 which deposed Perón.

provinces became clear and the years of stagnation began to end. The dominance of Buenos Aires was subordinated to the needs of the Argentine worker everywhere in the nation. Perón, however, was cheated in the end: he only succeeded in creating a revolutionary situation against himself. As the provinces began a process of development, they wanted change more rapidly and so became disenchanted with the slowdown in reforms by the early fifties. It was no accident that the revolution against Perón began in Córdoba.

Epilogue

MARK FALCOFF

When the Castillo regime fell in June 1943, it was widely assumed in most foreign capitals, particularly in Washington, that Argentina had before her but two political choices. Either she could return to some form of liberal democracy, presumably under the leadership of the Radical party (or of a Radical-Socialist coalition), or she would inevitably move towards some form of right-wing authoritarianism. In the first case she would proffer to the Allies all that aid and moral support which up till now she had jealously withheld; in the second, she would align herself with the Axis, whose declining fortunes were still unperceived by many neutrals.

While this assumption was accurate insofar as it summarized divisions among traditional political forces within the country, it was based on far too limited an understanding of Argentine reality. For one thing, the changed conditions of the world economy—and consequently, of Argentine society itself—made doubtful the restoration of the kind of "liberal" regime that had existed in the 1920s. For another, the very notion of conventional parliamentary politics had been irreparably weakened by the abuses committed in its name during the previous thirteen years. Many felt, as the writer Ernesto Sábato was to put it some years later, that in Argentina words like liberty and democracy "beg[an] in capital letters, eventually descend[ed] to the lower case, and invariably conclude[d] in pejorative quotation-marks."[1] As for Argentine fascism, in 1943 it remained a quasi-literary movement, still awaiting a leader, fearful of the masses whom he would presumably lead, and hopelessly unable to harness popular discontent. What emerged, then, in the stead of both options was the unique synthesis that later became known as *Peronismo*.

Paradoxically, the author of that synthesis, destined to become one of the most celebrated political figures of the century, was virtually unknown to the Argentine public on the morning of June 5, 1943. Yet he was by no means a stranger to the corridors of power or to the tangled web of Argentine military politics. Born to an impoverished middle-class family in the Argentine countryside in 1895, Juan Perón had entered the army at age 15 and had served for many years in unrewarding assignments in provincial garrisons. His career began to blossom in 1930 when, as a captain on General Uriburu's revolutionary general staff, he had his first taste of successful barracks intrigue. His reward throughout the rest of the decade was a succession of progressively more responsible assignments: Private Secretary and Aide-de-Camp to the Minister of War (1930-1935); Professor of Military History at the Escuela Superior de Guerra (1930-1936); Military Attaché in Chile (1936-1937); Professor of Combined Operations in the Escuela de Guerra Naval (1938); on a mission of study and observation in Italy (1939-1941); command of Argentina's Andean ski troops in Mendoza province (1941-1942). For several months before the Revolution of 1943 he had been serving as Director-General of Civil Aviation.[2]

An early association with right-wing nationalist groups (particularly the Argentine Patriotic League), participation in the Uriburu coup of 1930, and an extended stay in Mussolini's Italy might well have commended Perón to those who would replicate fascism in Argentina. But the colonel proved far too serious about the pursuit of power to allow himself to be confined by the framework of any given political doctrine. Further, his experience in the Uriburu movement and his observations in Italy convinced him of the fundamentally precarious nature of authoritarian regimes lacking an authentic base of popular support.

And his passage home through Spain in 1941 imbued him with a deep horror of social civil war.[3] Finally, Perón was a shrewd and imaginative strategist who appreciated that the social and economic changes produced in Argentina by the Depression had fundamentally altered the political landscape and had produced a serious leadership vacuum, which he now proceeded to fill.

The secret of his success was an early recognition that a new, majoritarian coalition could be assembled by appealing both to the groups that had emerged since 1930 and to the established elements that harbored long-standing grievances against the old order. From his first post as Secretary of Labor and Social Welfare he addressed himself to the working class, which had expanded enormously in size during the years 1936-1943, and whose newest members, migrants from the interior, remained unincorporated by the existing trade union movement. Then, from the War Ministry and Vice-Presidency, he reached out to the provincials, to the rural lower classes, to the "Young Turks" of the Radical party (and through them, to the middle class which had been largely disenfranchised throughout the thirties), even to the Roman Catholic Church.[4] In contrast, the traditional parties of the center and right (combined with the Socialists and the Communists), acted as if the Argentina of 1928 remained virtually intact, blithely ignored social and economic questions, and concentrated the whole of their attack on the dangers to democracy of Perón's alleged connections to "nazism." The elections of 1946 should thus be regarded not as a confrontation between left and right, but between an "old" politics and a "new."

For the next nine years Argentina experienced a regime that appeared in many respects to be the reverse-image of the one analyzed throughout this book. In its cultivation—some would say adulation, others, exploitation—of the working classes, in its open hostility to the United States and Great Britain, in its exhaltation of creole values and its cultural xenophobia, in its hostility to the landowning classes and its promotion of indus- trialization, above all in its sense of social ferment, the Perón government drastically altered the tone and mood of Argentine life. As V. S. Naipaul—so wrong generally about Argentina—has correctly observed, Perón "brought out and made strident the immigrant proletarian reality of a country where, in the women's magazines, the myth still reigns of 'old' families and polo and romance down on the estancia. He showed the country its unacknowledged Indian face. And by imposing his women on Argentina, first Evita, then Isabelita, one an actress, the other a cabaret dancer, both provincials . . . he did the roughest kind of justice on a society still ruled by degenerate machismo."[5]

Yet for all of its dramatic flourishes, Peronismo was less a revolution than a revolt, a momentary insurgency that, once spent, left Argentina's structures of power and property substantially intact.[6] For example, there was much talk about settling scores with imperialism, but except for verbal explosions in public meetings, foreign capital was treated with considerable solicitude. The British railroads were "repatriated" in 1948 for a remarkably generous sum, and Kaiser Industries and (at the end of the period) Standard Oil of California found Argentina a remunerative field of endeavor. And in spite of the vaunted "Third Position" in world affairs, presumably establishing independence from both American and Soviet blocs, Argentina subscribed to all the postwar continental defense treaties sponsored by the United States and remained active in the Organization of American States.

The local collaborators of Anglo-American imperialism, the hated "oligarchy," fared no worse: in spite of abundant vilification by the President's wife, Eva Duarte de Perón, and several "symbolic" expropriations, it survived the new dispensation largely unscathed. During Perón's first government (1946-1952) the great *estancieros* were compelled to sell their harvests to a government agency at artificially low prices—an indirect, but devastating, land tax—but even that practice was suspended in the second term when worsening international market conditions encouraged a policy of conciliation with the rural establishment. In reality the most grievous loss sustained by the traditional elite was its privileged sanctuary, the Jockey Club, burned by *Peronista* mobs on the night of June 16, 1955, that—and two intangibles—*élan* and self-assurance.

Nor did Peronismo definitively resolve two other problems passionately discussed throughout the thirties—the regional distribution (or rather, maldistribution) of national wealth and the need for a truly Argentine culture. With respect to the former, as chapter 7 makes clear, there was certainly a significant increase in social investment in the interior provinces during the Perón years, but several score more roads, schools and hospitals—however necessary and welcome—provided no permanent solution to the problem of rural unemployment. Hence the strong current of migration towards the provinces of the Littoral (particularly Buenos Aires) during the thirties continued unabated in the forties and fifties.

Of course the fault did not lie wholly with Perón: he had inherited a situation in which nearly half of the industrial plant was concentrated in the capital and its environs; the economic geography of Argentina could not be redrawn overnight. But little was done to reverse the trend, and this fact, combined with the government's support of the urban trade union movement, made relocation in Buenos Aires an irresistible alternative to the disinherited of the Argentine countryside. The prospect was rendered all the more appealing by the practice of bringing in trainloads of *provincianos* each year on Peronist "Loyalty Day" (October 17) to cheer the President and his wife in the Plaza de Mayo. After a day or two in the Paris of South America at government expense, few wished to return to La Rioja, Catamarca, or Santiago del Estero, and many never did. By the time Perón was overthrown in 1955, it was clear that the preponderant weight of Buenos Aires in the economic and social life of the nation—once based on its role as an entrepôt in the meat and grain trade—would continue into the era of Argentina's industrial development.

The cultural harvest of the Perón years was mixed, but far from revolutionary. Although Peronismo articulated many of the themes that had agitated Argentine letters in the thirties and early forties, it evoked but little support from the intellectual community as a whole.[7] Creative writers either opposed Perón outright or attempted to ignore him; the established literati, more conservative politically, turned their backs not only on the government, but on Argentine themes generally; younger writers, who were left-of-center, found it difficult to support a regime that, though pro-labor and anti-American, was intolerant of dissent, anti-intellectual, and (by its own definition) anti-Marxist.[8] Government intervention in the universities in 1946 and 1947 inflicted irreparable damage upon the structure of Argentine scholarship: the wholesale dismissal of rectors, deans, and professors led many distinguished academics to take up permanent residence in the United States and Europe. Lacking an intelligentsia of his own, Perón substituted right-wing nationalist lawyers, whose support of his government was tentative at best, and whose contributions to its political and social theories were minimal. Thus, except for a quasi-military style of architecture ("Mussolini modern"), the cultural impress of the regime was restricted to the film, the tango, radio, and the popular press, forms that were necessarily ephemeral.

What Perón did do, however, was to unsettle permanently the foundations of Argentine politics by forging a new consensus. Although elements of the victorious coalition of 1946 gradually fell away during the early fifties, even after Perón's overthrow in 1955 it was apparent that no one could rule Argentina without reassembling it in one form or another. Much subsequent history can be understood as a series of attempts to "integrate" (that is, de-Peronize) the organized working class and join it to a middle-class constituency, all under the rubric of Argentine nationalism. In the failure of these attempts is to be found the origins of the perennial instability that has afflicted the nation's politics for the last two decades.

The optimism that pervaded Argentine life at the turn of the century was partly inspired by the belief that the nation would soon attain the same standards of civilization and well-being as Europe and the United States—but without having to pay the social price of industrialization. Instead, through an excruciating irony of history, she has come to suffer from all the classic maladies of industrial society without experiencing many of its benefits.

Up to 1914 the world economic order seemed organized to satisfy this basic Argentine aspiration, but even in the "golden twenties," as Professor Villanueva demonstrates, the ground beneath the republic was shifting in ominous ways. By the 1930s it was clear that the changed international environment could no longer be ignored: Argentina would have to undergo serious adjustments in order to survive. Since that date her policymakers have applied, broadly speaking, one of two models of development. The first presupposes that the nation should continue in her basic role as an exporter of foodstuffs and industrial raw materials, buying time, as it were, to make the transition to industrialization. Those who have advocated this course have been extremely respectful of foreign capital, whose presence, they have hoped, will hasten the process of primary accumulation. An alternative model rests on the belief that the principal problem in Argentina is the distribution of political and social power and the revision of the terms under which the nation does business with her industrial customers. The first model corresponds roughly to the economic program applied by the Conservatives between 1930 and 1943 and for intermittent periods after 1955. The second is a picture (somewhat distorted for heuristic purposes) of the policies pursued by Perón.

Unfortunately neither model has proved workable. The Conservatives have attempted to carry out their "modernization" in a political vacuum. Concretely, in the thirties this meant that the presence of a large and politically conscious middle class had to be circumvented through effective annulment of the franchise. And in the fifties and sixties, confronted by a militant working class loyal to Perón, it was believed necessary to do away with constitutional government altogether. Both steps proved destructive of the very stability necessary to attract foreign investors, who stayed away from Argentina, as one commentator remarked in the sixties, in droves. Nor did the rural sector flourish during these years. Failure to apply new techniques and new investment in the countryside has meant that an increasingly less efficient agriculture has been forced to support a greater and greater number of Argentines.[9]

Nor did the Peronist alternative prove notably successful. During the late forties and early fifties, Argentina experienced an important redistribution of political and economic power, but the total amount of wealth and investment did not significantly increase. Perón assumed—incorrectly, as it turned out—that his country was in a position to dictate the terms of trade to the outside world. This held true only for a brief period following the Second World War, when European agriculture was still unsettled by the ravages of conflict. With regard to internal policies, a massive inflation of the budget for public works and social welfare—combined with the enlargement of the bureaucracy—doubtless won the regime many friends, but eventually bankrupted the treasury. When world agricultural prices dropped in the early fifties, the government found it necessary to come to terms with the rural sector, and Perón's working-class constituency was abruptly abandoned. (His vaunted economic nationalism met with the same fate; foreign investors were suddenly greeted with unwonted cordiality.) It was only after the fall of the leader in 1955 that his followers began to remember his years of power as a lost golden age. In time the myth of Perón became so powerful that it engulfed even its subject, who spoke in Spanish exile of his ouster as the product of an "unholy alliance" between Argentine oligarchs and Anglo-American imperialists.[10]

Writing in 1971, a distinguished economist argued that Argentina's problem consisted of a paradox: that the "right" policies for economic recovery were the "wrong" policies for political and social harmony.[11] But many wondered how programs that were pragmatically unworkable could lead to the nation's recovery, except in a laboratory.[12] In the seventies she remained a victim of her past successes, a country suspended, as one businessman remarked to this writer, "in a cloud of historicism." One of the few points upon which Argentines agreed seemed to be that the nation had taken the wrong turn in 1930, and that the return of Perón—or a government acting in his name—would rectify more than two generations of error. This judgment awaits the verdict of events.

Notes

CHAPTER 2: POLITICAL DEVELOPMENTS

1. This chapter does not pretend to be the fruit of original research so much as an attempt to synthesize and interpret some of the more recent materials and studies on the political life of the period. Particularly useful in its preparation have been the following: Alberto Ciria, *Partidos y poder en la Argentina moderna, 1930-46* (Buenos Aires, 1964; English trans., Albany, N. Y., 1974); Torcuato S. di Tella et al., *Argentina, sociedad de masas* (Buenos Aires, 1965); Alfredo Galletti, *La política y los partidos* (México-Buenos Aires, 1961); Marvin Goldwert, "The Argentine Revolution of 1930," Unpublished Ph.D. dissertation (University of Texas, 1964); Félix Luna, *Alvear* (Buenos Aires, 1958); Marysa Navarro Gerassi, *Los nacionalistas* (Buenos Aires, 1968); Robert Potash, *The Army and Politics in Argentina: From Yrigoyen to Perón* (Stanford, Calif., 1969), and Peter H. Smith, *Politics and Beef in Argentina* (New York, 1968). (Unfortunately Professor Smith's new (1974) work, *Argentina and the Failure of Democracy* appeared too late to be included.) Also useful is the symposium organized by the Extensión Universitaria de la Facultad de Derecho y Ciencias Sociales (FUBA), *Tres revoluciones* (Buenos Aires, 1959) and the special number dedicated to "La crisis del 1930" of the *Revista de Historia*, I, 3 (1958).

2. For Uriburu's political ideas, see *La palabra del General Uriburu: discursos, manifiestos, declaraciones y cartas publicadas durante su gobierno* (Buenos Aires, 1933).

3. The Argentine novelist Ernesto Sábato has written that during the 1930s "it was difficult to find students who still believed in the older generation of political leaders. . . . With the exception of a few who participated in 'pure' minoritarian parties, [most] inclined towards one of two

opposing forces: nationalism and revolutionary movements of the left. From my own experience as a Communist student between 1930 and 1935, I recall our reluctance to use words like 'fatherland' and 'liberty' . . . so frequently had they been prostituted on the lips of public thieves." *El otro rostro del Peronismo* (Buenos Aires, 1956), p. 17.

4. Ysabel Fisk Rennie, *The Argentine Republic* (New York, 1945), pp. 305-306. Mrs. Rennie spent much time in the Argentine Northwest during 1941-1942.

5. Apart from a lack of documentary evidence, this point of view flies in the face of the nationalist petroleum policies pursued by Uriburu and the governments that followed him. The fact that many of the general's cabinet ministers had previously received legal retainers from Standard Oil is not in itself very significant, for most of the important foreign contracts were concentrated in a few law firms. In short, if Standard paid for the Revolution, the latter proved one of its poorer investments.

6. See the interesting analysis and comparison of the cabinets of Yrigoyen and Alvear in Peter H. Smith's "Los radicales argentinos y la defensa de los intereses ganaderos," *Desarrollo Económico,* VII, 25 (1967), pp. 802-806.

7. Interview with *La Razón* (Buenos Aires), September 8, 1930, re-printed in Luna, op. cit., pp. 75-76.

8. This section relies on the material presented in Potash, op. cit., especially chapters 1 and 2.

9. Quoted in J. M. Espigares Moreno, *Lo que me dijo el General Uriburu* (Buenos Aires, 1933), p. 83.

10. Manuel Gálvez, *Vida de Hipólito Yrigoyen* (1936), in *Biografías completas* (Buenos Aires, 1962), I, pp. 377-378. Waldo Frank, who visited Yrigoyen shortly before his overthrow, records a similar impression in his *América Hispana* (New York and London, 1931), pp. 122-125.

11. Felix Weil, *Argentine Riddle* (New York, 1944), pp. 36-37.

12. The writers base this comment on discussions with a number of individuals from diverse walks of life who had occasion to deal with government agencies both before and after September 6, 1930.

13. Quoted in *Review of the River Plate* (Buenos Aires), March 24, 1933.

14. In 1936 the Vice-President was a very important landholder in both Buenos Aires and Córdoba provinces; the President of the Senate was the principal rural figure in Salta; the Minister of Agriculture was one of the most important cattlemen in Córdoba, as was his successor with respect to the province of Corrientes. José Luis de Imaz, *Los que mandan,* translated by Carlos A. Astiz (Albany, N. Y., 1970), p. 36.

15. For an exposition of the Plan and its subsequent difficulties, see Weil, op. cit., pp. 157-174. The text of the Plan and a section of the senatorial debate on its merits appears in Ministerio de Hacienda de la Nación, *El Plan de Reactivación Económica ante el Honorable Senado* (Buenos Aires, 1940).

16. The Radicals attempt to explain away their opposition on grounds of

principle, not very convincingly, in a special issue of their "theoretical" journal *Hechos e ideas*, VI, 38-39 (1941), pp. 314 et seq.

17. Imaz, op. cit., p. 15.

18. Ibid, pp. 23-24.

19. The reference is to Alejandro Ruiz-Guiñazú, *La Argentina ante sí misma: reflexiones sobre una revolución necesaria* (Buenos Aires, 1942).

20. Imaz, op. cit., p. 16.

CHAPTER 3: ECONOMIC DEVELOPMENT

1. J. A. Hobson, *The Evolution of Modern Capitalism* (London, 1914). According to the estimates presented in this work, Argentina occupied second place, after the United States. Hobson seemed not at all surprised at his findings, which affords an idea of the way in which Argentine development was viewed from abroad during the years immediately prior to the First World War.

2. Héctor Dieguéz, "Crecimiento e inestabilidad de las exportaciones argentinas," *Desarrollo económico*, XII, 46 (1972), pp. 333-349.

3. In 1913, 47.4 percent of the total fixed capital in Argentina was foreign. ONU, Comisión Económica para América Latina, *El desarrollo económico argentino* (Santiago de Chile, 1958), Anexo Estadístico (mimeo), V, pp. 341 et seq.

4. Ibid.

5. "The list of byproducts and derivates (especially those of meat-packing houses) had become so extensive that it was a commonplace to say that instead of fulfilling their original objective, they had become manufacturers of soap, cheese, ice cream, butter, cream, vegetable oils, margarines, and of preserved sweets, fruits, eggs, poultry, etc." Ricardo M. Ortiz, *Historia económica de la Argentina* (Buenos Aires, 1955), p. 25.

6. Real rate of growth as indicated by total added value.
   Annual average:

	1900-1904/1910-1914	1910-1914/1925-1929
GNP, at factor cost	6.3 percent	3.5 percent

Source: *El desarrollo económico argentino*, V, pp. 341 et. seq.

7. Bunge had pointed out clearly in 1927 that the economic model of the "generation of '80" had ceased to operate in 1908 and especially since 1914. See his "Una crisis de las fuerzas creadoras" in *Una nueva Argentina* (Buenos Aires, 1940). Much the same impression was perceived from a less narrowly economic point of view by the eminent pensador Alejandro Korn in his *Nuevas bases* (Buenos Aires, 1925).

8. "By 1910 . . . Chicago-based packinghouses were shipping over half the chilled beef that was exported from the Plate." Peter H. Smith, *Politics and Beef in Argentina* (New York, 1968), p. 58.

9. Julio Irazusta, *Balance del siglo y medio* (Buenos Aires, 1966), p. 109.

10. These quotes are taken from Arturo O'Connell, "The D'Abernon Mission and the Convention of Reciprocal Trade and Credits," Unpublished paper (University of Cambridge, 1970).

11. Lord D'Abernon to *The Times* (London), September 9, 1929.

12. H. S. Ferns indicates that this shows that the exchange control system tended to support Argentine industry. See his *Argentina* (New York and London, 1969), p. 162.

13. Ibid., p. 163.

14. In the Argentine senate the representatives of the smaller and middle-sized ranchers who were not particularly benefited by the Pact found the opportunity to express their disagreement with those who had concluded it. For them it was a treaty made in the exclusive interest of the great breeders and fatteners of the Province of Buenos Aires. On this issue see Smith, *Politics and Beef,* pp. 170-222.

15. Around 54 percent of the imports from Great Britain entered duty-free.

16. The accord of 1933 was renewed three years later along very similar lines. The second version added new restrictions to the previous agreement.

17. The idea was to maintain a difference of 20 percent between both markets.

18. Guido di Tella and Manuel Zymelman, *Las etapas del desarrollo económico argentino* (Buenos Aires, 1967), p. 440.

19. Banco Central de la República Argentina, *Memoria, 1936,* p. 1.

20. Di Tella and Zymelman, op. cit., p. 425.

21. Trabajo de Historia Oral, Instituto Torcuato S. di Tella, Buenos Aires, 1972.

22. See Javier Villanueva, "Aspectos de la estrategia de industrialización argentina" in *Los fragmentos del poder,* Torcuato S. di Tella and Tulio Halperín Donghi, eds., (Buenos Aires, 1969) and "El orígen de la industrialización argentina," *Desarrollo Económico,* XII, 47 (1972), pp. 451-476; also Alberto Petrecolla, *Prices, Import Substitution, and Investment in the Argentine Textile Industry (1920-1930)* (Buenos Aires, 1968) and Ricardo M. Ortiz, "El aspecto económico-social de la crisis del 1930," *Revista de Historia,* I, 3 (1958), pp. 41-72.

23. Di Tella and Zymelman, op. cit., p. 428.

24. On this see Carl Solberg, "The Tariff and Politics in Argentina", *Hispanic American Historical Review,* LIII, 2 (1973), pp. 260-284. The essence of Alvear's tariff reform in 1924 was an upward revision of the *tarifa de aváluos,* or valuations schedule. Based on prices prevailing in 1909, this schedule naturally became increasingly useless during the inflationary period following 1914.

25. Luis Duhau, "La crisis y las industrias nacionales," *Revista de Economía Argentina,* XXXII, 187 (1934), pp. 13-15. See also Juan J. Llach, *Intereses económicos dominantes y los orígenes del peronismo* (Buenos Aires, 1972) (mimeo).

26. Cited in Eduardo F. Jorge, *Industria y concentración económica* (Buenos Aires, 1971), pp. 115 et seq.

27. Roberto Cortés Conde, "Los años finales de la coyuntura de guerra, 1943-45," Unpublished MS, Buenos Aires, 1972.

28. Banco Central de la República Argentina, *Memoria, 1939,* pp. 1 et seq.

29. Cortes Conde, MS cited; also, Banco Central de la República Argentina, *Memoria, 1942*, pp. 1-10, which indicates that manufacturing enterprises functioned at full capacity; others enlarged their plants. A great number of small and middle-sized establishments also sprang up.

30. On a visit to the United States shortly thereafter, Pinedo told a group of New York financiers that since the historic reasons for Argentina's exclusively European orientation had come to an end, it was time to create a closer economic relationship with the United States. At the same time he warned his listeners that in the absence of a close commercial understanding, Argentina might be compelled to turn to Germany. [Speech to the New York Banker's Club, June, 1941]. To his fellow Argentines he likewise admonished that they were "too few in number and too small to carve out for ourselves a place in the postwar world without links to the greater associations of people who will hold economic predominance in it." [Speech to Acción Argentina, June, 1942]. Both reprinted in *Argentina en la vorágine* (Buenos Aires, 1943).

31. The Pinedo Plan was supported in part by the Unión Industrial; it obtained the benevolent neutrality of the Rural Society and the Buenos Aires Stock Exchange; it was strongly opposed by the Radicals and the cattlemen from the relatively nonprivileged zones of the Northern Littoral.

32. Conferencia Americana de Asociaciones de Comercio y Producción, Delegación Argentina, *El movimiento de capitales en el comercio exterior de las naciones americanas* (Buenos Aires-Montevideo, 1941). Among the final resolutions of that conference was one that recommended, among other things, "the attraction of foreign capital to countries of Latin America to assure in them the production of basic articles and the adequate industrialization of the economy."

33. Banco Central de la República Argentina, *Memoria, 1942*, pp. 29 et seq.

34. The Unión Industrial was divided: on one hand there were those who supported the idea of industrialization for export on the basis of local raw materials. On the other, there were those who supposed that the essential thing was to defend what already existed in the industrial field. Those who supported the former line of thought indicated that, after all, the industries based on local raw materials were not the only "natural" ones that might be considered. To argue thus would amount to saying that England should not have developed a cotton textile industry nor the United States her rubber industry.

35. Jorge Fodor and Arturo O'Connell, "La Argentina y la economía atlántica en la primera mitad del siglo XX," *Desarrollo Económico*, XIII, 49 (1973), pp. 3-65.

36. *Hacia un mayor y mejor conocimiento de la verdadera situación económica argentina* (Buenos Aires, 1950), p. 37.

37. Import substitution through adequate tariff protection; concentration upon the local market; external participation through imported capital, technology, equipment, and raw materials.

CHAPTER 4: FOREIGN RELATIONS

1. On the South American balance of power, see Robert N. Burr, "The Balance of Power in Nineteenth Century South America: An Exploratory Essay," *Hispanic American Historical Review*, XXXV, 1 (1955), pp. 37-60. The best statement of the foreign policy implications of the liberal model is Thomas F. McGann, *Argentina, The United States, and the Inter-American System, 1880-1914* (Cambridge, Mass., 1957).

2. This episode is reported in National Archives Record Group 165, Records of the Military Intelligence Division, File Number 2657-L-125/1, May 4, 1935. (Hereinafter these records are cited by RG 165, with file number and date.)

3. Some may argue that the concern for exports reflects the oligarchy's interests and not that of the nation as a whole. This argument has an appealing ring but it simply does not stand up under empirical scrutiny.

4. On the D'Abernon mission see the Records of the Foreign Office in the Public Records Office, London, file number A5964/3931/51, D'Abernon's telegram September 7, 1929; Robertson's dispatch June 17, 1929, file number A4751/52/2. (Hereinafter these records are cited by FO, the file number, and the date.) On the Argentine position at the Wheat Conference, see *La Prensa* (Buenos Aires), May 19, 1930, and May 24, 1930. Argentine fear of United States penetration and the preference for the British is expressed in RG 165, 2657-L-91/3, September 8, 1929; FO A7314 /3931/51, Minutes, October 25, 1929; A3967/52/2, Robertson's May 16, 1929; A3968/52/2, Robertson's May 16, 1929; and A4751/52/2, Robertson's June 17, 1929.

5. On Foreign Office pessimism, see FO A4751/52/2, various Minutes July and August, 1929; A4929/1480/2, Minutes to Macleay's dispatch, June 24, 1930. The comments in Commons and the press are reported in *The Times* (London), February 1, 1930; February 6, 1930; February 18, 1930; March 13, 1930. On the British economy and the organization of the government see FO A4751/52/2, Minutes, 1929; and, generally, Dereck H. Aldcroft and Harry W. Richardson, *The British Economy, 1870-1939* (London, 1969); Frederic Benham, *Great Britain Under Protection* (New York, 1941); Sidney Pollard, *The Development of the British Economy, 1914-1967* (London, 2d edition, 1969); and A. J. Youngson, *Britain's Economic Growth, 1920-1966* (New York, 1967).

6. Records of the Department of State, National Archives, Record Group 59, Decimal File 835.00 Revolutions/2, from Bliss, September 7, 1930, and 835.00 Revolutions/3, from Bliss, September 8, 1930. (Hereinafter cited by RG 59, the file number and the date.) The U. S. Military Attaché seconded the Ambassador's plea; see MID report October 9, 1930, RG 165, 2657-L-100/2. Some of the relevant documents are published in *Papers Relating to the Foreign Relations of the United States, 1930*, I, pp. 378-389 (Washington, 1945). (Hereinafter this series cited by FRUS, the year, and the volume.) British Ambassador Macleay reported the American

businessmen as "jubilant" at the revolution, FO A6008/666/2, September 10, 1930.

7. FO A6006/666/2, Lindsay's September 10, 1930.

8. RG 59, 835.00 Revolutions/11, Atherton's September 16, 1930 (from London); FO A5824/66/2, Minutes; and FO A5898/666/2, Macleay's September 7, 1930.

9. Compare Macleay's September 13, 1930, FO A6658/666/2 and Lindsay's September 26, 1930, FO A6474/1480/2 with the MID report July 1, 1930, RG 165, 2515—L-21/1 and the Bliss telegram August 16, 1930, RG 59, 611.353 Corn/19 or any of the RG 59 files dealing with agricultural matters, 611.353.

10. The debate can be followed in the files of *La Fronda, La Prensa,* and *La Nación* (Buenos Aires), and in the influential *Revista de Economía Argentina.* Other observations are in FO A7540/2/2, November 19, 1930, Minutes; *The Times,* February 8, 1930; *Crítica* (Buenos Aires), February 6, 1930, and February 7, 1930.

11. A fascinating account of the economic team developed by Alejandro Bunge and led by Raúl Prebisch is in the Instituto Torcuato S. di Tella Oral History Project, Interview with Enrique Malaccorto, August 24, 1971.

12. For example, see *The Times,* August 26, 1931; *La Prensa,* February 1, 1931; and Bunge's articles in the *Revista de Economía Argentina,* XXV (1930), XXVI (1931), XXVII (1931).

13. The Argentine nervousness and demands for direct government intervention in the export trade are in *Revista de Economía Argentina,* XXVII (1931), pp. 169-194 and XXVIII (1932), pp. 181-199, 265-269, 329-357, 453-470; *La Fronda,* November 21, 1931, and November 30, 1931; *La Prensa,* March 4, 1931, and May 2, 1931. The exchange developments are in RG 59, 835.5151 passim, and Virgil Salera, *Exchange Control and the Argentine Market* (New York, 1941), pp. 13-68. Macleay's warning is in FO A4931/9/2.

14. An example of the bullish forecasts is Carlos Tornquist, "El balance del año comercial," *Revista de Economía Argentina,* XXVIII (1932). pp. 471-484. Ambassador Malbran's talks with Sir John Simon are in FO A7013/7013/2 and A7022/7013/2. The flurry of activity at the end of 1931 is reported in *The Times,* December 4, 1931, and March 24, 1932; Daniel Drosdoff, *El gobierno de las vacas (1933-56): Tratado Roca-Runciman* (Buenos Aires, 1972), pp. 14-15; RG 59, 611.3531/105 from Bliss, July 6, 1932; *La Fronda,* December 16, 1931.

15. FO A4751/52/2 June 17, 1929. The same sentiments were expressed again by Robertson in 1932, *The Times,* January 27, 1932; and by Sir William Morris, Chairman of the National Council of Industry and Commerce, *The Times,* April 10, 1931. *The Times* was sympathetic to the Anglo-Argentine Committee and published articles supporting its position throughout 1930, 1931, and into the early months of 1932. For example, see December 23, 1930; February 18, 1931; and March 16, 1932.

16. *La Prensa,* February 13, 1932; also January 29, 1932.

17. RG 59, 611.3531/105 and 106, July 6 and 25, 1932; FO A4814/ 4453/2, July 22, 1932. See also FO A4691/1040/2, June 6, 1932, and *The Times,* July 2, 1932.

18. Malbran's offer, Macleay's report, the Foreign Office policy, and the rejection are in FO A4565/1040/2. For a general review of the Ottawa proceedings, see Benham, op. cit., pp. 62-95; Youngson, op. cit., pp. 87-88; and A. J. P. Taylor, *English History, 1914-45* (Oxford, 1965), pp. 332-339.

19. FO A6262/1040/2, Macleay's September 6, 1932.

20. The documentation on the preliminary negotiations is in FO 371/ 15789 and 16531, files 48/2 and 1040/2.

21. Malbran's depression is described in FO A110/48/2, Craigie's Minute, January 22, 1933. The same desperation is reflected by RG 59, 635.4131/ 65, from Bliss, November 4, 1932. Argentine anger with Great Britain is in *La Fronda,* December 29, 1932; *The Times,* November 3, 1932; *La Prensa,* November 29, 1932; and the British Embassy's Annual Report for 1932, FO A1713/1713/2, February 6, 1933. The final compromise and the Foreign Office sympathy for Argentina are in FO A7192/1040/2, Macleay's October 15, 1932, with Minutes, and A1033/48/2, Minute, February 9, 1933.

22. This agreement was mainly for show and had questionable results. Its terms violated the most-favored-nation treaties that Argentina already had with other nations. The United States was particularly upset and lodged strong protests in Buenos Aires and with the Argentine ambassador in Washington, Felipe Espil. Saavedra Lamas merely ignored the protests, as was his wont. Espil, unofficially, admitted his government's gaffe and asked the Department of State not to insist upon its protest, to hold its treaty rights in abeyance. *FRUS, 1933,* IV, pp. 683-721.

23. FO A765/4453/2, Lindsay's November 12, 1932, with Minutes; RG 59, 835.5151/72 1/2, from Bliss, November 25, 1932, and 835.5151/91 from Bliss, March 17, 1933. On the mission to Italy, see FO A3109/47/2, Macleay's April 15, 1933; and Ezequiel Ramos Mexía, *Mis memorias, 1853-1935* (Buenos Aires, 1937).

24. *FRUS, 1933,* IV, pp. 642-682; RG 59, 835.5151/99, from Bliss, April 4, 1933. Saavedra Lamas tried to bluff the British on the basis of Espil's talks with the Department of State but the British saw through it; FO A2983/48/2, Macleay's April 17, 1933.

25. The treaty negotiations can be reconstructed from FO file 48/2, volumes FO 371/16531-16535, and are summarized in Drosdoff, op. cit., pp. 24-36.

26. Roger Gravil, "State Intervention in Argentina's Export Trade Between the Wars," *Journal of Latin American Studies,* II, 2 (1971), pp. 147-173.

27. Roger Gravil, "British Retail Trade in Argentina, 1900-1940," *Inter-American Economic Affairs,* XXIV, 2 (1970), pp. 3-26.

28. Drosdoff, op. cit., pp. 42-43.

29. Benham, op. cit., p. 138; FO A4580/122/2, Macleay's July 12, 1932; A7041/52/2, Minute, August 29, 1934.

30. Foreign Office Minute, FO A838/27/2, January 21, 1935.

31. Foreign Office Minute, FO A9720/27/2, November 15, 1935. On the composition of forces within the British government, see FO A376/359/2, Minute, January 11, 1934, and A760/359/2, January 23, 1934.

32. Ambassador Henderson summarized the dilemma for the Argentines and the Foreign Office in A10328/111/2, December 5, 1935:

I am convinced that the Argentine government are thoroughly frightened and desperately anxious to secure themselves as soon as possible against further adverse developments in the United Kingdom market for their meat [and] will concede nothing tangible except in exchange for definite assurances on this angle. For this reason it is doubtful whether any satisfactory result from the present conversations will be obtainable and the question arises whether the moment has not arrived for His Majesty's Government to obtain the best possible bargain covering the whole ground of United Kingdom interests in this country. . . .

The issue seems unavoidably to resolve itself into a choice between protecting the vast United Kingdom capital and trade interests in this country, and sacrificing those interests in favour of the home farmer and imperial trade. Though I am obviously not in a position to ascertain exactly where the balance of advantages and disadvantages lies, I consider it my duty to point out the impossibility of negotiating satisfactory conditions for local United Kingdom interests unless Argentina's own particular interests can be generously treated by drawing a line to protect her from further encroachments on her trade such as have taken place in the form of 'experimental shipments' from the Dominions and the unrestricted increase of home production. The time for appealing to sentiment is past and nothing less than a definite and calculable trade advantage will have any weight with Argentine government and public opinion here. If however something really tangible could be held out as a bait the present moment appears psychologically favourable for extracting the maximum quid pro quo.

Generally speaking I would ask His Majesty's Government to consider whether in view of the vast amount of British capital invested here, greater in fact than in most of the Dominions, Argentina should not . . . for economic purposes, be treated as part of the British Empire.

For Argentine efforts to benefit from this, see FO A3772/359/2, April 27, 1934; A4961/111/2, May 28, 1935.

33. Winthrop R. Wright, "Foreign Owned Railways in Argentina: A Case Study of Economic Nationalism," *Business History Review*, XLI, 3 (1967), pp. 62-93; FO A4446/65/2, Henderson's April 30, 1936; Drosdoff, op. cit., pp. 94-116. British capital may not have been as captive as was supposed. The British firms reacted to exchange restrictions by altering their corporate financial strategies, removing their reserves to London, diversifying their activities in other markets, and converting their currency surplus into other assets. These measures undoubtedly inhibited reinvestment and curtailed the circulation of currency. See Gravil, "Retail Trade"; *The Times*, January 30, 1934; FO A2903/111/2, Commercial Secretary's report, March 18, 1935.

34. The aftosa question is discussed in E. Louise Peffer, "Foot and Mouth

Disease in United States Policy," *Food Research Institute Studies*, III, 2 (1962), pp. 141-180, and in Manuel A. Machado, Jr., *Aftosa: A Historical Survey of Foot-and-Mouth Disease and Inter-American Relations* (Albany, N. Y., 1969).

35. *FRUS, 1933*, V, pp. 650-51; *FRUS, 1934*, IV, pp. 329-422; *FRUS, 1935*, IV, pp. 278-280; RG 59, 611.3531/285, November 2, 1934.

36. RG 59, 611.3531/270, Welles' Memorandum, September 6, 1934.

37. *FRUS, 1936*, V, p. 176.

38. *FRUS, 1937*, V, pp. 231-232.

39. RG 59, 611.3531/221, Wallace to the Secretary of State, December 1, 1933.

40. RG 59 611.3531/229, Sayre to Roosevelt, December 27, 1933, and Latin American Division Memorandum, no date.

41. RG 59, 611.353 Linseed/23, Economic Adviser's Memorandum, August 9, 1934.

42. RG 59, 611.3531/304 1/2, Memorandum, January 16, 1935; and 611.3531/314 1/2 Memorandum, March 19, 1935.

43. RG 59, 611.353 Corn/33, Memorandum, undated.

44. RG 59, 611.353 Corn/34, Hull's Memorandum, April 14, 1936.

45. RG 59, 611.353 Linseed/73, Trade Agreements Division Memorandum, February 18, 1937. In the corn question, farm interests on both coasts opposed all restrictions on imports, as did several trade councils and some representatives of banking interests who favored liberalization of trade to help Argentina meet its external debt obligations. These interests were no match for the solid midwest farm bloc.

46. RG 59, 835.5151/694, June 14, 1937.

47. See, for example, *La Prensa*, March 13, 1934, and *La Fronda*, August 9, 1934.

48. *The Times*, July 9, 1936; November 7, 1936; November 28, 1936; Drosdoff, op. cit., pp. 60-61 and 80-92; FO A7153/76/2, Henderson's August 28, 1936, noting inflamed public opinion against the onerous conditions imposed on Argentina by Great Britain. On the changes in the Argentine economy see chapter 3 above and Carlos Díaz-Alejandro, *Essays on the Economic History of the Argentine Republic* (New Haven, Conn., 1970), chapters 2-4; Aldo Ferrer, *The Argentine Economy* (Berkeley and Los Angeles, Calif., 1967), especially Part IV; Alejandro E. Bunge, *Una nueva Argentina* (Buenos Aires, 1940), and Federico Pinedo, *En tiempos de la república* (Buenos Aires, 1946-1948), 5 vols.

49. *La Prensa*, July 7, 1936; *La Vanguardia* (Buenos Aires), January 27, 1937; in FO A1286/122/2, February 16, 1937.

50. For a detailed discussion of the nonbelligerency pact and the broad popular disenchantment with the Allies and the willing acceptance of neutrality, see Joseph S. Tulchin, "The Argentine Proposal for Non-Belligerency, April, 1940," *Journal of Inter-American Studies*, XI, 4 (1969), pp. 571-604.

51. FO 420/293 (Confidential Print), Hadow's July 12 and August 5, 1940.

Hadow's October 22, 1940, in the same file, explains how cattlemen, individually sympathetic to the Allies, came to support the policy of neutrality and nationalist alternatives in government. The Brazilians learned the lesson of self-interest earlier and with happier results, as shown in Stanley E. Hilton's "Brazil and Great Power Trade Rivalry in South America, 1934-1939," Ph.D. diss. (University of Texas, 1969).

CHAPTER 5: INTELLECTUAL CURRENTS

1. *South American Journey* (New York, 1943), pp. 63, 174.

2. "Intimidades" (1930), *Obras completas* (Madrid, 3rd edition, 1954), II, pp. 639, 645.

3. Juan José Sebreli, *Martínez Estrada, una rebelión inútil* (Buenos Aires, 2d edition, 1962), pp. 10, 39.

4. Ernesto Palacio, *La historia falsificada* (Buenos Aires, 1939), p. 51.

5. Hector Sáenz y Quesada, *Elegía de Buenos Aires*, quoted in Jorge Abelardo Ramos, *Revolución y contrarevolución en la Argentina* (Buenos Aires, 3rd edition, 1965), II, p. 551.

6. Quoted in José Luis Romero, *El desarrollo de las ideas en la sociedad argentina del siglo XX* (México-Buenos Aires, 1965), p. 135.

7. "Rosas, el marxismo, y la política contemporánea," *Revista del Instituto de Investigaciones Históricas "Juan Manuel de Rosas,"* I, 3 (1940).

8. Romero, op. cit., p. 140.

9. "La guerra y nuestro porvenir," *Nosotros,* May-June, 1940, p. 397. An English translation of this article appeared in *Living Age,* CCCLIX, 4488 (1940), pp. 48-51.

10. Federico Pinedo, address to the British Chamber of Commerce, text in *Review of the River Plate* (Buenos Aires), August 10, 1940.

11. Ibid., June 7, 1940.

12. Quoted in José Luis Torres, *Algunas maneras de vender la patria* (Buenos Aires, 1940), p. 16.

CHAPTER 6: POPULAR CULTURE

1. The creole sainete, or popular sketch, accurately records this process as it appeared in the first decades of the twentieth century. The evolution of creole-immigrant relations is perhaps best depicted in the works of Nemesio Trejo, Enrique García Velloso, Carlos M. Pacheco, Alberto Novión, José González Castillo, and Enrique Buttaro. The subject is best treated in Tulio Carella, ed., *El sainete criollo* (Buenos Aires, 1957), Blas Raúl Gallo, *Historia del sainete nacional* (Buenos Aires, 1959), and Luis Ordaz, *El teatro en el Río de la Plata* (Buenos Aires, 1962).

2. Jorge Luis Borges, the archetypical representative of this aristocratic official culture, selects only the folkloric aspects of our great popular creations, like *Martín Fierro,* and purposely ignores their obvious social content. This distortion of history and of popular culture provides a thoroughly picturesque—but very incomplete—image of the gaucho and the

compadrito. See Borges's "Evaristo Carriego" in *Obras completas* (Buenos Aires, 1966), I.

3. Hernández Arregui addresses himself specifically to the cultural problem in *Imperialismo y cultura* (Buenos Aires, 2d edition, 1964).

4. Horacio Ferrer, *El tango, su historia y evolución* (Buenos Aires, 1960).

5. Various tangos deal with Leandro N. Alem, founder of the Radical Party, President Hipólito Yrigoyen, Socialist deputy Alfredo L. Palacios, and other turn-of-the-century political leaders. This was but a passing phase of the form and left no important legacies to the art. By the 1930s it had completely disappeared.

6. Cf. Hernández Arregui, *Imperialismo y cultura.*

7. "Tres Esquinas," tango by Enrique Cadícamo.

8. In addition to composing tangos, Discépolo was a very popular personality in the thirties and forties through his extensive activities as an actor, film director, playwright, and radio commentator. A close friend of General Perón—who regarded him as "Argentina's greatest popular poet"—and of Eva Duarte de Perón, the general's wife, he became one of the most lucid propagandists of the Peronista movement.

9. *Buenos Aires, vida cotidiana y alienación* (Buenos Aires, 1965).

10. Since Argentine intellectuals find it difficult to admit the primacy of the Gardelian myth, they frequently disparage it by comparing it to that of Yrigoyen. For example, Ezequiel Martínez Estrada writes in *La cabeza de Goliat* (1943) that "Buenos Aires has had but one idol: Yrigoyen. The others are his legitimate children, but they only reflect the essence of the city."

11. Domingo Di Núbila, *Historia del cine argentino* (Buenos Aires, 1959).

12. The sentimental rascal interpreted by Luis Sandrini and the heroines persecuted by fate (who appeared in the tangos of Libertad Lamarque) were archetypes that later found their way into the popular culture of Latin America, where Sandrini and Lamarque enjoyed an impact similar to that of Chaplin in the United States.

13. Interview with Mario Soffici, 1970.

14. A humble background and broad human experience are frequent characteristics of the Argentine film director. Soffici held an incredible variety of jobs before turning to motion pictures: from truck driver to office employee, news vendor to circus performer—storing up the vital and broad experience he would later use in making his pictures.

15. An attempt to illustrate the complexities of Peronista culture will be found in Ernesto Goldar's "La literatura peronista," in Gonzalo Cárdenas et al., *El Peronismo* (Buenos Aires, 1969).

CHAPTER 7: THE PROVINCES

1. Alejandro E. Bunge, *Una nueva Argentina* (Buenos Aires, 1940), p. 251.

2. Of course, some provinces enjoyed periods of prosperity and progress through the production of certain staples of relative value, such as wheat in Santa Fe or sugar in Tucumán, but little benefit accrued to the provinces

themselves over the long run. This point is demonstrated in James R. Scobie's *Revolution on the Pampas: A Social History of Argentine Wheat, 1860-1910* (Austin, Tex., 1964), pp. 159-163.

3. The use of "Buenos Aires" without stipulation of province or city will refer to the complex formed by both together.

4. See Preston E. James, *Latin America* (New York, 4th edition, 1969), pp. 601-667.

5. Geographers and statistical journals divide the republic into different zones according to various criteria. The division used here is one which seemed most suitable for the thirties.

6. José Acre, ed., *La constitución argentina en la teoría y la práctica* (Buenos Aires, 1961), discussion of Article 5 of the Constitution of the Argentine Republic (1853), pp. 11-13.

7. Ibid., discussion of Article 6, pp. 13-16.

8. Víctor H. Martínez, "Federalismo y política centralista," in *Federalismo y centralismo,* Juan Carlos Agulla, ed. (Buenos Aires, 1967), p. 75.

9. James R. Scobie, *Argentina: A City and a Nation* (New York, 1964), p. 147. This work contains an excellent summary of the historic condition of the provinces.

10. See the discussion in Carl C. Taylor's *Rural Life in Argentina* (Baton Rouge, La., 1948), pp. 209-255. This study shows the effects of rural isolation and the resultant social problems.

11. Memoirs of this eminent Conservative figure, *La historia que yo he vivido* (Buenos Aires, 1955), pp. 16-22. Carlos Ibarguren was related on his mother's side to the Uriburu family of Salta, from which came two presidents, including the leader of the Revolution of 1930.

12. See the cogent discussion, still significant, although dated, in Felix J. Weil's *Argentine Riddle* (New York, 1944), p. 154.

13. Only about 73,000. Gino Germani, *Política y sociedad en una época de transición* (Buenos Aires, 1962), p. 182.

14. Zulma L. Recchini de Lattes and Alfredo E. Lattes, *Migraciones en la Argentina: estudio de las migraciones internas y internacionales, basado en datos censales, 1869-1960* (Buenos Aires, 1969). See particularly the first part on "Methodological Aspects."

15. Bunge, op. cit., pp. 223-28.

16. Figures are for 1946-1947 in Departamento de Sociología de la Fundación Bariloche, *Datos comparativos de las provincias argentinas* (San Carlos de Bariloche, 1970), I. For table on industrial establishments, p. 123; for economically active population, p. 27; and for infant mortality, p. 86.

17. Bunge, op. cit., pp. 409-412.

18. Editorial, March 21, 1940.

19. See the discussion of provincial politics in Richard Robert Strout's *The Recruitment of Candidates in Mendoza Province, Argentina* (Chapel Hill, N. C., 1968), pp. 1-37.

20. Alfredo Galletti, *La política y los partidos* (México-Buenos Aires, 1961), p. 105.

21. Editorial, November 1, 1935.

22. The appearance of guide books met this need, and a sense of the nature of this growing tourism can be found in Arturo Capdevila's, *Tierra mía* (Madrid, 1934).

23. *El Pampero* (Buenos Aires), January 17, 1943, for example.

24. Statistics can be found in *Datos comparativos de las provincias argentinas,* mostly for the late forties, pp. 108-124 passim. Generalizations about comparisons of economic development between Buenos Aires and Córdoba deal mainly with relative industrial growth.

25. Emilio E. Sánchez, *Del pasado cordobés en la vida argentina* (Córdoba, 1968), p. 19.

26. This record of accomplishment is well documented in Manuel A. Fresco's *Como encaré la política obrera durante mi gobierno* (La Plata, 1940), 2 vols.

27. Ibarguren, op. cit., pp. 379, 439.

28. *La Fronda* (Buenos Aires), September 29, 1933, and October 1, 1933.

29. Although Córdoba was somewhat more than one-half the size of Buenos Aires, it had about the same number of landowners. See Galletti, op. cit., p. 109.

30. For a laudatory biography of Sabattini, see Angel A. Vargas's, *Vida de Amadeo Sabattini* (Buenos Aires, 1966), especially pp. 41-85.

31. See *La Fronda,* May 31, 1936; August 26, 1936; and October 21, 1936.

EPILOGUE

1. "Palabras, palabras, palabras" (1960) in *Claves políticas* (Buenos Aires, 1971), p. 95.

2. These data are taken from a semi-official biography in *Quien es quien en la Argentina* (Buenos Aires, 1955), pp. 493-494.

3. Here I am summarizing the account of his intellectual and political development given to me by General Perón himself in an oral history interview taped at his home in Madrid on July 27, 1968.

4. Although the national church of Argentina, the Roman Catholic Church was shorn of its educational privileges in the 1880s. Laws apparently enacted in imitation of French practices forbade the Church from administering her own schools and also outlawed religious instruction in public institutions. The military junta reintroduced religious instruction in public schools in 1943, and it was Perón's pledge not to overturn this decree, which won him the tacit support of the Argentine hierarchy.

5. "Argentina: The Brothels Behind the Graveyard," *New York Review of Books,* XII, 14 (September 19, 1974), p. 13.

6. This is not to suggest that *Peronismo* did not make a major impact upon Argentine society, but rather, that in terms of the public issues of the thirties, its contributions were minimal. For the unique transformations worked upon Argentine society by Perón, see, inter alia, Mark Falcoff, "What Was Peronismo, 1946-55?" in Roger Cuniff, ed., *Latin America: Power and Poverty* (San Diego, Calif., 1975).

7. The late Arturo Jauretche once sought to disprove assertions of this type by compiling a list of Peronist intellectuals (in his *Los profetas del odio y la yapa* [Buenos Aires, 1967], p. 254n.) Extending the category to its broadest limits, he produced 36 names, the majority of whom were tango composers, film scenarists, or journalists. Notable exceptions were historians Ernesto Palacio and Raúl Scalabrini Ortiz, novelists Manuel Gálvez and Leopoldo Marechal, essayists Manuel Ugarte, Leonardo Castellani, and Arturo Cambours Ocampo. Taken as a whole it is not an impressive list, given the size and quality of the Argentine intellectual community.

8. Cf. Martin Stabb, "Argentine Letters and the Peronato: An Overview," *Journal of Inter-American Studies and World Affairs,* XII, 3-4 (1971), pp. 434-453.

9. Carlos Díaz-Alejandro, *Essays on the Economic History of the Argentine Republic* (New Haven, Conn., 1971), pp. 189-205.

10. Interview with Perón, previously cited.

11. Díaz-Alejandro, op. cit., pp. 351-390.

12. Cf. my review of Díaz-Alejandro in the *Hispanic American Historical Review,* LI, 4 (1971), pp. 679-782.

Bibliographical Note

CONTEMPORARY SOURCES, DOCUMENTS, MEMOIRS

As the thirties witnessed a significant change in the trends of Argentine thought and letters, an important development occurred in the publishing industry. Until this time a great many books for the Argentine market were produced in Europe, but the Depression made it profitable to manufacture paper and publish works in Buenos Aires, a trend much accelerated by the import restrictions of the Second World War. Hence, an "explosion" of publications took place for the Argentine reading public, which was of course extensive because of the high literacy rate. This increase encouraged a burgeoning group of Argentine writers, many of whom expressed the growing frustration of the average citizen. Although some scholarly works of economic and social commentary did appear, the characteristic form became the introspective essay and the polemic. Since so much of this kind of literature has been discussed in the body of the book, the editors have confined themselves to a representative sample; at the same time, they have rather arbitrarily selected certain other works—particularly documents and memoirs—that fill out some of the more complex shadings of the period. Works mentioned in either the body of the text or the notes have, in most cases, been purposely omitted.

The Revolution of 1930 and General Uriburu

The essential documentary source is República Argentina, Ministerio del Interior, *Documentos iniciales de la revolución* (Buenos Aires, 1932). A detailed account of the preparations of the Uriburu movement and the atmosphere in which it developed will be found in Diez Periodistas Porteños, *Al margen de la conspiración* (Buenos Aires, 1930). The "inside story" of the Uriburu government and its outflanking by General Justo and the Conservatives is told in General José María Sarobe, *Memorias sobre la revolución del 6 de septiembre de 1930: al servicio de la democracia* (Buenos Aires, 1957). Attached is an appendix by then-Captain Juan Perón describing his own participation in the movement and the lessons he derived from it. The Uriburu regime as it wished to appear before history is resumed in an anonymous volume published on the eve of the 1931 elections, *La obra de la revolución: reseña sintética de la labor desarrollada, 6 de septiembre, 1930-31* (Buenos Aires, 1931).

The Presidential Regimes

Any study of the Justo years must begin with the impressive República Argentina, *Poder Ejecutivo Nacional, Período 1932-38* (Buenos Aires, 1938), 10 volumes. Herein are contained the essential documents and legislation on finance, public works, law enforcement, armed forces, foreign relations, education, and agriculture, arranged topically and cross-indexed. The recent acquisition by the Archivo General de la Nación, Buenos Aires, of the private papers of General Justo may presage a further enrichment of published materials on his administration. Meanwhile we also have the memoirs of his son Liborio (pen name "Quebracho"), in *Prontuario* (Buenos Aires, 2d edition, 1957). Apart from revealing with rare authority the private man, this book has the added interest of being the testimony of a militant Trotskyist who became disillusioned with the Argentine left.

Unfortunately, when we turn to Justo's successors, the materials begin to dry up. Some insight can be derived from Roberto M. Ortiz, *Ideario democrático (a través de la república)* (Buenos Aires, 1937), campaign speeches from the 1937 elections. Light on both the Justo and Ortiz regimes is shed by Federico Pinedo, *En tiempos de la república* (Buenos Aires, 1946-1948), 5 volumes. The first volume consists of the finance minister's memoirs; the subsequent volumes are a collage of newspaper accounts, parliamentary debates, and documents. On the Castillo period there is a minimal amount of official documentation, and even the memoir literature is sparse.

The Nationalists and the Radicals

A major documentary source on Argentine nationalism is Federico Ibarguren, *Los orígenes del nacionalismo argentino, 1927-37* (Buenos Aires, 1970). Unfortunately the author's commentary tends to blur the distinctions between nationalists of the left and right, but it does provide some orientation through the mass of materials. Two good examples of right-wing nationalist "doctrinal" journalism are Bonafacio Lastra, *Bajo el signo del nacionalismo* (Buenos Aires, 1944), and Marcelo Sánchez Sorondo, *La revolución que anunciamos* (Buenos Aires, 1945). The left-wing variant is well represented in the documents and commentary of Arturo Jauretche, *FORJA y la década infame* (Buenos Aires, 1962). A leading figure in

nationalist politics who tells of his "conversion" and subsequent disillusionment is Juan Carulla, *Al filo del medio siglo* (Buenos Aires, 2d edition,
1964). How the nationalists viewed issues on a day-to-day basis can be
seen in their various periodicals, particularly *Nueva Política* and *Sol y Luna*
for the right, *Víspera* and *Reconquista* from the left.

Although the Radicals have their "official" history in Gabriel del Mazo's
El Radicalismo (Buenos Aires, 1957), 3 volumes, probably the best contemporary source for the thirties is the party's theoretical journal, *Hechos
e ideas.* Also useful are Alvear's speeches, published as *Democracia* (Buenos
Aires, 1936) and *¡Argentinos! Acción Cívica* (Buenos Aires, 1940). The
story of the paramilitary conspiracies to overthrow Justo during 1931-1933
is told by a leading participant in Lt. Col. Atilio E. Cattáneo's *Plan 1932*
(Buenos Aires, 1959), while the inside struggle in the Radical party is
revealed by Alvear's private secretary, Manuel Goldstraj, in *Años y errores*
(Buenos Aires, 1957). A thoroughgoing critique of the Radical party by
one of its most distinguished members is *El radicalismo de mañana* by
Ricardo Rojas (Buenos Aires, 1932).

The Economy and the Imbalances of Society

The major sources on the economy are Alejandro Bunge's excellent periodical,
Revista de Economía Argentina and the *Revista Económica del Banco de
la Nación,* which was edited by Raúl Prebisch. The views of the foreign
investment community are articulated by the First National Bank of
Boston, Buenos Aires Branch, in *The Situation in Argentina* (from 1938)
and by the *Review of the River Plate,* semi-official organ of the British
Chamber of Commerce. Although general censuses are lacking between
1914 and 1947, very useful specialized statistical data can be found in
government sources such as the *Censo nacional agropecuario de 1937*
(Buenos Aires, 1939) and the *Estadística industrial de 1939* (Buenos Aires,
1942).

The economic plan of the Pinedo team is outlined in República Argentina, Ministerios de Hacienda y Agricultura de la Nación, *El plan de
acción ecónomica ante el Congreso Nacional* (Buenos Aires, 1934). Although
somewhat prior to the period, quite useful in understanding many of its
problems is *La economía argentina* by Alejandro Bunge (Buenos Aires,
1928-1930), 4 volumes. This work has great value in anticipating many of
the structural problems of the thirties. Military perspectives on economic
development are provided by General José María Sarobe in *Política ecónomica argentina* (Buenos Aires, 1942) and by General Enrique Mosconi in
Obras, edited by Raúl Larra and Gregorio Weinberg (Buenos Aires, 1958),
2 volumes.

The literature on regional imbalances has already been extensively discussed in chapters 5 and 7. To this the editors might add F. Pedro Marotta's
Tierra y patria (Buenos Aires, 1932), which advocates a program of re-
settlement of Argentines on the land and, consequently, a thoroughgoing
agrarian reform; Juan Antonio Solari's *Parias argentinos* (Buenos Aires, 1940),

a heartrending study of the exploitation of rural workers in the Argentine north; and two works by the irascible if sometimes brilliant Senator Benjamín Villafañe of Jujuy, *La miseria de un país rico* (Buenos Aires, 1927), and *La tragedia argentina* (Buenos Aires, 1943). The plight of the urban working class is detailed by Alfredo L. Palacios in *La defensa del valor humano* (Buenos Aires, 1939), which also contains some of the social legislation this Socialist senator proposed during the thirties. Changes that occurred in the economic status of the urban workers are documented in República Argentina, Dirección de Estadística Social, *Nivel de vida de la familia obrera: su evolución durante la segunda guerra mundial* (Buenos Aires, 1945). And, finally, research on institutions can best be pursued from contemporary interest-oriented journals, such as *Estudios* for the Roman Catholic Church and *Revista Militar* for the Army.

LATER SOURCES

The thirties continue to exercise a fascination on Argentine and foreign writers because, as pointed out in the Preface, today it is clear that therein lie the origins of the Perón regime. Indeed, most of the works on Peronism or the post-Perón years take their point of departure from the Revolution of 1930, and many Argentines continue to search the period 1930-1943 for a way out of their present dilemma. While various works published since 1943 have been thoughtful and analytic, there has been no stemming the tide of polemics. Listed below is a sample of works arranged according to major topics; once again, except in the first sub-section, the editors have usually omitted mention of works cited or discussed in the text or notes.

The Economy and Society

Until very recently most of the literature on economic development during the thirties took its cue from Felix Weil, *Argentine Riddle* (New York, 1944), which stresses the "lost opportunities" for industrialization during the period. Such industry as did grow, Weil argues, did so by accident or as the unintended result of policies designed to favor agriculture and stock-raising. Much the same view has been advanced with Marxist variations by Leopoldo Portnoy in *Analisis crítico de la economía argentina* (México-Buenos Aires, 1961), and by Guido di Tella and Manuel Zymelman, *Las etapas del desarrollo económico argentino* (Buenos Aires, 1967), and by Aldo Ferrer, *The Argentine Economy* (Berkeley and Los Angeles, 1967). Since the publication of Carlos Díaz-Alejandro, *Essays on the Economic History of the Argentine Republic* (New Haven, 1971), the debate has taken a new turn. Díaz-Alejandro praises the Argentine elite of the thirties for its flexible and "realistic" responses to the crisis and to changes in the world economy, and credits it with a prescient policy of industrialization. He also shows that the most fruitful periods of Argentine industrial development have generally coincided with boom periods in the agro-export economy. The conservative political implications of this book are, needless to say, quite clear, especially since the author concludes with a devastating critique of Perón's economic policies, which, he says, undermined industry instead of enhancing its further development. Interestingly, Díaz-Alejandro's views are shared (although other lessons are drawn from them) by the more dogmatic, that is to say, more intransigently anti-Perón, members of the Marxist community, as shown by Gustavo Polit, "The Argentine Industrialists," in *Latin America, Reform or Revolution?* Maurice Zeitlin and James Petras, editors, (Greenwich, Conn., 1968). An attempt to clear neutral ground between the two warring camps has been made by Javier Villanueva, "Aspectos de la estrategia de industrialización argentina," in *Los fragmentos del poder,* Torcuato S. di Tella and Tulio Halperín Donghi, editors, (Buenos Aires, 1969).

Since the study of sociology, at least as it is known in Europe and the United States, is a recent innovation in Argentine universities, there have been as yet few studies on the social developments of the period. Gino Germani has produced two ground-breaking works, *Estructura social de la Argentina* (Buenos Aires, 1955) and *Política y sociedad en una época de transición* (Buenos Aires, 1962). Both are useful for an understanding of the transformations of the thirties and forties, although more recent sociological scholarship has looked toward revising many of Germani's conclusions. Two examples are the work of Mario Margulis, *Migración y marginalidad en la sociedad argentina* (Buenos Aires, 1968) and Miguel Murmis and Juan Carlos Portantiero, *Estudios sobre los orígenes del peronismo* (Buenos Aires, 1972). Somewhat outdated, but still a worthwhile source for the thirties and forties, is *Materiales para el estudio de la clase media en Latinoamérica,* R. Cravenna, editor, (Washington, D. C., 1950), Volume I, Argentina and Uruguay. The political history of Argentine labor from the First World War to the late Perón period is the subject of Samuel L. Baily, *Labor, Nationalism and Politics in Argentina* (New Brunswick, N. J., 1967), which, in spite of some conceptual difficulties, is a vast improvement over earlier literature; much of the story concentrates precisely on the period that is the subject of this book. Although covering a somewhat longer period, *Argentina, 1930-60,* Jorge Paita, ed. (Buenos Aires, 1961), is full of useful and interesting materials on social structure and political institutions.

The Spiritual Crisis

The most complete (and widely read) intellectual history of the period is Juan José Hernández Arregui's *La formación de la conciencia nacional* (Buenos Aires, 1960, and subsequent editions). A philosopher by training, a Peronist in politics, Hernández Arregui has produced a volume extraordinary in its insights and remarkable in the richness of its data. Its strong polemical tone should not lead to an underestimation of its intellectual value. And its impact upon younger Argentines has been so important as to give it a life of its own; perhaps more than any single document it has shaped an entirely new generation of Peronist pensadores. Almost half this lengthy volume advances hypotheses on the decade of the thirties.

Apart from Hernández Arregui there are few satisfactory attempts to explore the intellectual contours of the period as a whole. One such effort is the important doctoral dissertation of David C. Jordan, "Argentina's Nationalist Movements and the Political Parties (1930-63): A Study of Conflict" (University of Pennsylvania, 1964). Additionally, some fine monographic studies on individual thinkers and writers have been appearing in recent years. Among them are *Genio y figura de Leopoldo Lugones* (Buenos Aires, 1969), by Julio Irazusta, a close friend and political collaborator who is also a distinguished historian and man of letters; Peter G. Earle's *Prophet in the Wilderness* (Austin, 1971), a major study of Ezequiel Martínez Estrada; Norberto Galasso's *Vida de Scalabrini Ortiz* (Buenos Aires, 1970), based on private papers; and Mark Falcoff's "Raúl Scalabrini Ortiz, The Making of an Argentine Nationalist," *Hispanic American Historical Review*, LII, 1 (1972), pp. 74-101, which stresses Scalabrini's FORJA years. The best source on Manuel Gálvez is the man himself, as he appears in the third volume of his autobiography, *Entre la novela y la historia* (Buenos Aires, 1962), covering the years 1928-1938. For those ignorant of Spanish there is *Manuel Gálvez*, by Myron I. Lichtblau (New York, 1972). The only important study of Hugo Wast is by Juan Carlos Moreno, *Genio y figura de Hugo Wast* (Buenos Aires, 1969), which suffers from all the defects of a family-commissioned biography. On Aníbal Ponce there is only the boring exegesis of Emilio Troise, *Aníbal Ponce* (Buenos Aires, 1969). As yet there are no studies on Benjamín Villafañe, Alejandro Bunge, or Alfredo L. Palacios.

The standard sources on historical revisionism are Joseph Barager, "The Historiography of the Río de la Plata Area Since 1830," *Hispanic American Historical Review*, XXXIX, 4 (1959), pp. 588-642, and Clifton B. Kroeber, "Rosas and the Revision of Argentine History, 1880-1955," *Revista Interamericana de Bibliografía*, X, 1 (1960), pp. 3-25. An attempt to bring these articles up to date and place the subject in broader perspective is Tulio Haperín Donghi's *El revisionismo histórico argentino* (México, 1971). For those wishing to plunge *in media res,* there is from 1940 the *Revista del Instituto de Estudios Históricos "Juan Manuel de Rosas."*

Much of the tone and mood of the late years of the Conservative Restoration has been magnificently captured in a work of fiction by Eduardo Mallea, "Fiesta in November" [1938], in *All Green Shall Perish and Other Novellas and Stories* (New York, 1966).

Politics and The Military

Because in so many ways the crisis of contemporary Argentina is political in nature, much of the literature on the 1930's has dwelt upon the collapse of consensus and the entry of the military into the decision-making centers of government. Note 1, chapter 2 lists a number of the important monographs that have appeared in recent years. In general, the prevailing trend in the historiography of the thirties has been set by a neo-Marxist school whose members, many of them ex-Communists, take their former comrades to task for failing to appreciate the "revolutionary" nature of Argentine nationalism and consequently missing the boat of history (captained by Perón). Examples of this kind of writing, which has had a significant effect on the Peronization of Argentine students, are by Rodolfo Puiggrós, *Historia crítica de los partidos políticos argentinos* (Buenos Aires, 1956 and subsequent editions) and *La democracia fraudulenta* (Buenos Aires, 1968), which deals specifically with the thirties; also, Juan José Real's *30 años de historia argentina* (Buenos Aires, 1962).

The unrevolutionary nature of the Argentine Communist Party has been exposed for all to see by Trotskyist-Peronist Jorge Abelardo Ramos in *El partido comunista argentino: su historia y su crítica* (Buenos Aires, 1962), recently reissued as *Historia del stalinismo en la Argentina* (1970). It is doubtful that the Party will ever be as damaged by CIA conduits as much as it has been by this entertaining and devastating little book. Félix Luna, a Radical subsequently friendly to Peronism, has chronicled the transition from *década infame* to *Peronato* in *El 45* (Buenos Aires, 1969), a political history of the year 1945, based on interviews with many surviving participants. Old-fashioned (but nonetheless valuable) contributions to the political history of the thirties are the memoirs of Socialist deputy Nicolás Repetto, *Mi paso por la política: de Uriburu a Perón* (Buenos Aires, 1957), while Carlos Fayt has assembled some interesting materials on the period 1939-1943 in a book rather inappropriately titled *La naturaleza del peronismo* (Buenos Aires, 1967).

Although the military has received a good deal of attention from observers of the Argentine scene in recent decades, only in the last five or so years have we begun to see the appearance of serious studies. The work of Potash is obviously fundamental, supplemented by that of Jorge Abelardo Ramos, *Historia política del ejército argentino* (Buenos Aires, 1959), Juan V. Orona, *La logia militar que enfrentó a Yrigoyen* (Buenos Aires, 1966) and *La logia militar que derrocó a Castillo* (Buenos Aires, 1967), Enrique Díaz Araujo, *La conspiración del 43: el GOU, una experiencia militarista en la Argentina* (Buenos Aires, 1971), and Marvin Goldwert, *Democracy, Militarism and Nationalism in Argentina, 1930-66* (Austin, 1972). A pioneering work of Argentine sociology is Dario Cantón's *La política de los militares argentinos, 1900-1971* (Buenos Aires, 1971); whatever one may think of the author's conclusions, he does at least make available data of enormous value to researchers. A biography that deals extensively with the military phase of Perón's career is Enrique Pavón Pereyra's *Perón, preparación de una vida para el mando, 1895-1945* (Buenos Aires, 1965).

Index